COASTAL TRAILS
OF NORTHERN
CALIFORNIA

Pigeon Point Lighthouse

COASTAL TRAILS OF NORTHERN CALIFORNIA

INCLUDING BEST DOG FRIENDLY BEACHES

Linda and David Mullally

FALCONGUIDES

GUILFORD, CONNECTICUT

We dedicate this book to each other as coauthors and soul mates
who share the joys and challenges of cocreativity.

FALCONGUIDES®

An imprint of Rowman & Littlefield

Falcon and FalconGuides are registered trademarks and Make Adventure Your Story is a trademark of Rowman & Littlefield.

Distributed by NATIONAL BOOK NETWORK

Copyright © 2017 by Rowman & Littlefield

Maps by Melissa Baker © Rowman & Littlefield

All photos by David Mullally unless noted otherwise.

Printed in the United States of America

British Library Cataloguing-in-Publication Information available

Library of Congress Cataloging-in-Publication Data available

ISBN 978-1-4930-2603-6 (paperback)

ISBN 978-1-4930-2604-3 (e-book)

∞™ The paper used in this publication meets the minimum requirements of American National Standard for Information Sciences—Permanence of Paper for Printed Library Materials, ANSI/NISO Z39.48-1992.

The authors and Rowman & Littlefield assume no liability for accidents happening to, or injuries sustained by, readers who engage in the activities described in this book.

THE HIKES

Map and Icon Legends

ICON LEGEND

 BEST PHOTOS

 FAMILY FRIENDLY

 BEACH ACCESS

 DOG FRIENDLY

 FINDING SOLITUDE

NAVIGATION

Carry relevant maps and know how to read a topographic map so you can anticipate difficulty, shady spots, water sources, and suitability for your dog. It will help you pack and pace yourself.

USGS quad map(s) with a scale of 1:24,000 and a compass are the traditional means of navigation. Consider taking a navigation workshop at a local outdoor recreation store like REI or a local community college.

A good GPS (global positioning system) or maybe a smartphone with a good map app should enable you to determine your approximate location along the trail. Usually, a GPS more accurately shows latitude and longitude. Reception may be limited. Remember to fully charge your devices and carry spare batteries.

280	Interstate Highway	Bench	
101	US Highway	Boat Launch	
1	State Road	Building/Point of Interest	
	Railroad	Campground	
	Tunnel	Gate	
	Featured Trail	Info Panel/Visitor Center	
	Trail	Lighthouse	
	Featured Trail on Roads	Parking	
	Bridge	Picnic Area	
	Boardwalk/Steps	Recycling	
	Body of Water	Restroom	
	Marsh	Scenic View	
	River/Creek	Stables	
	Intermittent Stream	Telephone	
	National Park/Forest	Town	
	National Monument/ Wilderness Area	Trailhead	
	State/County Park	Trash	
		Water	

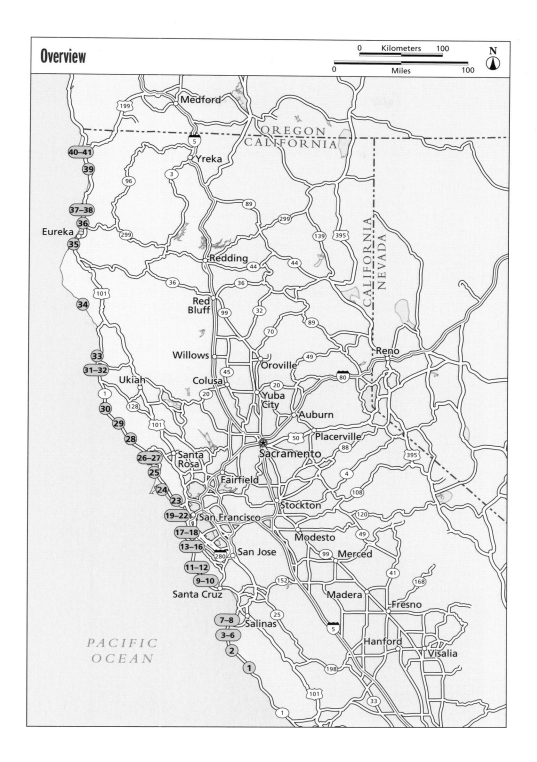

Overview

0 Kilometers 100
0 Miles 100

N

Medford

OREGON
CALIFORNIA

40–41
39

199

5

Yreka

3

96

37–38
36

89

299

139 395

Eureka

35

299

Redding

44

44

36

36

CALIFORNIA
NEVADA

34

101

Red
Bluff

99

32

70

89

33
31–32

Willows

45

Oroville

49

Reno

80

Ukiah

1

128

Colusa

20

Yuba
City

30

101

20

29
28

Auburn

50

Placerville

88

26–27
25

Santa
Rosa

Fairfield

Sacramento

4

395

24
23

108

19–22

San Francisco

Stockton

120

17–18

Modesto

49

13–16

280

San Jose

99

Merced

41

11–12
9–10

152

Madera

168

Fresno

Santa Cruz

25

7–8

Salinas

5

Hanford

3–6
2

Visalia

1

198

PACIFIC
OCEAN

101

33

1

MEET YOUR GUIDES

Quebec-born **LINDA MULLALLY** and native Californian **DAVID MULLALLY** have been a wife-and-husband team adventuring around the globe and cocreating with her writing and his photography for more than 30 years. She, a travel columnist/author and "doggie nanny," and he, an attorney/photographer, share their passion for travel, hiking, and dogs through articles, books, and multimedia presentations. Linda's *Monterey Herald* travel column Away We Go inspires readers to explore the world's bounty of natural and cultural treasures on bike and on foot. David and Linda divide their home time at base camps in the best of both outdoors worlds—a pad in Carmel on California's Central Coast and a mountain cabin at Mammoth Lakes in the Eastern Sierra. Gem, a young Siberian husky and enthusiastic member of their pack, inspires and enhances their life at home, on the road, and on the trail hiking, biking, kayaking, and paddleboarding. *Coastal Trails of Northern California Including Best Dog Friendly Beaches* is their eighth book, with more titles in progress. Visit your guides at lindabmullally.com and falcon.com.

ACKNOWLEDGMENTS

David and I could not have imagined spending time working on a more exhilarating project in a more inspiring setting than the Northern California coast. In addition to the sublime natural beauty, the openness and friendliness of the local people we encountered in parks and campgrounds along the way made every base camp feel like home. Rangers, docents, volunteers, fellow hikers and campers, dog lovers, shopkeepers, business owners, and employees expressed enthusiasm and desire to contribute to make *Coastal Trails of Northern California Including Best Dog Friendly Beaches* a superb guidebook. We are grateful for their local knowledge and generous spirits.

Cheers to Merideth Canham-Nelson at beergeeks.com for her extensive knowledge of brews and breweries.

The California Coastal Trail is at the heart of what makes this a unique guide filled with information and resources to give readers at home or on the trail a rich experience. There would be no purpose or inspiration for this book if not for the dedication of the nonprofit California Coastal Trail Association (CCTA), its staff, and volunteers. The CCTA continues to further the vision of Bill and Lucy Kortum and the original group of Coastwalkers, who spearheaded the idea of a trail reaching from the Oregon border to the Mexican border. Much has been accomplished since 1983 when an organized group of seventy walkers journeyed 60 miles from Gualala to Bodega Bay to create awareness about the value of public coastal access for the purpose of enjoying and protecting the California coastline's wealth of beauty. Local residents and visitors are increasingly enjoying stitches of multiuse trails in their cities and communities as a result of citizen activism raising funds, passing bond acts, and pushing for government-sponsored grants. These individual trail projects benefit communities economically, recreationally, and environmentally while playing a vital role in helping fulfill the dream of connecting the California coast with a continuous walking trail for the public's enjoyment as well as fostering appreciation and protection of this natural treasure.

We thank all the visionary citizens, politicians, agencies, and the battalions of volunteers whose efforts and successes are the reason David and I had the privilege of living an extraordinary several-month adventure walking along some of Northern California's most magnificent stretches of coastline and sampling the miles of fabulous beaches we share in this book. Those dog-loving lawmakers at the national, state, county, and local level who realize how important to our daily quality of life our four-legged pals have become deserve a note of gratitude and extra tail wagging for setting up guidelines that allow us to share many of California's coastal trails and beaches with our precious furry family members. Hopefully responsible dog owners will make their voices heard so more coastal trails and beaches welcome well-behaved canine citizens.

HOW TO USE THIS GUIDE

The book uses Big Sur in Monterey County north to Crescent City in Del Norte County as the boundaries for the coastal trails and dog friendly beaches of Northern California. The **Trail Finder** helps you sort hikes by five categories: best photos, family friendly, beach access, dog friendly, and finding solitude. The Top 5 Hikes are family friendly and sprinkled from south to north as samples of the Northern California coast's most stunning scenery.

Before You Hit the Trail gives you an overview of Northern California's coastal ecology and history and the future of the California Coastal Trail. It also includes sections that underline the area's highlights and hazards and information to help you prepare for the trail and enhance your excursion with or without a dog.

The hikes are categorized by coastal counties, of which there are nine from south to north: Monterey, Santa Cruz, San Mateo, San Francisco, Marin, Sonoma, Mendocino, Humboldt, and Del Norte. Each set of hikes is introduced with a brief profile of the county.

The trails were chosen primarily for their close proximity to the shore and convenient accessibility from a major paved road for the whole family's maximum enjoyment of a coastal experience. Some segments of coastal trail along the Lost Coast and the shoreline of Redwood National Park in southern Humboldt County were deliberately omitted because of their extreme isolation and difficult access along seasonally impassable rugged dirt roads. Other factors considered were the precariousness of routes on narrow strips of sand in extremely tide-sensitive areas as well as higher risk of Roosevelt elk encounters on some remote trails, when these regal but powerful members of the deer family are more aggressive and unpredictable during the fall rut (males/bulls engage in mating rituals to compete with other bulls in attracting the females/cows to their harem) from late summer though late fall. Cows can also be dangerous when protecting their young during calving season from late spring into early summer. There are several safe viewing areas to observe and admire the elk as you drive through Redwood National Park along the Newton Drury Scenic Parkway. Although elk may appear tame, rangers remind park visitors that "it isn't so, Joe." They advise tourists to give elk the space, respect, and attention they deserve.

The hikes vary in distances based on the extent of the trail development, points of interest, and the overall appeal of the setting. Most of the hikes are out and back, which allows you to choose your turnaround point based on available time and physical condition. Unless otherwise specified, the access roads are paved.

The distances were calculated using area-specific maps in tandem with a GPS unit for maximum accuracy. It is not uncommon for some coastal trails to suffer from erosion during severe winter storms or other natural events. Sections of trails may be closed, modified, or rerouted. Call the managing agency to confirm the status of the trail.

The Rundown below the **Why Go?** hike overview is designed to help you select and prepare for the hike. Features include:

Distance, which is listed as the total round-trip from the trailhead. Generally the hike will be an out-and-back, loop, or lollipop.

Start specifies the exact location where the hike begins.

Nearest town helps orient you to the location of the trail.

Hiking time is based on approximately a 2-mile-per-hour pace with snack and photo breaks.

Fees and permits apply to day-use and parking fees and any special permit process.

Conveniences tell you about trail amenities, including visitor centers, restrooms, and picnic areas.

Beach access lets you know if there is an accessible beach from the trail. Some of the most sublime beaches are at the foot of precipitous cliffs with no safe access. If a beach is accessible and dog compatible, "on leash" or "under voice control" will be specified. No mention of dogs implies that dogs are not allowed.

Trail users lists those with whom you may share the trail. On multi-recreational trails, this can include horses and bicycles. If dogs are allowed, it will specify "dogs

Tidytips and goldfields

on leash" or "under voice control." No mention of dogs implies that dogs are not allowed.

Trailhead elevation and **Highest point** help you determine if there is any significant elevation change on the trail.

Trail surface helps you anticipate the best footwear, depending on whether you'll be walking on pavement, dirt or rocky path, or sandy beaches.

Difficulty rates the hike as easy, moderate, or strenuous. Distance and terrain are factored into the rating.

Seasonal highlights focuses on natural seasonal attractions, including vegetation and wildlife. Whale watching is the most popular spring and fall attraction on coastal trails.

Managing agency is the contact source for information about the trail's condition, rerouting or closure of the trail, and current policies. Policies, especially rules concerning dogs, are always subject to change without notice.

Finding the trailhead provides directions to the trail from the major highway closest to the coast, which in Northern California is either CA 1 or US 101.

What to See includes some historical information related to the trail along with details on the points of interest and in some cases optional shorter routes or suggested extensions. **Miles and Directions** is a concise summary of key junctions and significant landmarks along the trail.

Bakeries, Breweries, Eats, and Sleeps lists any nearby bakeries and breweries. Places to eat and sleep with unique characteristics or local flavor were given preference when available. In some instances chain hotels and restaurants are the only game in town for convenience. The listings specify whether the establishment is dog friendly. All campgrounds listed are dog friendly.

Since not all trails described in the book are "dog friendly," there is a list of some of the best **Dog Friendly Beaches** at the end of each county chapter; they're also shown on the map at the beginning of each chapter. A brief description of the beach is included, along with the leash policy and the contact information for the beach's managing agency. If the beach listed happens to be one of the featured coastal trail hikes in that county or is referenced in one of the hikes, the listing will refer you to that particular coastal trail by hike number.

The **Coastal Attractions** section following "Dog Friendly Beaches" at the end of each county chapter complement the highlights mentioned in the hikes. The listings specify if the attraction is dog friendly. This list of additional places and/or activities of interest includes some of the best coastal farmers' markets, which are fresh and fun venues to stock up on camping and picnicking provisions.

	BEST PHOTOS	FAMILY FRIENDLY	BEACH ACCESSS	DOG FRIENDLY	FINDING SOLITUDE
MONTEREY COUNTY					
1. McWay Falls	•	•			
2. Brazil Ranch	•			•	•
3. Soberanes Point	•	•			•
4. Point Lobos	•	•	•		
5. Carmel Meadows	•	•	•	•	
6. Carmel Beach Bluff	•	•	•	•	
7. Asilomar to Bird Rock	•	•	•	•	
8. Old Fisherman's Wharf to Pacific Grove Marine Refuge	•	•	•	•	
SANTA CRUZ COUNTY					
9. West Cliff Trail	•	•	•	•	
10. Cove-Bluff Trail			•		•
SAN MATEO COUNTY					
11. Franklin Point		•			•
12. Bean Hollow		•	•	•	
13. Cowell-Purisima Trail		•			•
14. Half Moon Bay State Beach to Ritz-Carleton			•	•	
15. Half Moon Bay State Beach to Pillar Point Harbor		•	•	•	
16. Pillar Point Bluff		•		•	•

	BEST PHOTOS	FAMILY FRIENDLY	BEACH ACCESS	DOG FRIENDLY	FINDING SOLITUDE
SAN MATEO COUNTY					
17. Devil's Slide		•		•	
18. Pacifica State Beach to Pier			•	•	
SAN FRANCISCO COUNTY					
19. Fort Funston		•	•	•	
20. Lands End	•	•	•	•	
21. Fisherman's Wharf to Golden Gate Bridge	•	•	•	•	
MARIN COUNTY					
22. Golden Gate Bridge to Marin Headlands Visitor Center	•		•	•	•
23. Stinson Beach to Bolinas Lagoon		•	•	•	
24. Limantour Dunes		•	•	•	•
25. Tomales Point	•	•			•
SONOMA COUNTY					
26. Bodega Head	•	•			
27. Kortum Trail to Russian River			•		•
28. Salt Point to Sentinel Rock	•		•		•
29. Bluff Top Trail to Walk-On Beach	•	•	•	•	•

	BEST PHOTOS	FAMILY FRIENDLY	BEACH ACCESS	DOG FRIENDLY	FINDING SOLITUDE
MENDOCINO COUNTY					
30. Stornetta	•	•		•	•
31. Mendocino Headlands	•	•	•	•	
32. Point Cabrillo	•	•	•	•	
33. Haul Road		•	•	•	
HUMBOLDT COUNTY					
34. Black Sands Beach		•	•	•	•
35. Eureka Waterfront Trail		•	•	•	
36. Hammond Trail		•	•	•	
37. Trinidad Head	•	•	•	•	
38. Rim Trail	•	•	•		
DEL NORTE COUNTY					
39. Lagoon Creek to Klamath Overlook					•
40. Enderts Beach		•	•		
41. Point St. George	•	•	•	•	•

1. MCWAY FALLS

2. POINT LOBOS

1. MCWAY FALLS. This is the shortest family friendly hike, to a unique and stunning coastal waterfall—California's only major falls that plummets into the Pacific Ocean.

2. POINT LOBOS. This spectacular family friendly coastal trail is the "crown jewel" of California's state park system and a must-do.

3. LANDS END. This family and dog friendly trail is a nature oasis on the edge of moody San Francisco Bay.

4. TRINIDAD HEAD. Trinidad Head's relatively short, rugged trail blends breathtaking views of an untamed sea stack dotted with shoreline on one side and the hidden cove's lush Caribbean feel on the other.

5. RIM TRAIL. Patrick's Point State Park's gem traces the forested cliffs with access paths to rocky pocket beaches and promontories.

3. LANDS END

4. TRINIDAD HEAD

5. RIM TRAIL

BEFORE YOU HIT THE TRAIL

CALIFORNIA BOASTS OVER 3,000 MILES OF PACIFIC OCEAN SHORELINE between the Mexican and Oregon borders, and its coastline is one of the most famous and popular scenic routes in the world. CA 1 and US 101 serve to connect the coastal communities on a vehicular route. But there are many stitches of hiking trails and multiuse pathways along the coast that are meant to be nonmotorized networks to connect communities by foot, bicycle, and/or horseback. These individual stitches on or close enough to the coast to see, hear, or smell the ocean with some segments on the beach are part of the California Coastal Trail (CCT), which when completed to include coastal inlets and bays will form a 1,200-mile-long thread spanning from Oregon to Mexico. As of 2016 the CCT vision was two-thirds completed.

We can look back to 1769 and the Portolá Expedition for some of the earliest accounts of land explorers along the California coast. Juan Bautista de Anza was another Spanish explorer who left his mark along the coast. To this day there are sections of the Juan Bautista de Anza National Historic Trail that overlap the California Coastal Trail route.

The 1972 Coastal Initiative was the modern-day step to formalize the establishment of a coastal trail system. But the seed for implementing protection of public access to the coastline and propelling the vision of a recognized coastal trail was planted by the founding of the nonprofit organization Coastwalk. Bill and Lucy Kortum's desire to draw attention to the need to create and promote public access to the California coast and protect this natural treasure began in 1982 with their ambitious idea to gather 1,000 people for a walk along the Sonoma Coast. The following year a more logistically feasible version involved seventy coast walkers in an organized seven-day/60-mile trek from Gualala to Bodega Bay.

In 1999 the CCT got another boost when Governor Gray Davis and the Millennium Trail Council designated the California Coastal Trail as California's Millennium Legacy Trail. Between the 2000 Parks Bond Act and the 2001 Coastal Trail bill, the CCT was destined to become a reality. The cooperation and commitment of the State Coastal Conservancy, Coastwalk, and various state programs, as well as partnerships with local and federal agencies, has accomplished much. But environmental and habitat protection, funding obstacles, and land ownership issues, as well as Mother Nature's relentless sculpting of beaches, bluffs, and cliffs, present additional challenges and stumbling blocks. Public support and participation is necessary to

CCT logo

keep the momentum of connecting existing trails with new stitches until the coastal tapestry is complete. Newly posted CCT plaques with the blue-and-white wave logo at trailheads are always a welcome sight and reason to cheer that the vision is alive and progressing.

The Northern California coastline as defined in this book begins in Big Sur south of Carmel-by-the-Sea in Monterey County and stretches north through nine counties to Crescent City in Del Norte County. Many of the trails described in the book are vital stitches in the California Coastal Trail system.

The Northern California coastline is as rich in nature, culture, and history as it is stunning. From Native American roots and Russian influence to Spanish and Mexican heritage, the imprint of these cultures can still be seen and felt in the communities that dot the coast. Fishing, hunting, whaling, mining, logging, ranching, and farming industries have all feasted, at times to excess, on the coast's natural resources. Grassroots environmental movements were born here and have played historic roles in preserving some of the world's most amazing natural treasures.

The North Coast boasts a string of county and state parks, preserves, and national parks as well as marine sanctuaries—all created to combine habitat protection and preservation of our natural and cultural heritage with education and recreation

The California Coastal National Monument protects habitats on offshore rocks and small islands.

for the enrichment and pleasure of generations to come. Unique in the national monument system, the California Coastal National Monument was established by presidential proclamation in 2000. This monument protects the various habitats dependent on the offshore rocks and small islands along 1,100 miles of California coastline. Many stitches of the California Coastal Trail offer breathtaking views of the sea stacks and islands, with a front-row seat to observe the marine and bird life dependent on the safety of the monument as home and refuge.

The coast is about the wonders of the ocean, the fascinating intertidal world that thrives between the sandy beaches, river mouths, and the surf. It's the portal to prairie, meadow, dune, forest, and mountainous wilderness, with a 500-mile belt of ancient redwoods being the most awesome sentinels of the northern coastal realm.

Walking a coastal trail in Northern California is an intimate experience with unadulterated beauty, sometimes tame and subdued and sometimes fiercely wild. Since dogs have become increasingly more important family members in recent years, it's fortunate that many coastal trails welcome the canine pals so many of us consider our four-legged furry children. The Northern California coast boasts over

Spring brings fluttering swallowtail butterflies to the coast.

Hovering hawks are common along coastal trails.

A heron hunts in the kelp beds.

one hundred beaches, many of which you can explore with your dog. Most require dogs be on leash, but a few special surf-and-sand playgrounds let your pooch gallivant under voice control.

On the cultural side, the coast's land, maritime, and human history has been preserved in park visitor centers and the many lighthouse museums, as well as on trail interpretive panels and exhibits.

The North Coast's past is fascinating, but its present inspires a promise for the future with its abundance of businesses echoing the message to support "local and

Dogs are welcome on many Northern California beaches.

Spring attracts photographers to coastal meadows.

sustainable." Nowhere else can you so easily gorge on scenery along a coastal trail between feasting on fresh seafood and produce, artisan cheese, handcrafted baked goods, and locally brewed beer.

Almost 200 years after pioneers followed the siren call to California's Garden of Eden, the Northern California coast, from its urbanized shores to its most remote hamlets, continues to overwhelm and impress visitors with its bounty of attractions—natural as well as those nurtured by human hands and creativity.

A DYNAMIC COASTLINE

Movement of the earth's crust (plate tectonics) along the Pacific and North American plates continues to play a major role in the shaping of the California coast. California is subject to the activity in the Ring of Fire's 25,000-mile horseshoe-shaped field of volcanic activity in the basin of the Pacific Ocean. More than 75 percent of the world's active and dormant volcanoes are concentrated in this seismic cauldron bubbling with volcanic eruptions and earthquakes as a result of the plate movements that scrape, push, poke, and rise. The land in motion triggers regular small earthquakes, most of which are too subtle to be felt. But in Northern California, the famous and very active San Andreas Fault extending from San Francisco north to Cape Mendocino is the primary player when the coastal landscape has a bout of severe shaking, rattling, and rolling.

Although a seismic sea or tidal wave, known as a tsunami (Japanese for "harbor wave"), can be triggered by a variety of events that displace enormous volumes of

Mother Nature continuously sculpts the California coastline.

Crumbling beach bluff

water, such as massive landslides, glacier calving, or underwater detonations, the majority of tsunamis occur within the geologically dynamic Ring of Fire as a result of an abrupt plate shift and the domino effect of deep-sea quakes, slips, or eruptions. Tsunami waves can travel across the Pacific at jet speeds, and a foot-high tsunami wave on the ocean floor can reach devastating height and force as it slows and amplifies closer to shallow water at the shoreline.

Not all tsunamis are devastators. Historically, either recorded or reconstructed from as far back as the 1700s, California shores have been hit by up to one hundred tsunamis. Damage and casualties depend on how populated and developed the affected coastal communities are as well as the effectiveness of the warning system. Northern California's offshore faults and steep underwater slopes compound to make it the most vulnerable coastline to tsunamis in the continental United States. Of the thirty-four recorded on the North Coast, five caused damage. The most publicized tsunami affected Crescent City in 1964. The surge of water generated by a 9.2 earthquake off the coast of Alaska flooded 29 city blocks and killed twelve people. The 2011 9.0-magnitude earthquake was a disaster for Japan, but even the 2- to 3-foot surges that rolled into harbors like Santa Cruz caused millions of dollars of damage to boats and docks. At least one person lured to the shore to take photos was swept away.

Respect trail rules.

DOGS ON LEASH ONLY
HORSES ON DESIGNATED
TRAIL ONLY
BIKES ON ROADWAY ONLY
NO VEHICLES, FIRES
OR CAMPING

CLOSED 10 PM – 6 AM

Mother Nature continuously sculpts the coastline. Less dramatic but still powerful elements like the wind blows across the ocean, shaping water into swells of waves that crash against the shoreline. Waves, wind, and rain slough, scoop, and erode soil and rock, while runoff from rivers and streams carries sediment to the shore for ocean currents to retool, create, and reshape beaches. Ocean tides influenced by the gravitational pull of the moon cause the ocean's water to rise and fall, from a few inches to 6 or 8 feet. At high tide, especially if accompanied by winter's stormy weather, elements give the shoreline seasonal makeovers.

Climate change is a serious factor in forecasting changes along the Northern California coast. California was one of the first states to track indicators of climate change impacts. The Golden Gate tide gauge at Crissy Field in San Francisco reveals that sea levels have already increased by an average of 7 inches over the last century. The rising sea levels compounded by winter storm surges will accelerate cliff and beach erosion. The chemistry of seawater is becoming more acidic as the ocean absorbs the increased carbon dioxide released from human causes. The acidic water compromises the integrity of some marine life's protective shells, which in turn affects the food supply for marine life and seabirds as well as land mammals that depend on salmon populations and their cycle of sea to stream. Higher air temperatures also affect the migratory patterns of birds. In short, climate change from a coastal perspective exacerbates the disruption of the food chain as well as contributes to the redesigning of the topography.

The bigger picture for coast walkers paints the Northern California coastline as a work of art in perpetual progress, its canvas highlighted by pebbled coves in the

TSUNAMI WARNINGS TO HEAD TO HIGHER GROUND

wcatwc.arh.noaa.gov; tsunami.gov

- If you are in a low-lying coastal area and feel an earthquake, move immediately to higher ground. If you can't get to higher ground, retreat to the highest floor of a concrete building.
- Listen for tsunami warning sirens.
- Tsunamis are a series of waves that can be hours apart. Stay away from the shore until authorities declare it safe.
- If you see a sudden rise and fall of water mimicking the tide, this is your warning to head to higher ground, as a tsunami is on the way.
- Large tsunamis usually announce themselves with a loud roar resembling a train or aircraft. At night, this is your warning to get to safe high ground.
- Small tsunami waves on one beach can mean disaster at another. Be safe and head for higher ground.
- Never get lured to the beach to watch a tsunami. If you see the wave, it's too late to escape.

shadow of jagged sea stacks, jutting headlands, and chiseled precipitous cliffs interrupted by gentle slopes of soft, sandy beaches tracing coastal plains.

Be wary and don't let the coastline's visual magnificence and visceral stirring hypnotize you. Always stay a safe distance from the edge of bluffs, ridges, and surf lines as you enjoy the bountiful beauty of the Northern California coast.

SAFETY BY THE SEA

There's a seductive wild beauty and a hypnotic quality to the rugged North Coast's vast seascape as waves swell and sculpt the sand, rock, and bluffs along the shoreline. But wildness can also mean unpredictability and the need for additional caution by the water. Some coastal trails and especially sections of the California Coastal Trail skirt beaches, which make some stretches of trail tide sensitive and hazardous at certain times of the day. It is important to check the tide chart before setting off on a beach trail, as the surf line can change quickly, leaving you stranded or vulnerable to being swept out to sea. A seemingly wide stretch of sand can become impassable at high tide. Click on "North Coast" at ca.usharbors.com/california-tide-charts to find a tide chart for the closest harbor to your trail.

Conditions can vary along different sections of the coast, making some beaches more appropriate for swimming and wading than others. Some of the most mesmerizing beaches and dramatic coastlines can be the most inappropriate and dangerous for recreating. Steep drop-offs with pounding surf and undertow, rogue waves, and rip currents combined with cold water can be deadly. On bluffs, large waves can undermine and crumble the earth under your feet.

Below are ten tips for safe, happy trails along the coast.

1. Check the local tides to avoid being stranded or swept out.

2. Respect posted signs on water conditions and watch for High Surf Advisories issued by the National Weather Service.

3. Never turn your back on the ocean. Rogue waves can sneak up on you anytime.

4. Wet sand is easier but riskier to walk on. Walk and picnic on dry sand higher up from the surf line.

5. Keep children close.

6. When in doubt, leash your dog. Even good swimmers are vulnerable to dangerous surf conditions and hypothermia.

7. Stay off slippery rocks and wear a life jacket when engaged in distracting activities like fishing or tidepooling.

8. Stay away from the edge of bluffs.

9. In a rescue situation, throw something the person can grab onto rather than going in the water. Most rescue attempts with someone going in after the distressed person end up in double tragedies.

10. In the rare event of a tsunami or earthquake, head inland to higher ground.

Hand in hand for safety along the shore

Harbor seals sunbathing

WHAT'S OUT THERE?

The North Coast is less populated with more open undeveloped space for wildlife habitat on land and sea. At the shore and out to sea, depending on the time of year, you'll have the privilege of hearing and seeing harbor seals, sea lions, elephant seals, otters, migrating whales, and various colonies of shore- and seabirds. Seagulls, pelicans, and cormorants swoop the surf and perch on sea stacks.

The western snowy plover is a small shorebird listed as threatened under the federal Endangered Species Act and a "species of special concern" by the State of California. These little white-bellied birds with dark bills and black legs migrate to Northern California beaches to breed and nest. Unfortunately their nesting season, March through September, overlaps peak beach activity between Memorial Day and Labor Day. An effort to promote recovery by the state and the US Fish and Wildlife Service includes closure of some beach areas during the critical seasons; signs are posted and regulations are enforced. Recreational activity is limited, and dogs are banned from specific areas of the beaches and in some cases banned from the entire beach during this vulnerable period. The positive side effect of snowy plover

Cormorants scanning for a meal

Seagulls and vultures feasting
on a whale carcass

Respect snowy plover nesting areas.

protection measures will also benefit other shorebirds as well as marine mammals that use the beach.

Many of the plover nesting sites are on state park property, and rangers will also enforce regulations banning removal of natural features such as driftwood and shells, along with prohibiting horses, camping, motorized vehicles, fireworks, and fires on beaches. Even kites and Frisbees can cause nest abandonment. The overall goal is to enlist the public's cooperation in learning to "share the shore."

Tidepools are also rich in sea life. Be fascinated by the orange sea stars, purple sea urchins, sea cucumbers, anemones, hermit crabs, and clusters of barnacle–covered mussels as well as numerous tiny fish and organisms, but follow tidepool etiquette to

FEEDING WILDLIFE IS NOT A KINDNESS

Feeding wildlife is prohibited . . . for the well-being of both the animal and people. Some wildlife can transmit disease through fleas and ticks. Animals have a digestive system adapted to a particular diet in their natural environment. Human food can make them sick or worse. Animals that get accustomed to human food may become so dependent on handouts that their brazen behavior will make them a nuisance or even dangerous to hikers and campers. A "fed bear" from trash or provisions left by neglectful hikers and campers is destined to be a dead bear. Problem wildlife, whether it's a bear, coyote, deer, or squirrel, doesn't get rehabilitated or relocated. Even the most harmless roadside beggar eventually becomes roadkill.

Hermit crabs feeding in a tidepool

Be cautious while tidepooling.

minimize disturbance to these delicate marine residents in their home. Observe and explore mostly with your eyes. Be a considerate guest and gentle giant as you watch where you step and tread along the rocks.

There are forests on land and in the ocean. Northern California's kelp (a brown seaweed or algae) forests are anchored to the shallower ocean floor. Kelp consist of long (up to almost 300 feet) stems with flat leaflike blades with small gas-filled balls that serve as floatation bladders to keep the leaves near the surface. Kelp forests are marine habitats and food sources. Kelp is high in nutrients and harvested for human

WHO'S WHO

It is often difficult to tell one species of seal from another or even a seal from a sea otter when you're standing on the shore looking at the rocks or in the surf.

- Harbor seals are the pudgy ones with small flippers. They waddle on their bellies and scoot on land. They have a grayish to charcoal spotted coat and have flapless ears. Harbor seals often interrupt their offshore rock lounging to frolic around kayakers and divers. In the spring they give birth to a single pup on protected beaches.

- California sea lions are larger and are playful, nimble swimmers that like to huddle up against one another. Even if you can't see them, their loud barking lets you know they are under a pier or out on a jetty or rock outcrop in the area. They have a dark brown coat and visible earflaps. Sea lions use their flippers like feet to move on land. They hunt and hang out along the Northern California coast, but breed farther south.

- Elephant seals, named for the male's elephant-like nose, are exceptional divers and can feed on fish and squid offshore as deep as 1,800 feet. They migrate to islands and some beaches to rest, breed, and pup. The beaches in Ano Nuevo State Reserve in Santa Cruz County are a famous and important breeding/pupping ground. The males engage in fierce battles to protect territory and a harem of females during breeding season.

- Sea otters have cute, puppylike faces that you'll see poking out of the water and kelp beds while they're lounging on their backs. They use their small flippers like tools, tapping hard-shelled catches with small rocks to get at the meat. Females give birth to one pup between January and March.

The United States banned the hunting of marine mammals in 1972, which has helped the recovery of species that had almost been hunted to extinction for their blubber or fur. Federal law stipulates that humans stay at least 150 feet away to avoid stressing them and threatening their survival. BLM ranger and California Coastal National Monument manager Dave Ledig loves that Northern California offers so many opportunities to view and appreciate the coast and its marine and bird residents, but reminds visitors, "You are in their home. Be good guests. Back off and give them space."

Golden poppies are common along coastal trails.

Deer travel coastal trails too.

Towering redwoods

consumption. Different types of kelp have long been staples in Asian cuisine.

The coastal forests are shaped by redwood, Douglas fir, tan oak, and cypress trees with transition zones to maritime chaparral (manzanita and native ceanothus, among other shrubs), coastal grasslands, and scrub (bush lupine and coffeeberry, among others). The slope of the land, moisture (fog and rainfall), sun, and shade play a vital role in the health and diversity of life in the forests.

The North Coast is lush and Mother Nature does not discriminate, so expect to enjoy groves of giant redwood trees (California's state tree) as well as wildflower meadows showered in golden poppies (California's state flower), yellow mustard, and sweet honeysuckle. Canyons are draped in cascades of delicate ferns, and woodlands pop with pink azalea blossoms. California blackberry tangles are common, and poison oak's shiny green or red three-leaf stems happily mimic vines and bushes. Wear long pants and sleeves if you are sensitive to itchy skin breakouts from the plant's oil.

Ticks are an inevitable nuisance in the forest and grasses of the coastal plains, so check your skin along the hike. Strip and wash your clothes at the end of day to safeguard against both clingy ticks and poison oak residue. Bathe your dog, as the poison oak residue on his coat can rub off on you and whatever fabric he comes in contact with in the car and at home.

The coastal forests, woodlands, and prairies support deer, elk, bobcat, coyote, and other mammals. Larger predators include mountain lions and bears, both of which prefer avoidance rather than contact with humans. As far as human encounters, stay on designated developed trails and respect "private property" signs.

TO BRING OR NOT TO BRING YOUR FOUR-LEGGED PAL

As dog lovers, we have shared most of our lives and the majority of our road and trail adventures with a dog, including Gem, our new four-legged furry family member. We take her wherever she is welcome and hate to leave home without her. She enriches every aspect of our lives because she is 100 percent integrated into our lifestyle. Our pack represents a growing demographic of the North American population, who feel dogs have earned their status as family members.

Well-behaved and well-adjusted dogs are wonderful traveling companions. Good training starts at home, complemented by obedience and good manner classes. But it's also important to be exposed to the bigger world outside of home and back-yard to practice and reinforce these new skills and good behaviors. Expanding your

Many coastal trails welcome well-behaved dogs on leash.

Leave no trace and pack out your dog's waste.

dog's world and experiences is the added ingredient to help him or her develop into a well-adjusted dog and family member. "New" and "different" in safe environments is stimulating and necessary for a happier dog. Taking your dog along on your adventures is also an opportunity for additional quality bonding time. Even playing favorite games in new places makes everything old new again.

Having said that, it's important to consider a few things like your dog's age and fitness when deciding whether Fido would be happier on the trail or at home. Is your dog current on his vaccinations as well as tick, flea, and heartworm preventative medications or treatment? Does your dog have good trail manners? If your dog is a healthy, well-socialized hiking partner, make sure you choose a trail that is designated "dog friendly" and an appropriate length for his level of fitness. Read the description to make sure the trail has enough shade to keep your dog comfortable. Is there an accessible body of water (stream, creek, lagoon, ocean) for cooling off? Some trails are very exposed and dry and would be inappropriate for dogs that overheat more easily, especially dogs with thick or dark coats.

There are several dog friendly trails and beaches in this book, but unfortunately and arguably for valid reasons, state parks and national parks in particular do not have an open-arm policy toward canine visitors. Wildlife breeding, nesting, and pupping seasons pose additional problems for recreation management and protection of the species. Leaving your dog in the car, even in what you think are safe, shady, ventilated conditions, while you hike should never be an option. Also be aware that if you plan on camping, some campgrounds have breed and size exceptions. Study the trail descriptions carefully for canine compatibility. Take the time to call ahead for complete information about rules and seasonal restrictions. Policies change and vary on public lands as well as private property. Plan and pack accordingly for a tail-wagging time.

Five Fido must-haves for the trail:

1. Collar or preferably a harness with identification tag (name, phone number, and address) and leash
2. Proof of current vaccinations, including rabies certificate
3. Drinking water (8 ounces per hour or 2 miles of trail)
4. Energy-boosting treats and snacks
5. Biodegradable dog-waste bags so pooch only leaves paw prints behind

GEARING UP FOR COMFORT AND SAFETY

One of the most variable factors when visiting the North Coast is weather. Proper clothing can make all the difference between an enjoyable day and a miserable day out on the coastal trails. It is not uncommon to experience fog, cold, wind, sun, and heat within an hour. Layers are the key, and never leave home without a windbreaker, hat, and sunblock and sandals for streams and surf. During the winter months, pack your rain gear and wear waterproof hiking boots.

Proper clothing keeps you comfortable even in blustery coastal winds.

Abide by posted warnings.

If you take Bowser along, remember you are solely responsible for your dog's safety and well-being on the trail, as well as his behavior in every situation along the way. Leash your dog even in off-leash areas if you are not 100 percent confident that you have him under voice control. Chasing wildlife, which need their energy for survival, is not a game. Running amok in areas designated for protecting endangered animal and plant species is not cool. Abide by the regulations posted during critical seasons. Carry proof of vaccinations and rabies innoculations in your pack. Don't litter wildlife's home. Carry out your dog's waste in biodegradable bags.

Contact the managing agency for a current status of the trail you plan to hike, both trail condition and dog policy. Make sure your cellphone, camera, and GPS batteries are charged. Stock your daypack with plenty of water, snacks, and a first-aid kit (see Appendix A).

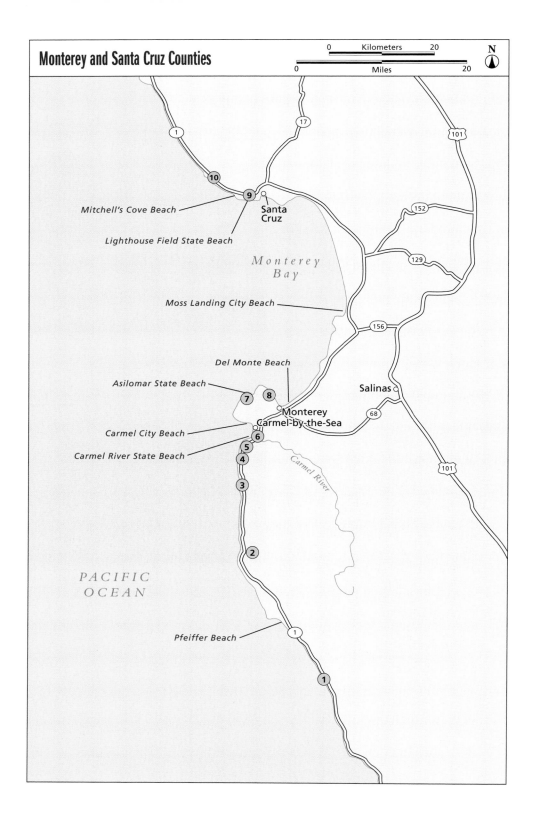

Monterey and Santa Cruz Counties

0 Kilometers 20

0 Miles 20

N

Mitchell's Cove Beach

Santa Cruz

Lighthouse Field State Beach

Monterey Bay

Moss Landing City Beach

Del Monte Beach

Asilomar State Beach

Salinas

Monterey
Carmel-by-the-Sea

Carmel City Beach

Carmel River State Beach

Carmel River

PACIFIC OCEAN

Pfeiffer Beach

MONTEREY COUNTY

Although "Salad Bowl of the World," Steinbeck classics, Cannery Row, and fresh artichokes often come to mind when talking about **MONTEREY COUNTY**, it's Big Sur and the 17-mile drive through exclusive Pebble Beach that conjure up visions of panoramic ocean views along a highway that traces the base of redwood canyons where the mountains meet the sea on the edge of precipitous rocky cliffs. Because of the steepness of the terrain, CA 1 has been chiseled to cling to the face of the cliffs on the Big Sur coast at the southern end of Monterey County. Little land is safe from the sea's erosion assault in these parts, and coastal trails are only possible if they thread the ridges on the east side of CA 1.

Farther north, between Carmel and Marina, a gentler topography and higher population have helped develop a more extensive network of coastal trails consisting of nearly 30 miles of paved multiuse pathways. Thanks to the establishment of the Monterey Bay National Marine Sanctuary—the largest marine sanctuary in the country, established in 1992 to protect almost 300 miles of shoreline (San Luis Obispo County north to Marin County) and over 6,000 square miles of ocean embracing the Monterey Bay—no oil rig will ever blemish the pristine views on coastal trails along this stretch of coastline. The National Oceanic and Atmospheric Administration (NOAA) manages the country's thirteen national marine sanctuaries, four of which are in California.

1. MCWAY FALLS

WHY GO?

Only one word describes this short hike—surreal! You won't believe how easy it is to walk to the only major waterfall in California that plunges into the Pacific Ocean.

THE RUNDOWN

Distance: 0.6 mile out and back

Start: McWay Falls trail sign at stairs just past pay station across from restrooms

Nearest town: Carmel

Hiking time: About 30 minutes

Fees and permits: Parking fee; experienced scuba divers can obtain special permits to explore the underwater reserve.

Conveniences: Restroom with flush toilets, trash and recycling containers, and picnic tables

Beach access: No

Trail users: Hikers only

Trailhead elevation: 243 feet

Highest point: 243 feet

Trail surface: Dirt

Difficulty: Easy

Seasonal highlights: The waterfall is at its most voluminous after the winter and spring wet season. Condors have been known to peek down from the eucalyptus trees at the overlook.

Managing agency: California State Parks, parks.ca.gov; Julia Pfeiffer Burns State Park, Big Sur 93920, (831) 667-2315

FINDING THE TRAILHEAD

From Carmel at CA 1 and Rio Road, drive 36 miles south to Julia Pfeiffer Burns State Park/McWay Canyon. Turn left into the parking lot. **GPS:** N36 09.58' / W121 40.14'

WHAT TO SEE

McWay Falls 80-foot "tidefall" is the most well-known attraction in Julia Pfeiffer Burns State Park, established in 1962 and named after one of the early pioneers who came to the Big Sur area in the early twentieth century. Before the land originally known as Saddle Rock Ranch became a park, the McWay family homesteaded here in the 1870s. Lathrop Brown, a US representative, bought the ranch in 1924 and built one of the first houses to have electricity in Big Sur. McWay Creek was harnessed to supply the power. Julia Pfeiffer Burns was a close friend of the McWays,

Trail to McWay Falls overlook

and they honored her by naming the land in her memory when it was bequeathed to the State of California in 1961.

The waterfall continues to seduce photographers, artists, and writers with its almost "too beautiful to be real" setting. A fire and landslide in the mid-1980s changed the topography of McWay Cove, creating a visually enticing beach that is inaccessible from above. Now the falls plummet to kiss the ocean only at high tide.

The entrance to the 3,700-plus-acre park is narrow and access is limited. Trailers are not permitted to enter. The trailhead is accessible from the upper south parking lot and follows a trail under the bridge. The trail to the waterfall overlook is wheelchair accessible.

This hike starts at the trailhead closest to the park entrance across from the restrooms. Walk down a few steps, turn right, and walk through the tunnel under CA 1 and follow the level trail bearing right. If you go left, it takes you to the two environmental campsites.

The views immediately open to a turquoise cove beneath the precipitous granite cliffs. The cove is hugged by rocky monuments and highlighted by cypress trees

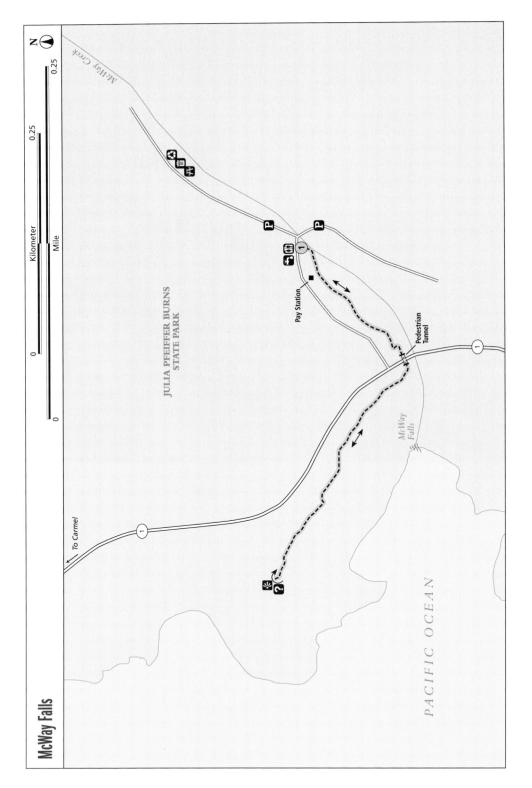

McWay Falls

JULIA PFEIFFER BURNS
STATE PARK

To Carmel

McWay Creek

Pay Station

Pedestrian
Tunnel

McWay
Falls

PACIFIC OCEAN

N

Kilometer

Mile

0   0.25
0   0.25

McWay Falls plunges into the Pacific.

and a single majestic palm tree. It's easy to understand why this park also protects a 1,600-acre underwater reserve. The path is braced by wooden fence rails and leads to a viewpoint. The waterfall draws you in every step of the way, offering serial photographic vantage points, each frame as surreal as the next. There are many natural wonders in California, and McWay Falls makes the top 10.

Once you've gorged on the scenery, enjoy the park's setting on the banks of McWay Creek with a snack in the picnic area. If waterfalls are your theme, you can walk up Canyon Trail 0.25 mile from the east parking area to a 60-foot waterfall on McWay Creek. Other park trails also boast redwood and tan oak stands between the ocean and the park's 3,000-foot ridges.

MILES AND DIRECTIONS

0.0 Start at the trail sign at the steps across from the restrooms. Turn right through the tunnel under CA 1 and bear right on the trail.

0.3 Arrive at the fenced-in viewpoint. Go back to the trailhead the way you came.

0.6 Arrive back at the trailhead.

BAKERIES, BREWERIES, EATS, AND SLEEPS

Big Sur Bakery, 47540 CA 1, Big Sur 93920; (831) 667-0520; bigsurbakery.com. The bakery/restaurant sits at the south end of the Big Sur community in a cozy historic ranch house. The expensive Morning Glory muffins are well worth the splurge. The bakery is open 7 days a week and serves breakfast, lunch, or brunch. Reservations are recommended for dinner Tues through Sun. House specialties utilize organic fresh ingredients and are wood fired and wood grilled.

Big Sur Tap House, 47520 CA 1, Big Sur 93920; (831) 667-2197; bigsurtap house.com. Rotation of 10 different craft beers; fresh daily tacos and daily pub-fare specials.

Big Sur Deli, 47520 CA 1, Big Sur 93920; (831) 667-2225; bigsurdeli.com.

Nepenthe, 48510 CA 1, Big Sur 93920; (831) 667-2345; nepenthebigsur.com. This is a family-operated Big Sur landmark since 1949. The outrageous views from the deck draw flocks of local and foreign visitors here year-round for lunch and dinner. Except for the undistinguished and expensively disappointing Ambrosia Burger, the menu is very satisfying and the desserts are mouthwatering good.

Deetjen's Big Sur Inn, 48865 CA 1, Big Sur 93920; (831) 667-2378; deetjens .com. A Norwegian immigrant came to Big Sur in the 1930s and the seed was planted for Deetjen's Big Sur Inn. The atmospheric rustic inn is on the National Register of Historic Places. Romantic, cozy guest rooms are a result of Grandpa Deetjen's Norwegian heritage and what is now known as "Big Sur style" architecture. The inn serves breakfast and dinner.

CAMPING

Riverside Campground & Cabins, 22 miles south of Carmel on CA 1, Big Sur 93920; (831) 667-2414; riversidecampground.com. Tent and RV sites as well as cabins; all are dog friendly.

Pfeiffer Big Sur State Park, 26 miles south of Carmel on CA 1, Big Sur 93920; parks.ca.gov. Tent and RV sites as well as lodge rooms and cottages, with a cafe and grocery store; dog friendly.

Julia Pfeiffer Burns State Park Walk-In Environmental Campground, 36 miles south of Carmel on CA 1, Big Sur 93920; (831) 667-2315.

2. BRAZIL RANCH

WHY GO?

This is the most readily accessed coastal trail in Los Padres National Forest. The climb to the ridge is a cardio workout. Hikers are rewarded with spectacular views of the coastline, with Pico Blanco lording over the undulating hills to the east.

THE RUNDOWN

Distance: 3.9-mile lollipop

Start: Trailhead on east side of road at information panel behind metal gate

Nearest town: Carmel

Hiking time: 2 hours

Fees and permits: None

Conveniences: None

Beach access: No

Trail users: Hikers and dogs under voice control. Dogs should be on leash to pass the cattle on the ridge and avoid potential conflicts that could cause injury to livestock or dog.

Trailhead elevation: 415 feet

Highest point: 1,526 feet

Trail surface: Pavement, dirt, and grass

Difficulty: Strenuous

Seasonal highlights: Wildflowers in the spring; whale watching from late fall to late spring

Managing agency: Los Padres National Forest, Monterey Ranger District, 406 South Mildred, King City 93930; (831) 385-3434; Resource Manager, (831) 667-1126; Big Sur Station, (831) 667-2315

FINDING THE TRAILHEAD

From Carmel at CA 1 and Rio Road, drive 13.5 miles south to the pullout on the west side of the road just past Bixby Bridge. **GPS:** N36 21.80′ / W121 53.99′

WHAT TO SEE

El Sur Grande (The Big South), south of Monterey Peninsula, has always been a rugged and spectacular swath of wilderness described as the "Greatest Meeting of Land and Sea." Ohlone, Esselen, and Salinan Native American tribes were the first to make this coastline a seasonal home. In 1769 a Spanish expedition led by Gaspar de Portolá set foot on the inhospitably steep shores before finally landing in Monterey in 1770. Monterey became the capital of Alta California, and the Spanish

Looking south toward
CA 1 and Point Sur

considered the big country of the south "impenetrable." Mexico's independence from Spain in 1821 turned California into Mexican territory until the Mexican-American War of 1848. The federal Homestead Act of 1862 lured hardy souls to settle in "Big Sur."

Many of the local sites retain the names of the early pioneers who persisted in building a life and making a living on the rugged coast long before the two-lane highway was opened in 1937 and became the first State Scenic Highway in 1965. Gold mining, lumbering, dairy farming, and ranching all have had their day on the Big Sur coast. Artists, writers, movie stars, naturalists, and spiritualists have always been inspired by Big Sur's wild solitary beauty, and many have made it home part of the time alongside the descendants of early pioneer families. The coast has remained mostly unchanged, drawing tourists who enjoy the scenic drive and hikers who travel the trails of Los Padres National Forest and the Ventana Wilderness where streams, hot springs, waterfalls, and redwood sanctuaries rule.

The Brazil Ranch was named after its original owners, the Brazil family. Over the years the property operated as a farm, dairy, and ranch. In 1977 the ranch was sold

Looking north along
the Big Sur coast

to Allen Funt, creator of the *Candid Camera* television show. Following his death, the estate sold the land to a developer in 2000. In 2002 the Trust for Public Lands acquired the 1,255 acres at the northern end of the Big Sur coast, saving it from development and permanently protecting that stretch of California coastline. The land was transferred to Los Padres National Forest, and a hiking trail was opened to the public. Currently a caretaker who was awarded a "stewardship contract" occupies the ranch buildings and is responsible for the care of the land in exchange for permission to graze cattle.

When the Brazil Ranch was first opened to hikers, the trail started on the paved section of the ranch road just off CA 1 for 0.5 mile before turning right on a dirt trail. The hike now follows the paved road for just 0.1 mile before turning right onto a dirt trail that sweeps uphill across the slope for about 0.5 mile. Wooden signs with a white arrow lead hikers left at a trail junction at 0.3 mile and right at 0.6 mile, where it joins the original trail to complete the haul up to the ridge.

Park rangers have come across hikers who have been misled into thinking that Brazil Ranch is part of a connected matrix of trails through Big Sur. Brazil Ranch is

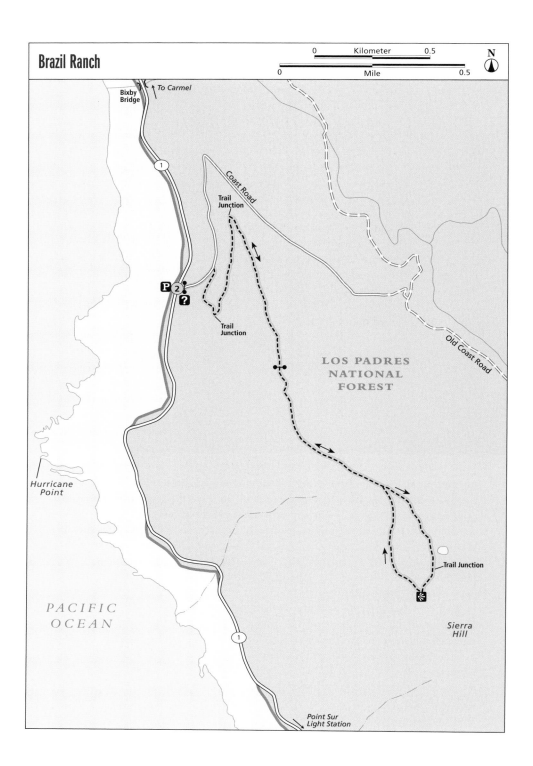

Brazil Ranch

Kilometer
0   0.5
Mile
0   0.5

N

To Carmel

Bixby
Bridge

1

Coast Road

Trail
Junction

P 2

?

Trail
Junction

LOS PADRES
NATIONAL
FOREST

Old Coast Road

Hurricane
Point

PACIFIC
OCEAN

Trail Junction

1

Sierra
Hill

Point Sur
Light Station

an island bordered by private land. This single, albeit spectacular, stitch of trail is not a portal into Los Padres National Forest or the Ventana Wilderness.

At 1.0 mile you come to a cattle gate with a walk-in gate on the right. Make sure you latch the walk-in gate closed behind you. At 1.6 miles you leave the view of the coastline briefly to bear left on the backside of the knoll. The expansive views of the Santa Lucia Range and Pico Blanco to the east are breathtaking. The land undulates and swells in the shadow of the canyon-sliced range. Add a couple of bells to the roaming cattle munching on the spring green, and this could be "Switzerland by the sea."

At 1.8 miles you come to an unmarked trail junction. Bear right and walk uphill. Just a short huff and you're back on the ridge also known as Sierra Hill, overlooking the Pacific and Hurricane Point with Point Sur Light Station to the southwest sitting on the bump of land at the edge of the long curving beach. This is a superb vantage point to appreciate the magnificence of the land and seascape. Bear right along the ridge, following the faded tracks marking an old ranch road until you rejoin the main trail at 2.3 miles. Close the lollipop and continue walking north back to the trailhead the way you came.

MILES AND DIRECTIONS

0.0 Start at the information panel behind the gate on the east side of CA 1.

0.1 Turn right at the trail sign and leave the paved road.

0.3 Come to a T junction and turn left.

0.6 Come to a T junction and turn right.

1.0 Arrive at a cattle gate and walk-in gate on the right.

1.6 Come to a trail junction and bear left to begin the lollipop.

1.8 Come to an unmarked trail junction and walk uphill, staying on the right.

1.9 Arrive on the ridge and bear right.

2.3 Rejoin the main trail and close the lollipop. Continue walking north back to the trailhead the way you came.

3.9 Arrive back at the trailhead.

BAKERIES, BREWERIES, EATS, AND SLEEPS

The Brazil Ranch hike is smack between Carmel and Big Sur, which makes services a "toss-up" and allows hikers to have a foot in the best of both worlds.

BIG SUR

Big Sur Bakery, 47540 CA 1, Big Sur 93920; (831) 667-0520; bigsurbakery.com. The bakery/restaurant sits at the south end of the Big Sur community in a cozy historic ranch house. The expensive Morning Glory muffins are well worth the splurge. The bakery is open 7 days a week and serves breakfast, lunch, or brunch. Reservations are recommended for dinner Tues through Sun. House specialties utilize organic fresh ingredients and are wood fired and wood grilled.

Big Sur Tap House, 47520 CA 1, Big Sur 93920; (831) 667-2197; bigsurtaphouse .com. Rotation of 10 different craft beers; fresh daily tacos and daily pub-fare specials.

Big Sur Deli, 47520 CA 1, Big Sur 93920; (831) 667-2225; bigsurdeli.com.

Nepenthe, 48510 CA 1, Big Sur 93920; (831) 667-2345; nepenthebigsur.com. This is a family-operated Big Sur landmark since 1949. The outrageous views from the deck draw flocks of local and foreign visitors here year-round for lunch and dinner. Except for the undistinguished and expensively disappointing Ambrosia Burger, the menu is very satisfying and the desserts are mouthwatering good.

Deetjen's Big Sur Inn, 48865 CA 1, Big Sur 93920; (831) 667-2378; deetjens .com. A Norwegian immigrant came to Big Sur in the 1930s and the seed was planted for Deetjen's Big Sur Inn. The atmospheric rustic inn is on the National Register of Historic Places. Romantic, cozy guest rooms are a result of Grandpa Deetjen's Norwegian heritage and what is now known as "Big Sur style" architecture. The inn serves breakfast and dinner.

CARMEL

Lafayette Bakery, 3659 The Barnyard, Unit 22, Carmel 93923; lafayettebakery .com. Everything an authentic French bakery should be, with great almond croissants, fondant au chocolat, and mini chocolate éclairs in addition to traditional baguettes. Dogs are welcome on the front patio and back courtyard.

Carmel Valley Coffee Roasting Company at The Crossroads, 246 Crossroads Blvd., Carmel 93923; carmelcoffeeroasters.com. Coffee connoisseurs will appreciate that this local organic coffee company has served handcrafted coffee since 1994.

California Market at the Highlands Inn, 120 Highlands Dr., Carmel 93923; (831) 622-5050. This is a casual, intimate spot for breakfast and lunch in an exclusive setting. The dog friendly outdoor deck perch with ocean views makes every bite taste that much better.

Carmel River Inn, 26600 Oliver Rd., Carmel 93923; (831) 624-1575; carmel riverinn.com. The rustic cottages are set in a private, tranquil setting, and the motel rooms are dog friendly.

CAMPING

Riverside Campground & Cabins, 22 miles south of Carmel on CA 1, Big Sur 93920; (831) 667-2414; riversidecampground.com. Tent and RV sites as well as cabins; all are dog friendly.

Pfeiffer Big Sur State Park, 26 miles south of Carmel on CA 1, Big Sur 93920; (831) 667-2315, (831) 667-3100; parks.ca.gov. Tent and RV sites as well as lodge rooms and cottages, with a cafe and grocery store; dog friendly.

3. SOBERANES POINT

WHY GO?

This scenic hike along the windswept headlands of Garrapata State Park epitomizes the rugged splendor of the California coast. It boasts a picturesque wooden footbridge over a creek, a wildflower bonanza in springtime, and two dramatic viewpoints on twin knolls. Soberanes Point is the portal to the big, beautiful Big Sur coast.

THE RUNDOWN

Distance: 2-mile lollipop

Start: West side of road at top of stairs

Nearest town: Carmel

Hiking time: About 1 hour

Fees and permits: None

Conveniences: None

Beach access: No

Trail users: Hikers only

Trailhead elevation: 92 feet

Highest point: 286 feet

Trail surface: Dirt

Difficulty: Easy

Seasonal highlights: Abundance of wildflowers in the spring; whale watching from late fall to late spring

Managing agency: Garrapata State Park, (831) 624-4909, parks.ca.gov

FINDING THE TRAILHEAD

From Carmel at CA 1 and Rio Road, drive 6.5 miles south on CA 1. Turn into the pullout on the right, and you will see the trailhead and a wooden footbridge on the west side of the road. **GPS:** N36 27.39' / W121 55.45'

WHAT TO SEE

This is a superb coastal sampler. The wooden footbridge above Soberanes Creek sets the tone for a hike on a trail developed to do justice to the panorama. Shortly after setting off from the trailhead, you come to a trail junction. The trail to the right is about 0.2 mile long and leads to a viewpoint. If time permits, you can explore that stitch either at the beginning of your hike or when you return to the trailhead at the end of this hike.

To continue on the hike described here, walk straight past the spur. There is a cypress tunnel through a clearing just ahead. At 0.4 mile you come to a trail

Whale Peak and the rugged Big Sur coast

junction. You will return from the trail on the left to close the lollipop on the way back to the trailhead. Continue walking straight, with the Pacific on your right. The trail narrows as you trace the base of the knoll. You will pass a few narrow, obscure trails heading down on the headlands closer to the bluff's edge. The coast is subject to erosion, so stay on the main trail and respect the signs warning you about the steep cliffs.

At 0.8 mile you come to a fork. Bear right on the trail across a headland meadow exploding with a variety of grasses and coastal chaparral vines. In the spring this meadow is a wild garden of mustard, purple periwinkle, morning glory, poppies, yarrow, sage, and poison oak.

At 1.0 mile the trail winds back to the left around the knoll and parallels CA 1. Just ahead you will come to a trail junction. Turn left and walk uphill to Whale Peak and the T junction with a trail that goes to the unmarked north and the south peaks. Both short trails lead to viewpoints for stunning photos, and each has a wooden bench for lingering and drinking up the views of the powerful surf forever sculpting and reshaping cliffs and shoreline. It can be very windy on the hilltop, but on days

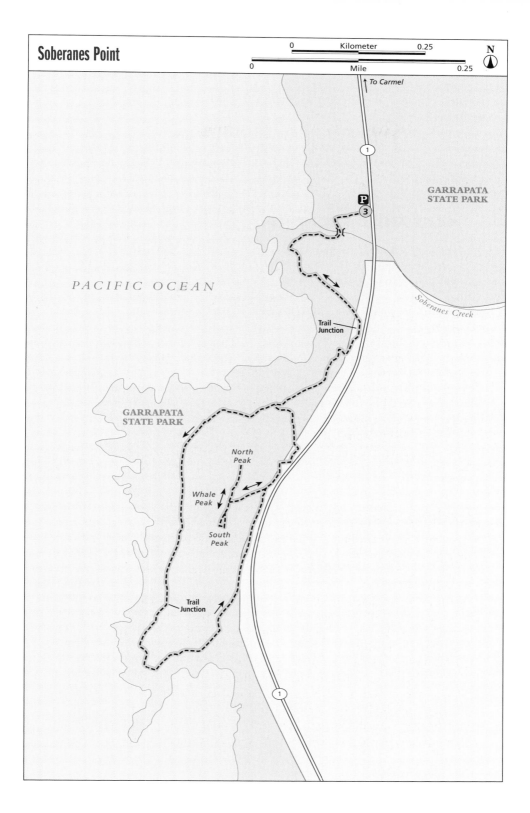

Soberanes Point

0   Kilometer   0.25

0   Mile   0.25

N

↑ *To Carmel*

GARRAPATA
STATE PARK

P
③

PACIFIC OCEAN

Soberanes Creek

Trail
Junction

GARRAPATA
STATE PARK

*North
Peak*

*Whale
Peak*

*South
Peak*

Trail
Junction

when the breeze is dialed down to gentle, either bench makes an ideal spot for a picnic break.

Go back down to the trail junction when you've scanned both viewpoints and bear left with CA 1 on your right. You close the lollipop at the trail junction at 1.6 miles. Turn right and walk 0.4 mile back to the trailhead the way you came. The Pacific is on your left.

MILES AND DIRECTIONS

0.0 Start at the stairs on the west side of the road. Walk past the spur trail on the right and across the wooden footbridge over Soberanes Creek.

0.3 Come to a spur road on the left. Continue walking straight.

0.4 Come to a trail junction. The trail coming in from the left is where you will return to close the lollipop. Continue walking straight.

0.8 Come to a fork. Bear right.

1.2 Come to a T junction and turn left uphill. In about 250 feet, arrive at another T junction and turn left to the viewpoint at unmarked South Whale Peak.

1.3 Arrive at the viewpoint. Go back to the T junction and walk past the junction uphill to the viewpoint on unmarked North Whale Peak.

1.4 Arrive at the viewpoint. Go back to the T junction, walk downhill toward CA 1, and turn left. CA 1 will be on your right. Continue to the trail junction 0.2 mile ahead. Turn right to close the lollipop and return to the trailhead the way you came.

2.0 Arrive back at the trailhead.

BAKERIES, BREWERIES, EATS, AND SLEEPS

On the outskirts of Carmel-by-the-Sea conveniently off CA 1 are two small, singular outdoor shopping malls, The Crossroads and The Barnyard. Both have lively local establishments to fuel up on drinks and food.

Lafayette Bakery, 3659 The Barnyard, Unit 22, Carmel 93923; lafayettebakery .com. Everything an authentic French bakery should be, with great almond croissants, fondant au chocolat, and mini chocolate éclairs in addition to traditional baguettes. Dogs are welcome on the front patio and back courtyard.

Carmel Valley Coffee Roasting Company at The Crossroads, 246 Crossroads Blvd., Carmel 93923; carmelcoffeeroasters.com. Coffee connoisseurs will appreciate that this local organic coffee company has served handcrafted coffee since 1994.

McIntyre Vineyards at The Crossroads, 161 Crossroads Blvd. at CA 1 and Rio Rd., Carmel 93923; (831) 626-6268. Carmel is still more into grapes than hops,

Footbridge across Soberanes Creek

so you are more likely to stumble on a wine barrel than a keg of beer for your post-hike libations. This tasting room is open Tues through Sun.

Island Taco at The Crossroads, 173 Crossroads Blvd. at CA 1 and Rio Rd., Carmel 93923; (831) 624-8454; islandtaco.com. Savor tasty grilled mahi-mahi tacos with a south of the border brew at one of the indoor tables or on the patio with pooch.

Rio Grill Bar and Restaurant at The Crossroads, 101 Crossroads Blvd. at CA 1 and Rio Rd., Carmel 93923; (831) 625-5436; riogrill.com. With its South-western decor and creative menu, this has been a happening place since 1983. Carb addicts come to gorge on the warm, crusty sourdough baguette with a lather of butter. There's nothing pedestrian about the Rio's burger and the Chinese chicken salad, but these two staple entrees are perfect for simpler palates.

Sea Harvest Fish Market and Restaurant at The Crossroads, 100 Cross-roads Blvd. at CA 1 and Rio Rd., Carmel 93923; (831) 626-3636. The decor is simple, and the lunch and dinner menu is loaded with fresh selections. There are a couple of outdoor tables for diners with dogs.

Crab feeding on mussels during low tide

Lugano Swiss Bistro, 3670 The Barnyard, Carmel 93923; (831) 626-3779; swissbistro.com. Lunch and dinner Tues through Sun. The menu and the decor are pure Switzerland. Dogs are welcome on the patio.

Sur at The Barnyard, 3601 The Barnyard, Carmel 93923; (831) 275-2087. This is local restaurateur extraordinaire Billy Quon's latest venture. His fans celebrate his famous ciabatta cheese with corn and jalapeño bread, eclectic California main dishes, and famously decadent Arctic Bon Bon dessert. Dogs are welcome on the patio.

California Market at the Highlands Inn, 120 Highlands Dr., Carmel 93923; (831) 622-5050. This is a casual, intimate spot for breakfast and lunch in an exclusive setting. The dog friendly outdoor deck perch with ocean views makes every bite taste that much better.

Carmel River Inn, 26600 Oliver Rd., Carmel 93923; (831) 624-1575; carmelriverinn.com. The rustic cottages are set in a private, tranquil setting, and the motel rooms are dog friendly.

Carmel Mission Inn, 3665 Rio Rd., Carmel 93923; (831) 624-1841; carmelmissioninn.com. Dog friendly rooms.

4. POINT LOBOS

WHY GO?

From the minute you step onto this coastal trail, you will understand why Point Lobos is considered the "crown jewel" of California's state park system. Every view is a painting, and the landscape is as dynamic as the seascape. The park also boasts the country's first underwater reserve. Add a whaler's cabin built in the 1850s with an adjacent whaling station museum for some fascinating cultural history.

THE RUNDOWN

Distance: 4.9-mile circuit

Start: North Shore Trailhead at far end of Whalers Cove parking lot

Nearest town: Carmel

Hiking time: About 3 hours

Fees and permits: Parking fee (includes a park map). There is no parking fee if you choose to park on CA 1 and walk in.

Conveniences: Two restrooms with flush toilets at the trailhead, drinking fountain, picnic tables, trash and recycling containers, designated bicycle hitching post, boat launch ramp for divers and kayakers, interpretive panels including a 3-D underwater model and map to orient divers, and coordinates for a self-guided cellphone tour (castateparks .toursphere.com)

Beach access: Yes, but can be restricted in the spring during seal pupping season

Trail users: Hikers only. Dogs are not permitted anywhere in the park, including in your parked car.

Trailhead elevation: 11 feet

Highest point: 131 feet

Trail surface: Compacted dirt on the ADA trail segments, sand, shell fragments, rocks, and roots

Difficulty: Moderate

Seasonal highlights: Whale migration from late fall into early spring; seal pupping in the spring

Managing agency: California State Parks, Monterey District, 2211 Garden Rd., Monterey 93940; (831) 649-2836; parks.ca.gov. Point Lobos State Natural Reserve, Riley Ranch Road and CA 1/Cabrillo Highway, Carmel 93923; (831) 624-4909.

FINDING THE TRAILHEAD

 From Carmel at Rio Road and CA 1, drive 2 miles south on CA 1 and turn right into Point Lobos State Natural Reserve to the entrance booth for a map and to pay the parking fee. Follow the signs to Whalers Cove, which

is the first right turn on a paved road past the entrance booth. Drive downhill to the cul-de-sac and parking area. **GPS:** N36 31.24' / W121 56.44'

WHAT TO SEE

This is a magnificent showcase of protected California coastline with views galore. Point Lobos State Natural Reserve is historically significant as well as a pristine oasis of coastal and underwater habitat.

Rumsien native people, Chinese, Japanese, Portuguese, and Europeans all took their share from the area's bounty of land and sea resources. But by 1898 a local resident and visionary named A. M. Allan bought land in Point Lobos along with lots slated for residential development. Thanks to the Allans with the support of local residents and the Save-the-Redwoods League, Point Lobos became part of the state park system in 1933. The reserve was expanded over the years and includes the nation's first underwater reserve, part of the 5.4-square-mile Point Lobos State Marine Reserve since 2007.

This circuit hike traces almost the entire perimeter of the reserve on well-defined paths that are part of the California Coastal Trail, threading loops past a historic whaling cabin, several spectacular overlooks, trailside tidepools, and stairways to secluded sandy beaches lapped by turquoise water. In the spring the scent of blue ceanothus, also known as wild lilac, permeates the breeze. An occasional bench invites hikers to rest and contemplate Mother Nature's masterpiece, and the picnic areas are perfect for lingering and refueling on snacks.

Some of the local wildlife attractions include migrating gray whales between December and May, blue and humpback whales in the summer and fall, and resident sea otters and harbor seals, as well as the California sea lions after which the Spaniards named the area Punta de los Lobos Marinos, or "Point of the Sea Wolves." Black-tailed mule deer are regular grazers in the reserve's meadows.

The hike begins on the North Shore Trail up thirty-four stone steps looping around a promontory with views across Carmel Bay to the white strip of Carmel River State Beach, Carmel-by-the-Sea, and Pebble Beach golf course's green plateau. The North Shore Trail then meanders up seventy-three steps of railroad ties through a stand of Monterey pines. This first mile of trail is at times rugged, navigating knurly roots and uneven humps of rock.

At 0.3 mile you pass the junction for the Cabin Trail on the left and continue straight along the shady corridor, with dancing dappled lighting highlighting the kelp forest rocking in the surf below on your right. Several short spurs to the right along the way lead to overlooks where solitude is only interrupted by the sounds of gulls in the breeze overhead.

At 0.8 mile you come to a trail junction on the left. Continue walking straight through the cypress and pine woodland bordered by tangles of thriving poison oak. Terraced steps lead down to a more level dirt path with an information booth and volunteer docents describing exhibits and answering questions at the edge of the

Overlooking China Cove

park road and parking area. There are three restrooms here with flush toilets and drinking water. Take time to browse the exhibits and/or take advantage of the facilities before bearing right on the trail to the Allan Memorial Grove. This is a lollipop trail that will return to this junction. Visitors with limited time often overlook this amazing 0.5-mile extension around the cypress grove. Hikers are rewarded with unexpected views of rocky fingers of land and weather-sculpted cliffs with tenacious tapered cypress trees clinging to the stony crevices. The scene is wild, primeval, and breathtaking.

At 1.2 miles you walk over roots and rock and up more stone steps to the point where the trail veers left and views open southward ahead toward the Big Sur coast's scalloped signature profile. You close the lollipop at 1.6 miles and bear right through the parking lot to continue on the Sea Lion Point Trail. You leave the forest for a more exposed and tamer landscape as you continue to follow the coastal trail as it meanders southward. During spring pupping season, several of the spur trails to beaches, tidepools, and some viewpoints are closed to protect birthing seals and their vulnerable pups.

At 2.0 miles bear right to continue the hike on the South Shore Trail. Low tide exposes large sloping rock to the tidepools and access to Hidden Beach. Just ahead is the south-end parking lot with restrooms, picnic tables, a bicycle hitching post, and the trailhead for the Bird Island Trail. A gradual, sloping ADA trail on the left joins the main trail at the top of the fifty-one steps you climb to the bluff.

Walk past the access staircase down to China Beach at 3.2 miles and turn right at the trail junction to begin the lollipop on the ADA Bird Island Trail. Walk across the wooden footbridge and bear right to loop counterclockwise. In the spring, brilliant poppies bloom in abundance along this 0.4-mile stretch of path. Back at the junction, walk past Gibson Beach and follow the sign to the entrance along the South Plateau Trail. The trail rises into the forest away from the coast on a carpet of pine needles. You will hear traffic on CA 1 to the right as you walk northward to close your circuit.

At 4.0 miles you come to a trail junction for the Pine Ridge Trail to the left. Continue walking straight and you will come to the park entrance. Cross the road in the crosswalk. The entrance booth is on your right. Continue on the shady Carmelo Meadow Trail and the California Coastal Trail. You will come to a T junction 0.5 mile ahead at Whalers Cove and the Granite Point Trail. If you feel like an extra short jaunt, you can turn right and walk just under 1 mile on the Granite Point Trail and across a meadow to the reserve's northern boundary and fence line just above Monastery Beach before retracing your steps to this junction and walking back to the trailhead.

To complete this hike, however, turn left on the Granite Point Trail and walk past the Whalers Cabin toward the Whalers Cove parking lot and your trailhead. If time permits, take a look around the Whaling Station Museum in the Whalers Cabin. This is the only on-site whaling museum on the West Coast. There are interpretive exhibits with photographs, whaling tools, and equipment as well as whale vertebrae. Turn right at the Whalers Cabin and walk on the paved road down to the trailhead to close your circuit.

MILES AND DIRECTIONS

0.0 Start at the North Shore Trailhead in the Whalers Cove parking lot and turn right at the top of the stone steps.

0.1 Turn left to continue on the North Shore Trail.

0.3 Come to a trail junction for the Cabin Trail on the left. Continue walking straight.

0.4 Come to a trail junction for Whalers Knoll. Continue walking straight.

0.8 Come to a trail junction on the left. Continue walking straight to the next trail junction at the information booth and turn right onto the Cypress Grove Trail to the Allen Memorial Grove. Bear right at the fork to loop counterclockwise.

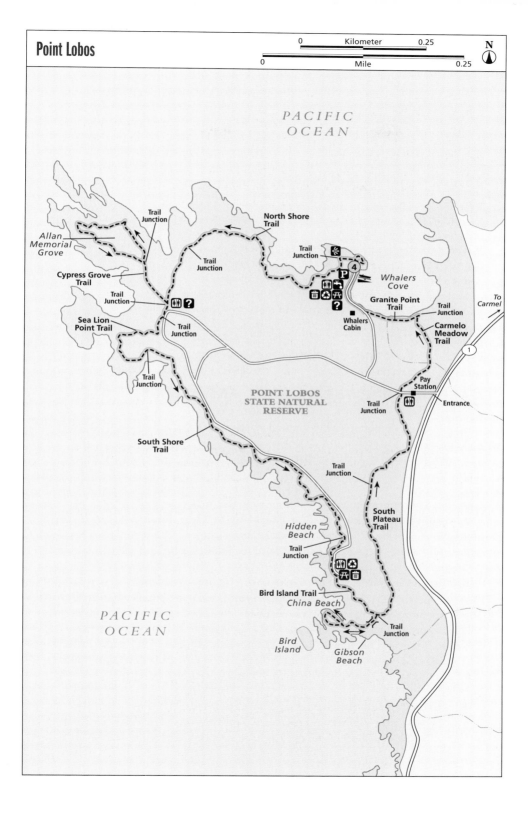

1.6 Close the loop and continue walking toward the information booth junction. Turn right through the parking lot to the Sea Lion Point Trail and bear right on the trail.

2.0 Come to a trail junction and bear right on the South Shore Trail.

2.9 Walk past Hidden Beach to the south parking lot and Bird Island Trail ahead. Walk up fifty-one steps to the bluff on the Bird Island Trail.

3.2 Come to China Beach below the bluff and continue on the trail to a junction. Turn right and walk across the wooden footbridge. Bear right and walk the Bird Island Trail counterclockwise back to the trail junction. Continue walking past Gibson Beach and bear left on the South Plateau Trail to the entrance.

4.0 Come to a trail junction for the Pine Ridge Trail on the left. Continue walking straight on the South Plateau Trail.

4.3 Arrive at the park entrance and a crosswalk. Walk across the road and continue on the Carmelo Meadow Trail.

4.5 Come to a T junction and the Granite Point Trail. Turn left on the Granite Point Trail to the paved road and the Whalers Cabin and Whaling Station Museum. Turn right on the paved road.

4.9 Arrive back at the trailhead.

BAKERIES, BREWERIES, EATS, AND SLEEPS

On the outskirts of Carmel-by-the-Sea conveniently off CA 1 are two small and unique outdoor shopping malls with great places to fuel up on drinks and food. Alas, no breweries in Carmel.

Lafayette Bakery, 3659 The Barnyard, Unit 22, Carmel 93923; lafayettebakery .com. Everything an authentic French bakery should be, with great almond croissants, fondant au chocolat, and mini chocolate éclairs in addition to traditional baguettes. Dogs are welcome on the front patio and back courtyard.

Carmel Valley Coffee Roasting Company at The Crossroads, 246 Crossroads Blvd., Carmel 93923; carmelcoffeeroasters.com. Coffee connoisseurs will appreciate that this local organic coffee company has served handcrafted coffee since 1994.

McIntyre Vineyards at The Crossroads, 161 Crossroads Blvd. at CA 1 and Rio Rd., Carmel 93923; (831) 626-6268. Carmel is still more into grapes than hops, so you are more likely to stumble on a wine barrel than a keg of beer for your post-hike libations. This tasting room is open Tues through Sun.

Island Taco at The Crossroads, 173 Crossroads Blvd. at CA 1 and Rio Rd., Carmel 93923; (831) 624-8454; islandtaco.com. Savor tasty grilled mahimahi tacos with a south of the border brew at one of the indoor tables or on the patio with pooch.

Rio Grill Bar and Restaurant at The Crossroads, 101 Crossroads Blvd. at CA 1 and Rio Rd., Carmel 93923; (831) 625-5436; riogrill.com. With its Southwestern decor and creative menu, this has been a happening place since 1983. Carb

Historic Whalers Cabin above Whalers Cove

addicts come to gorge on the warm, crusty sourdough baguette with a lather of butter. There's nothing pedestrian about the Rio's burger and the Chinese chicken salad, but these two staple entrees are perfect for simpler palates

Sea Harvest Fish Market and Restaurant at The Crossroads, 100 Crossroads Blvd. at CA 1 and Rio Rd., Carmel 93923; (831) 626-3636. The decor is simple and the lunch and dinner menu is loaded with fresh selections. There are a couple of outdoor tables for diners with dogs.

Lugano Swiss Bistro, 3670 The Barnyard, Carmel 93923; (831) 626-3779; swissbistro.com. Lunch and dinner Tues through Sun. The menu and the decor are pure Switzerland. Dogs are welcome on the patio.

Sur at The Barnyard, 3601 The Barnyard, Carmel 93923; (831) 275-2087. This is local restaurateur extraordinaire Billy Quon's latest venture. His fans celebrate his famous ciabatta cheese with corn and jalapeño bread, eclectic California main dishes, and famously decadent Arctic Bon Bon dessert. Dogs are welcome on the patio.

California Market at the Highlands Inn, 120 Highlands Dr., Carmel 93923; (831) 622-5050. This is a casual, intimate spot for breakfast and lunch in an exclusive

Baby otter takes a rest while mom feeds.

setting. The dog friendly outdoor deck perch with ocean views makes every bite taste that much better.

Carmel River Inn, 26600 Oliver Rd., Carmel, CA 93923; (831) 624-1575; carmelriverinn.com. The rustic cottages are set in a private, tranquil setting, and the motel rooms are dog friendly.

Carmel Mission Inn, 3665 Rio Rd., Carmel 93923; (831) 624-1841; carmel missioninn.com. Dog friendly rooms.

5. CARMEL MEADOWS

WHY GO?

This is one of the California coast's premier trails overlooking Carmel Bay, two beaches, the Monterey Bay National Marine Sanctuary, and Point Lobos. Views across the Carmel River lagoon's picturesque wetlands and east up the bucolic hill-cradled Carmel Valley only sweeten the panoramic pot.

THE RUNDOWN

Distance: 2-mile double lollipop

Start: Opening between metal gate and Public Trail sign and arrow

Nearest town: Carmel

Hiking time: About 1 hour

Fees and permits: None

Conveniences: None

Beach access: Yes

Trail users: Hikers, mountain bikers, and dogs on leash on the trail and beach

Trailhead elevation: 43 feet

Highest point: 100 feet

Trail surface: Dirt and sand

Difficulty: Easy

Seasonal highlights: Abundance of wildflowers in the spring; whale watching from late fall to late spring

Managing agency: California State Parks, Monterey District, 2211 Garden Rd., Monterey 93940; (831) 649-2836; parks.ca.gov

FINDING THE TRAILHEAD

 From Carmel at CA 1 and Rio Road, drive 1.2 miles south on CA 1 and turn right (sharp right) into the unmarked Bay School driveway. Park at the end of the paved road by the metal gate at the trailhead above the school parking lot on the left. **GPS:** N36 31.56' / W121 55.39'

WHAT TO SEE

Carmel may be a world-class destination for its vibrant Euro village vibe bloated with gourmet restaurants, art galleries, and exclusive shops, but its inimitable location tucked between the untamed Pacific and swaths of pristine vegetated habitat is what gives it unique appeal to nature lovers.

Just a couple miles south of the tourist mecca, the tone is set for hikers as they park their vehicle across the road from the cloistered Carmelite Monastery at the

Clear winter day at the Carmel River and State Beach

foot of Palo Corona Ranch, now 10,000 acres of protected open space as part of the Monterey Peninsula Regional Park District. The Monterey Bay marine canyon, deeper than the Grand Canyon, dives steeply at the edge of Monastery Beach at the south end of the trail, and the seasonal Carmel River nourishes the lagoon's wetlands reserve as it flows into Carmel Bay across Carmel River State Beach at the north end of the trail. Apart from a couple of quaint vacation cottages perched at the point of the rocky headland on the left and a cluster of mansions peering reverently from the bluff on the right, the panorama is pure Pacific rugged beauty highlighted by Point Lobos State Reserve's cypress and pine promontory to the south.

You begin this hike's double lollipop route shaded by a eucalyptus grove on a narrow dirt trail and walk across a meadow to the left of the metal gate. The sandy trail widens as an access road for park service vehicles as it parallels the coast above the beach, tidepools, and crashing surf. There are no conveniences at the trailhead, but a couple of trash cans can be found along the way to dispose of dog waste and other litter.

At 0.2 mile you pass an uphill spur trail on the right. This is the trail you will return on from the bluff to close the second lollipop. Beginning as early as February, the meadows become a phenomenal blooming garden of flowering ice plants, bouquets of purple wild radish, and streams of yellow mustard dotted with patches of golden poppies. Mother Nature goes wild with her paintbrush, as does the poison oak camouflaged among the California blackberry vines.

An occasional wooden bench invites you to sit and absorb the masterpiece. At 0.4 mile notice the wooden steps climbing up the slope to the bluff and a parking area. These are the steps you will climb on the way back for the second lollipop loop. Continue walking past the steps. The beach is on your left, and the string of mansions is above you on the right. At the fork on the trail just ahead past the houses, bear left and continue walking along the main trail. The trail narrows and curves right as you reach the Carmel River lagoon's wetlands natural reserve and a few wooden steps down to the beach. During the winter rains the Carmel River will breach the sand at this point and flow through the lagoon into the Pacific, making it impassable for hikers to walk beyond this point along the beach, especially at high tide.

At other times of year, when the river's flow is tame to dry, the water is contained in the lagoon and the surrounding wetlands, and hikers can explore the Carmel River State Beach along the lagoon across the beach to the parking lot and restrooms at the north end of the beach on Scenic Avenue. If you are there close to sunset, you will have a front-row view of the daily pageantry of geese flocking to the sanctuary for overnight shelter from inland predators.

To continue the hike, follow the trail as it curves right with the lagoon on the left. The trail rises gently up to the cross on a knoll at 1.0 mile. The cross was erected by the Spanish Crespi-Portolá land expedition of 1769 to signal the supply ship they had been waiting for. The ship, *San Jose*, never arrived, forcing the explorers to return to San Diego. You can easily imagine the landscape as the expedition saw it 250 years ago as you look eastward up the Carmel Valley and southward across the bay to Point Lobos.

Walk downhill 0.1 mile past the cross and the stone plaque commemorating the expedition. At the unmarked trail junction, continue walking straight back along the trail and close the first loop of the lollipops just ahead. The Pacific is on your right, and the bluff homes are on your left. At 1.4 miles turn left and walk up the 110 wooden steps to the bluff. Come to the dead end with a small parking area at the top. Turn right onto the bluff trail. There are a couple of wooden benches on the bluff and some rock outcroppings that make perfect picnic and photo stops.

At 1.7 miles the trail forks at a fence line and a wooden post with a faded arrow pointing left for the trail. You can turn right to a bench and a viewpoint a few yards up the trail before returning to the fork and bearing left for 0.1 mile on the mellow downhill grade back to the main trail to close the second loop of your double lollipop. Turn left at the bottom of the slope and go back to the trailhead the way you came, with the Pacific on your right.

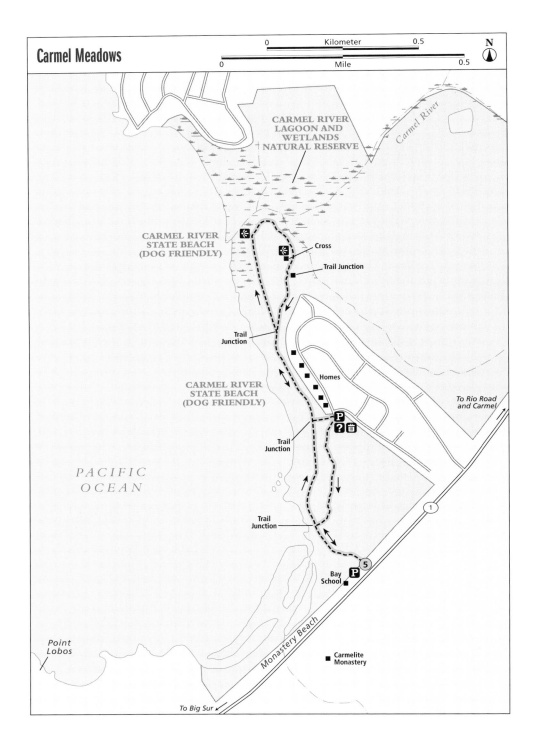

Carmel Meadows

0   Kilometer   0.5

0   Mile   0.5

N

CARMEL RIVER
LAGOON AND
WETLANDS
NATURAL RESERVE

Carmel River

CARMEL RIVER
STATE BEACH
(DOG FRIENDLY)

Cross

Trail Junction

Trail
Junction

CARMEL RIVER
STATE BEACH
(DOG FRIENDLY)

Homes

Trail
Junction

To Rio Road
and Carmel

P
?

PACIFIC
OCEAN

Trail
Junction

1

Trail
Junction

5

Bay
School

P

Point
Lobos

Monastery Beach

Carmelite
Monastery

To Big Sur

MILES AND DIRECTIONS

0.0 Start at the wooden gate and Public Trail sign.

0.2 Come to a spur trail on the right. This is one of the lollipop return loops. Continue walking straight.

0.4 Come to wooden steps going uphill on the right. You will go up these steps to the bluff on the return. Continue walking past the steps.

0.6 Come to a fork and bear left on the trail. This is the start of your lollipops.

0.8 Arrive at a viewpoint overlooking the dog friendly (on leash) Carmel River State Beach and lagoon. Follow the trail to the right. The lagoon is on your left.

1.0 Come to a cross on the knoll and walk downhill.

1.1 Come to an unmarked trail junction and continue walking straight. You will close one of the two lollipops and continue walking with the Pacific on your right until you come to the wooden steps on your left. Turn left up the 110 wooden steps to the bluff.

1.5 Turn right on the bluff and continue walking along the bluff with the Pacific below on your right. The trail will descend gently and rejoin the main trail 0.3 mile ahead to close the second loop of your double lollipops. Turn left at the bottom and go back to the trailhead the way you came.

2.0 Arrive back at the trailhead.

BAKERIES, BREWERIES, EATS, AND SLEEPS

On the outskirts of Carmel-by-the-Sea conveniently off CA 1 are two small, singular outdoor shopping malls, The Crossroads and The Barnyard. Both have lively local establishments to fuel up on drinks and food.

Lafayette Bakery, 3659 The Barnyard, Unit 22, Carmel 93923; lafayettebakery .com. Everything an authentic French bakery should be, with great almond croissants, fondant au chocolat, and mini chocolate éclairs in addition to traditional baguettes. Dogs are welcome on the front patio and back courtyard.

Carmel Valley Coffee Roasting Company at The Crossroads, 246 Crossroads Blvd., Carmel 93923; carmelcoffeeroasters.com. Coffee connoisseurs will appreciate that this local organic coffee company has served handcrafted coffee since 1994.

McIntyre Vineyards at The Crossroads, 161 Crossroads Blvd. at CA 1 and Rio Rd., Carmel 93923; (831) 626-6268. Carmel is still more into grapes than hops, so you are more likely to stumble on a wine barrel than a keg of beer for your post-hike libations. This tasting room is open Tues through Sun.

Island Taco at The Crossroads, 173 Crossroads Blvd. at CA 1 and Rio Rd., Carmel 93923; (831) 624-8454; islandtaco.com. Savor tasty grilled mahimahi tacos with a south of the border brew at one of the indoor tables or on the patio with pooch.

Rio Grill Bar and Restaurant at The Crossroads, 101 Crossroads Blvd. at CA 1 and Rio Rd., Carmel 93923; (831) 625-5436; riogrill.com. With its Southwestern decor and creative menu, this has been a happening place since 1983. Carb addicts come to gorge on the warm, crusty sourdough baguette with a lather of butter. There's nothing pedestrian about the Rio's burger and the Chinese chicken salad, but these two staple entrees are perfect for simpler palates

Sea Harvest Fish Market and Restaurant at The Crossroads, 100 Crossroads Blvd. at CA 1 and Rio Rd., Carmel 93923; (831) 626-3636. The decor is simple, and the lunch and dinner menu is loaded with fresh selections. There are a couple of outdoor tables for diners with dogs.

Lugano Swiss Bistro, 3670 The Barnyard, Carmel 93923; (831) 626-3779; swissbistro.com. Lunch and dinner Tues through Sun. The menu and the decor are pure Switzerland. Dogs are welcome on the patio.

Sur at The Barnyard, 3601 The Barnyard, Carmel 93923; (831) 275-2087. This is local restaurateur extraordinaire Billy Quon's latest venture. His fans celebrate his famous ciabatta cheese with corn and jalapeño bread, eclectic California main dishes, and famously decadent Arctic Bon Bon dessert. Dogs are welcome on the patio.

California Market at the Highlands Inn, 120 Highlands Dr., Carmel 93923; (831) 622-5050. This is a casual, intimate spot for breakfast and lunch in an exclusive setting. The dog friendly outdoor deck perch with ocean views makes every bite taste that much better.

Carmel River Inn, 26600 Oliver Rd., Carmel 93923; (831) 624-1575; carmel riverinn.com. The rustic cottages are set in a private, tranquil setting, and the motel rooms are dog friendly.

Carmel Mission Inn, 3665 Rio Rd., Carmel 93923; (831) 624-1841; carmel missioninn.com. Dog friendly rooms.

Walking south along Carmel River State Beach

6. CARMEL BEACH BLUFF

WHY GO?

This stretch of the California Coastal Trail along Carmel's Scenic Road overlooks Northern California's best dog friendly beach. This is the longest uninterrupted, dedicated stitch of the California Coastal Trail within Carmel-by-the-Sea's 1-square-mile city limits. The panoramic views sweep between two of the most iconic landmarks on the coast. Pebble Beach golf course dominates the canvas to the north, while your eyes rest on the only oceanfront house ever designed by Frank Lloyd Wright as you scan down the southern end of the beach.

THE RUNDOWN

Distance: 2.0 miles out and back

Start: Carmel Beach at bottom of Ocean Avenue

Nearest town: Carmel

Hiking time: About 1 hour

Fees and permits: None

Conveniences: Flush toilets, drinking fountain, trash and recycling containers, and dog waste bag dispenser at trailhead

Beach access: Yes; dogs under voice control

Trail users: Hikers and dogs on leash

Trailhead elevation: 54 feet

Highest point: 54 feet

Trail surface: Sand and dirt

Difficulty: Easy

Seasonal highlights: Whales migrating in the spring and fall

Managing agency: City of Carmel, Monte Verde Street between Ocean Avenue and 7th Avenue, Carmel-by-the-Sea; (831) 620-3000; ci.carmel.ca.us

FINDING THE TRAILHEAD

From Carmel at CA 1 and Ocean Avenue, drive west downhill 1 mile to the Carmel Beach parking area at the bottom of Ocean Avenue. **GPS:** N36 33.31' / W121 55.78'

WHAT TO SEE

The California Coastal Trail (CCT) has two segments developed as dedicated footpaths in Carmel, offering three options to walk the coast in Carmel-by-the-Sea. The northern stitch parallels San Antonio Avenue from the Carmel Gate at Pebble Beach

World-famous Pebble Beach golf course in the distance

to Ocean Avenue. Starting a hike from this point requires finding street parking in the residential neighborhoods. Parking in Carmel can be challenging to scarce during the holidays and on weekends, not to mention often limited to 90 minutes. The dedicated off-street footpath ends at the corner of San Antonio Avenue and Ocean Avenue, where hikers must transition to the sidewalk downhill on Ocean Avenue and turn south on Scenic Road. There is no sidewalk on Scenic Road, and you must walk 0.2 mile on the street until you connect to the coastal path at the foot of 8th Avenue.

Option number two is to connect to the Ocean Avenue sidewalk from the Carmel Gate at Pebble Beach on San Antonio Avenue and continue walking down to Carmel Beach. Walk south 0.2 mile on the beach rather than on the street to join the CCT segment at the foot of 8th Avenue.

The third option, described in this hike, avoids the parking dilemma and begins from the official and unlimited beach parking area (between 6 a.m. and midnight) at the bottom of Ocean Avenue. You walk south 0.2 mile on the beach above the high-tide mark to a discreet set of terraced stone steps on the left that lead you from

Sunset over Carmel Beach

the beach up to the coastal path at the foot of 8th Avenue on Scenic Road. This bluff path between 8th Avenue and Santa Lucia Avenue is sprinkled with benches, trash and recycling containers, and beach-access stairways as well as dog waste bag dispensers. This is the longest uninterrupted stretch of the CCT in Carmel-by-the-Sea. Some of the terraced beach-access stone stairways also have faucets to offer dogs drinking water partway down to the beach.

At 0.8 mile the restroom known as the "million dollar bathroom" was so successfully designed to fit into the organic forms of the hillside, you might walk right past it on the right at the bottom of Santa Lucia Avenue.

The breaking surf, cliff-top green golf fairways, and off-leash dogs gallivanting across the white sand is a pleasing spectacle as you fill your lungs with kelp-scented ocean air, whiffs of fragrant cypress trees, and garden blossoms. But the homes along Scenic Road are a special treat for hikers with an appreciation for architecture. From the original single-story historic Carmel charmers to contemporaries with Tuscan flair, your eyes will dance around the courtyards, decks, and turrets flaunting sculpted stone and glass facades

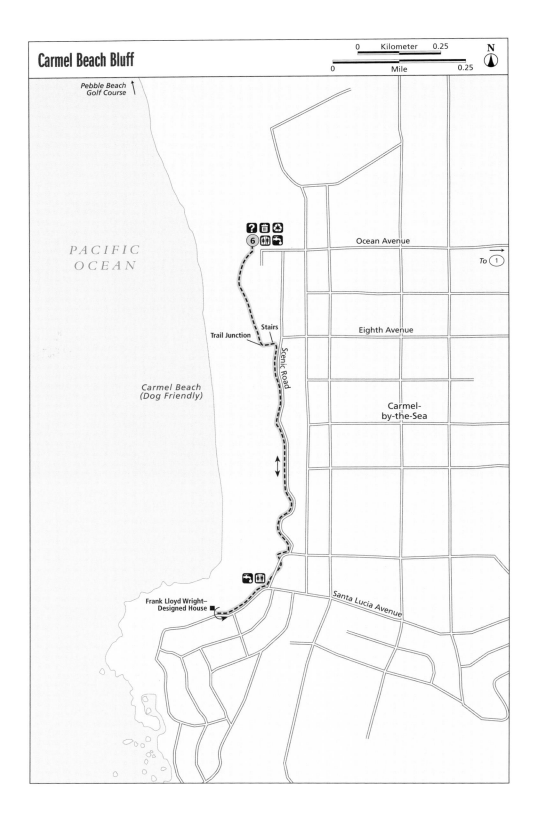

Carmel Beach Bluff

Pebble Beach
Golf Course

*PACIFIC
OCEAN*

*Carmel Beach
(Dog Friendly)*

Ocean Avenue

To (1)

Eighth Avenue

Trail Junction

Stairs

Scenic Road

Carmel-
by-the-Sea

Santa Lucia Avenue

Frank Lloyd Wright–
Designed House

The path ends at the southernmost wooden stairway at 1.0 mile just before the famous Frank Lloyd Wright–designed oceanfront house built in 1948 above the rocky cove that marks the south end of Carmel Beach. In the winter, Pacific storms bring higher tides and voluptuous swells that erode the sand and strip the beach, exposing large sandstone slabs. Some of the southern stairway (wood and stone) accesses to the beach can be closed.

Go back to the trailhead the way you came, or if tides permit, you can return to the trailhead on the beach for part or the entire length of the route. If you are journeying with a well-mannered four-legged furry family member, Carmel Beach is a perfect place for him or her to romp and make new pals.

MILES AND DIRECTIONS

0.0 Start on dog friendly (voice control) Carmel Beach at the bottom of Ocean Avenue and walk south.

0.2 Turn left and up the terraced stone steps to the coastal path and continue walking south.

0.8 Come to the restroom and drinking fountain on the right side of the path.

1.0 Come to the end of the path. Turn around and go back to the trailhead the way you came, or along the beach if tide permits.

2.0 Arrive back at the trailhead.

BAKERIES, BREWERIES, EATS, AND SLEEPS

Carmel Bakery, Ocean Ave. and Lincoln St., Carmel-by-the-Sea 93923; (831) 626-8885. The bakery has been in business since 1906, and their cookies are proof that practice makes perfect.

Patisserie Boissiere and Restaurant, Mission St. and Ocean Ave., Carmel-by-the-Sea 93923; (831) 624-5008. The old-world charm and flavors of this French establishment have been favorites of Carmelites for over 50 years.

400 Degrees, Mission St. and 7th Ave., Carmel-by-the-Sea 93923; (831) 244-0040; 400degrees.com. Top your hike or beach jaunt with a gourmet burger, fries, and a milk shake or craft beer at this casual contemporary eatery. Dogs are welcome on the heated patio.

Tuck Box, Dolores St. and 7th Ave., Carmel-by-the-Sea 93923; (831) 624-6365; tuckbox.com. It's a tiny tearoom with English charm wrapped in famous, historic Comstock "Carmel Charmer" architecture. The scones and preserves are divine. Pooches are welcome on the patio.

Dametra Cafe, Ocean Ave. at Lincoln St., Carmel-by-the-Sea 93921; (831) 622-7766. This cafe is everything Mediterranean, from the food and ambience to the welcoming hosts and impromptu entertainment.

La Bicyclette, 29 Dolores St., Carmel-by-the-Sea 93923; (831) 622-9899; la bicycletterestaurant.com. It's a bustling, cozy Euro bistro.

Terry's Restaurant at the Cypress Inn, Lincoln St. and 7th Ave., Carmel-by-the-Sea 93921; (831) 624-3871; carmelterrys.com. Dine with dogs in the lobby bar and on the patio.

Lula's Chocolates, Court of the Fountains on Mission St. at 7th Ave., Carmel-by-the-Sea 93923; (831) 624-5852; lulas.com. A tradition of family recipes for premium chocolate confections and a quality sugar boost for the trail.

Cypress Inn, Lincoln St. and 7th Ave., Carmel-by-the-Sea 93921; (831) 624-3871. Canine guests are VIPs (very important pooches) at this Doris Day establishment.

Pine Inn, Ocean Ave. between Lincoln St. and Monte Verde St., Carmel-by-the-Sea 93921; (831) 624-3851; pineinn.com. Carmel's historic hotel was the town's first inn. Built in 1889, the red velvet furniture in the foyer reflects the period elegance.

La Playa Hotel, Camino Real St. and 8th Ave., Carmel-by-the-Sea 93923; (800) 582-8900; laplayahotel.com. This Mediterranean mansion–style hotel is one of Carmel's prized landmarks. Built in 1905, it is a member of the Historic Hotels of America.

Happy Landing Inn, 3 Monte Verde St., Carmel-by-the-Sea 93923; (831) 624-7917; happylandinginn.com. This 7-room, cottage-style bed-and-breakfast inn is arguably the most romantic hideaway in downtown Carmel-by-the-Sea, and it welcomes your four-legged furry family member.

7. ASILOMAR TO BIRD ROCK

WHY GO?

This is a superb stretch of scenic coastline on a flat, sandy trail anchored by a unique state park facility and a world-class resort destination and private residential community.

THE RUNDOWN

Distance: 6.2 miles out and back

Start: Boardwalk at west end of grassy oval on Asilomar State Beach Conference Grounds, just beyond outdoor fire pit and picnic tables

Nearest town: Pacific Grove

Hiking time: About 3 hours

Fees and permits: None

Conveniences: Picnic tables, volleyball court, swimming pool, and bicycle rack and rentals. Restrooms, gift shop, and cafe inside main building. Crocker Dining Hall serves breakfast and dinner. Outdoor deck has tables and chairs and recycling and trash containers.

Beach access: Yes; dogs allowed on the beach on leash

Trail users: Hikers and dogs on leash. Dogs also allowed on the conference grounds, but not in the buildings and guest rooms.

Trailhead elevation: 36 feet

Highest point: 36 feet

Trail surface: Boardwalk, compacted dirt, and loose sand

Difficulty: Moderate because of distance but otherwise flat

Seasonal highlights: Whale migration from late fall into early spring

Managing agency: Asilomar State Beach and Conference Grounds, (831) 372-8016, www.visitasilomar.com; schedule of park-led tours, (831) 646-6443

FINDING THE TRAILHEAD

 From Monterey on CA 1, take exit 401A and follow the signs to Fisherman's Wharf. Drive 0.5 mile from the freeway exit and turn right on Camino El Estero. Drive 0.4 mile on Camino El Estero to Del Monte Avenue and turn left. Drive 1.6 miles on Del Monte Avenue to David Avenue; Del Monte Avenue becomes Lighthouse Avenue after the tunnel. Turn left on David Avenue uphill and immediately right at the traffic signal to continue on Lighthouse Avenue, which leaves the city of Monterey to enter Pacific Grove. Drive 1.8 miles on Lighthouse Avenue through downtown Pacific Grove and turn left on Asilomar Avenue. Drive 0.8 mile on Asilomar Avenue to the entrance to Asilomar State Beach and Conference Grounds on the right. There are several parking lots.

Drive to parking lot A for the most convenient access to the trailhead. **GPS:** N36 37.15' / W121 56.34'

WHAT TO SEE

Asilomar, true to its Spanish name, is a unique "refuge by the sea" and the Monterey Peninsula's best-kept secret. Asilomar State Beach and Conference Grounds became part of the California state park system in 1956. The ambiguous nature of this park's name is a matter of historical roots. In 1912 the YWCA (Young Women's Christian Association) was given an opportunity to establish a West Coast camp. The Pacific Improvement Company agreed to lease and subsequently deed 30 acres of ocean-front land to the YWCA as long as they made $35,000 worth of improvements to the property within 10 years and paid the annual $1-per-acre taxes.

Fortunately the YWCA West Coast branch had a "fairy godmother" named Phoebe Hearst, who was connected to San Francisco Bay's entourage of influential women. Within a few months, the real estate dream was a deal. Bay Area architect Julia Morgan, best known for the almost thirty-year Hearst Castle project, came on board to design what would become the first conference center owned by a women's organization in the United States. Morgan's Arts and Craft–style architecture highlighted by redwood, local stone, and glass is the foundation for the complex's harmony with the park's 107 acres of Monterey pines and restored dunes facing an ethereal stretch of pristine California coastline.

The YWCA was at the forefront of fighting for and promoting women's issues. Annual camp meetings on the Central Coast to provide "wholesome recreation and social enjoyment" for girls was a natural extension of the organization's mission. The camp's operating costs were covered by room-and-board charges and fees collected from groups utilizing the grounds. But the project's construction coffers relied on wealthy philanthropists as well as small donations from female supporters. Unfortunately generous benefactors became much scarcer during the Great Depression of the 1930s, and the YWCA National Board decided to put Asilomar on the market. For the next 20 years Asilomar's future bobbed along, floating on the visions of tenants and potential buyers while Friends of Asilomar volunteers kept it going.

By the early 1950s the YWCA was considering two deals, either of which could change Asilomar's destiny permanently. Word of the deals spurred a group of concerned Pacific Grove citizens to form the Save Asilomar committee and lobby the state to buy the property. Fortuitously the wind of coastal land protection was beginning to blow along California, and in 1952 California State Parks expressed interest in acquiring the conference grounds and neighboring dunes. Four years later the conference grounds officially became part of Asilomar State Beach Park.

Since then hospitality industry concessionaires have partnered with the state park to enhance this National Historic Landmark gem with expansions and renovations. Among the projects and upgrades initiated under Aramark's management banner since 2009, the 312 guest rooms have been refreshed with new carpeting, beds, and

Walking along south end of
Asilomar State Beach

linens. New construction and remodeling around the property has also included improved accessibility per the ADA (Americans with Disabilities Act).

The lofty Crocker Hall's cafeteria-style dining room features three-course seasonal menus focused on sustainability at breakfast, lunch, and dinner, while Phoebe's deck-front cafe is perfect for a light bite alongside a robust hot cup of coffee, glass of wine, or frothy beer. If you're in the mood for a little shopping, the well-stocked gift shop carries sundries and a variety of "must have" keepsakes. Soak up the relaxed, wholesome resort ambience by a roaring fire or on the sun-soaked deck. Test your skills at a game of pool or Ping-Pong, and enjoy a scenic stroll along the boardwalk and nature trails. Reflect on the day's activities over marshmallow-smothered s'mores at the nightly bonfire.

From the conference grounds you walk west on the boardwalk across the dunes to the crosswalk at Sunset Drive. Note that Asilomar State Beach goes in either direction from here. When tides permit, you can extend this hike by walking north 1 mile along a less-traveled narrow trail, dipping and undulating across the beach and rocks to a bench and arbor—the north gateway to Asilomar Beach State Park.

The hike described here takes you 3.1 miles south. It begins on the boardwalk across the dunes to the crosswalk across Sunset Drive to the Asilomar State Beach. You continue along another boardwalk between the beach and Spanish Bay Resort links golf course. The boardwalk drops onto the beach and you walk 0.1 mile and walk across the seasonal creek runoff before turning left up from the beach to rejoin the boardwalk. It is common for the beach sand to pile up and conceal parts of the boardwalk at the beginning of the trail. Winter storms also frequently erode the shoreline, and you will notice newer sections of boardwalk where the path dips closest to the beach. There are a couple of spurs to the left leading up to Spanish Bay Resort. Bear right at the spurs and keep hugging the coastline.

At 0.8 mile the boardwalk comes to a parking lot where sand has covered parts of the boardwalk. Walk a few yards on the blacktop and rejoin the boardwalk next to picnic tables. At 1.0 mile you will come to the south end of the parking lot and a trail sign for "Point Joe .5 Bird Rock 1.8." Follow the path as it meanders along the coast parallel to 17-Mile Drive and the golf courses. 17-Mile Drive is a private road within the gated community of Pebble Beach. Auto traffic must pay a fee at the entrance gates, but pedestrians and cyclists do not.

You will pass interpretive panels along the way and signs with large numbers at various points of interest detailed on the 17-Mile Drive auto tour map. Benches are sprinkled along the trail to rest, snack, or just gorge on the views and "feel good" negative ions. The telescopes at strategic locations along the coast invite hikers to scan for whales, otters, dolphins, and other marine life activity.

Except for a cluster of wind-tested cypress trees next to the small Spanish-style cottage owned by the Monterey Peninsula Golf Course and Country Club, the landscape is open and at the mercy of the elements. The trade-off means expansive unobstructed views from the forested hills of Del Monte Forest to the northeast across the plateau of golf greens and sand dunes to the rock-and-beach-lined Pacific's edge. The sun can be punishing on a warm day, especially in the spring and fall, when there is typically less chance of fog to throw a cool blanket over the coast. Mother Nature can be temperamental with sunny but windy days. Wear sunscreen and a hat, and carry a windbreaker. If you are hiking with a dog, make sure to carry plenty of water. There is no access to drinking water until you reach the restrooms at Bird Rock, 3.1 miles from the trailhead.

You come to Point Joe at 1.6 miles, the most exposed point on the peninsula, where a Chinese man once lived in a driftwood shack. China Rock is 0.3 mile ahead. Low tide reveals access to tidepools and idyllic patches of white sand in secluded coves, where you can retreat further from the road.

The roof of the restrooms and the outline of tour buses at Bird Rock will come into view as you approach the 3.1 miles of your hike destination. Bird Rock is a very popular stop, but you can find some solitude at the picnic tables at the far end of the parking lot. Make sure you refill your water before going back to the trailhead the way you came.

Sections of trail meander along golf holes and 17-Mile Drive.

All eyes are on Bird Rock.

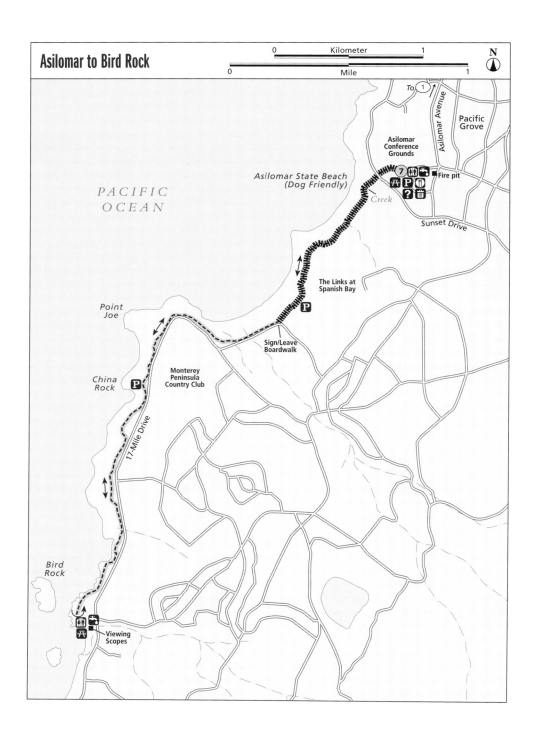

Asilomar to Bird Rock

PACIFIC OCEAN

Asilomar State Beach
(Dog Friendly)

Creek

Asilomar Conference Grounds

Fire pit

Pacific Grove

Asilomar Avenue

Sunset Drive

To 1

7

The Links at Spanish Bay

Point Joe

Sign/Leave Boardwalk

China Rock

Monterey Peninsula Country Club

17-Mile Drive

Bird Rock

Viewing Scopes

Kilometer
0   1

Mile
0   1

N

MILES AND DIRECTIONS

0.0 Start at the boardwalk at the west end of the grassy oval on the Asilomar State Beach Conference Grounds.

0.1 Walk across the road in the crosswalk to the dog friendly (on leash) beach along the boardwalk on the left.

0.2 Walk across the seasonal creek and rejoin the boardwalk up the slope between the cables that define the sandy path. Turn right on the boardwalk.

0.8 Come to the parking lot and follow the boardwalk by the picnic tables on the right.

1.0 Arrive at the trail sign for "Point Joe .5 Bird Rock 1.8." Continue walking on the trail between the road and the beach.

1.6 Come to Point Joe.

1.9 Come to China Rock.

3.1 Arrive at Bird Rock. Go back to the trailhead the way you came.

6.2 Arrive back at the trailhead.

BAKERIES, BREWERIES, EATS, AND SLEEPS

Pavel's Backerei, 219 Forest Ave., Pacific Grove 93950; (831) 643-2636. Get there early for the best chocolate chunk and peanut butter cookies.

Cannery Row Brewing Company, 95 Prescott Ave., Monterey 93940; (831) 643-2722; canneryrowbrewingcompany.com. It's technically not a "brewery" but boasts the second-largest selection of beers on tap, in Northern California, with over 75 kegs visible behind the glass bar. The burgers aren't bad either.

Goodies Delicatessen, 518 Lighthouse Ave., Pacific Grove 93950; (831) 655-3663. Good sandwiches, but great lemon bars.

The Fishwife, 1996 Sunset Dr., Pacific Grove 93950; (831) 375-7107; fishwife .com. Fresh seafood and pasta for lunch and dinner.

Asilomar State Beach Park and Conference Grounds, 800 Asilomar Ave., Pacific Grove 93950; (888) 635-5310; visitasilomar.com. The conference grounds have Phoebe's Cafe for snacks and the Crocker Dining Hall for breakfast, lunch, and dinner. You can bring your own snacks or order to go from Phoebe's and enjoy the outdoor deck with your dog.

Accommodations include the more-rustic historic rooms as well as contemporary rooms with balconies and fireplaces. There are no telephones or televisions in the rooms in keeping with the "retreat" atmosphere.

Bide-A-Wee Inn & Cottages, 221 Asilomar Ave., Pacific Grove 93950; (831) 372-2330; bideawee.com. Free continental breakfast and dog friendly.

The Inn at Spanish Bay, 2700 17-Mile Dr., Pebble Beach 93953; (831) 647-7500; pebblebeach.com. This is the place to stay if your post-hike experience has to include "luxury" and "exclusive."

8. OLD FISHERMAN'S WHARF TO PACIFIC GROVE MARINE REFUGE

WHY GO?

This popular recreational trail is a significant stitch in the California Coastal Trail. The hike goes through the heart of Monterey's marine history and along Pacific Grove's most scenic stretch of shoreline.

THE RUNDOWN

Distance: 7.2 miles out and back

Start: Monterey Bay Coastal Trail sign to the left of Old Fisherman's Wharf entrance and Harbor House sign

Nearest town: Monterey

Hiking time: About 3 hours

Fees and permits: Parking fee

Conveniences: Restroom partway down the wharf on the left side

Beach access: Yes; dogs allowed on leash on the tide-sensitive pocket beaches and Del Monte Beach (see map)

Trail users: Hikers; cyclists and in line skaters allowed on paved path to Lovers Point; dogs on leash

Trailhead elevation: 19 feet

Highest point: 45 feet

Trail surface: Paved multiuse path and compacted dirt shoulder

Difficulty: Moderate

Seasonal highlights: Migrating whales from late fall to early spring

Managing agency: City of Monterey, 580 Pacific St., Monterey 93940; (831) 646-3866; monterey.org. City of Pacific Grove, 300 Forest Ave., Pacific Grove 93950; (831) 648-3100; cityofpacificgrove.org.

FINDING THE TRAILHEAD

From Monterey on CA 1, take exit 401A and follow the signs to Fisherman's Wharf. Drive 0.5 mile to Camino El Estero and turn right. Drive 0.4 mile to Del Monte Boulevard and turn left on Del Monte Boulevard to the entrance to Fisherman's Wharf and parking lots on the right. Drive to the far end of the parking lot and follow the pedestrian path to Old Fisherman's Wharf. **GPS:** N36 36.22' / W121 53.62'

WHAT TO SEE

The blue curled wave emblem nailed on the lamppost at Shoreline Park just beyond the Custom House Plaza and Fisherman's Wharf is a discreet but thrilling reminder of the importance of the Monterey Bay Coastal Trail as a stitch in the ongoing commitment to complete the continuous 1,200-mile coastal ribbon for recreation and transportation known as the CCT (California Coastal Trail). The emblem officially identifies trails and paths as vital stitches in the grander scheme of coastal access and open-space conservation. The first mile of this trail buzzes with activity on weekends and holidays as divers, kayakers, cyclists, joggers, and strolling tourists enjoying the historical and recreational bounty of Monterey Bay.

At Drake Avenue and Wave Street, an interpretive plaque about Doc Rickett's fatal 1948 train collision marks the gateway to Cannery Row, with several more trailside signs and monuments between this intersection and the aquarium.

At 1.3 miles the trail crosses the last street just past the aquarium and you are greeted by the National Trail Network and Rails to Trails Conservancy sign as you leave Monterey city limits and enter the sedate, picturesque community of Pacific Grove. The next mile to Lovers Point boasts a rugged rocky shoreline on the right, with views across the bay toward Moss Landing and Santa Cruz. On the left, across the street, several stately Victorian inns will charm you with their towers and gables peering over the trail and bay.

Volunteer docents for the Monterey Bay Marine Sanctuary often post themselves with telescopes along the trail, inviting visitors to get a closer look at playful sea otters and dolphins, migrating whales, or harbor seals sunning themselves on the

The trail caresses Monterey Harbor.

rocks below. In the spring, stretches of the shore are screened with fencing to protect the pupping seals on the beaches below.

At 2.2 miles you come to Lovers Point Park and the beach's crescent sands in the typically calm cove. The park's grassy picnic area is a lovely spot for a break. There is a drinking fountain in the park. Unfortunately, if you are hiking with your furry friend, dogs are not allowed in this park. The public restrooms have an exterior entrance downstairs from the Beach House. There is a snack bar by the beach, and the Beach House restaurant overlooking the park and bay serves dinner. The paved multiuse trail ends here as you walk past the park and connect to the narrow dirt trail to continue the hike along this more tranquil stretch tucked between Ocean Boulevard's attractive homes and the untamed coastline, which is enhanced in the spring by a carpet of pink flowers.

At 3.6 miles you come to the sign for the Pacific Grove Shoreline Parkway Marine Refuge at the intersection of Asilomar Avenue. The Point Pinos Lighthouse is just a few hundred yards up the street and worth a side trip if you happen to hike when it is open to the public.

If you wish to continue farther, the next 2 miles to Asilomar State Beach Park and Conference Grounds offer reasonably pleasant coastal walking on dirt trails, except for some less peaceful stretches, where you must walk on the road and share the bicycle lane. The next uninterrupted stretch of coastal trail is a 3-mile stitch from the Asilomar State Beach Park Conference Grounds to Bird Rock.

The Pacific Grove Shoreline Parkway Marine Refuge at the intersection of Asilomar Avenue at 3.6 miles is the turnaround point for this hike.

MILES AND DIRECTIONS

0.0 Start on the Monterey Coastal Trail path at Old Fisherman's Wharf.

0.4 Walk across Cannery Row.

0.5 Walk across Reeside Avenue.

0.7 Walk across Drake Avenue and Wave Street.

0.9 Walk across Hoffman Avenue.

1.0 Walk across Prescott Avenue.

1.2 Walk across David Avenue.

1.3 Enter Pacific Grove at the sign.

2.2 Arrive at Lovers Point Park. Veer right on the sidewalk toward the water and bear left at the far end of the park to continue on the dirt trail paralleling the coast.

3.6 Come to Asilomar Avenue across Ocean View Boulevard and the sign for the Pacific Grove Shoreline Parkway Marine Refuge. Go back to the trailhead the way you came.

7.2 Arrive back at the trailhead.

Old Fisherman's Wharf to Pacific Grove Marine Refuge

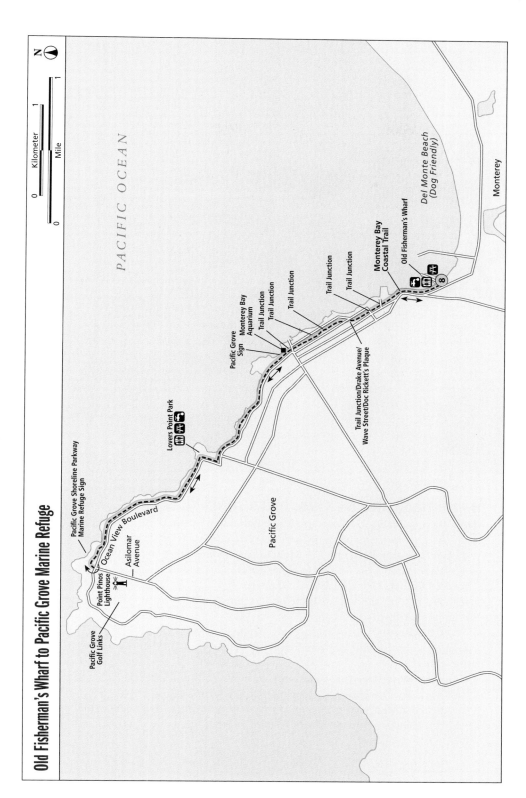

N

Kilometer
0   1

Mile
0   1

PACIFIC OCEAN

Pacific Grove Shoreline Parkway
Marine Refuge Sign

Ocean View Boulevard

Point Pinos
Lighthouse

Pacific Grove
Golf Links

Asilomar Avenue

Lovers Point Park

Pacific Grove

Pacific Grove
Sign

Monterey Bay
Aquarium

Trail Junction

Trail Junction

Trail Junction

Trail Junction

Trail Junction

Trail Junction/Drake Avenue/
Wave Street/Doc Rickett's Plaque

Monterey Bay
Coastal Trail

Old Fisherman's Wharf

Del Monte Beach
(Dog Friendly)

Monterey

Pacific Grove Victorians with Lovers Point in the distance

BAKERIES, BREWERIES, EATS, AND SLEEPS

Paris Bakery Cafe, 271 Bonifacio Place, Monterey 93940; (831) 646-1620; paris bakery.us. The French onion soup and chocolate éclairs scream Vive la France!

Parker Lusseau Pastries, 731 Munras Ave., Monterey 93940; (831) 641-9188; parkerlusseau.com. Treat yourself to some delicate petits fours.

Red's Donuts, 433 Alvarado St., Monterey 93940; (831) 372-9761; redsdonuts .com. It's a hole-in-the-wall with the best handmade donuts since 1950. Start your hike on a sugar high.

Peter B's Brew Pub, 2 Portola Plaza, Monterey 93940; (831) 649-2699; portola hotel.com. Great for pub food and locally brewed beer since 1996. The patio is dog friendly.

Cannery Row Brewing Company, 95 Prescott Ave., Monterey 93940; (831) 643-2722; canneryrowbrewingcompany.com. It's technically not a "brewery" but boasts the second-largest selection of beers on tap in Northern California, with over 75 kegs visible behind the glass bar. The burgers aren't bad either.

Beach House at Lover's Point, 620 Ocean View Blvd., Pacific Grove 93950; (831) 375-2345. Location, location for dinner with a view.

Point Pinos Grill, 79 Asilomar Ave., Pacific Grove 93950; (831) 648-5774; pointpinosgrill.com. It's on the Pacific Grove Golf Links, with a dog friendly deck perfect for enjoying the ocean view over breakfast, lunch, happy hour, or dinner.

Portola Hotel, 2 Portola Plaza, Monterey 93940; (888) 222-5851; portolahotel .com. The best Monterey location for access to Fisherman's Wharf.

Monterey Tides Resort, a Joie de Vivre hotel, 2600 Sand Dunes Dr., Monterey 93940; (831) 394-3321; jdvhotels.com. This oceanfront property is the only dog friendly hotel on Del Monte Beach, and you can walk 2 miles south to the trailhead along the beach or the multiuse paved recreational path.

Seven Gables Inn, 555 Ocean Avenue Blvd., Pacific Grove 93950; (831) 372-4341; sevengablesinn.com. This is one of several Victorian grandes dames in Pacific Grove. The bed-and-breakfast inn has a spectacular perch across the street from Pacific Grove's picturesque coastline.

HI Monterey Hostel, 778 Hawthorne St., Monterey 93940; (831) 649-0375; hiusa.org. Great location within walking distance of the coastal trail and Monterey/ Pacific Grove tourist attractions.

CAMPING

Veterans Memorial Park, Veterans Dr., Monterey 93940; (831) 646-3865; monterey.org. Clean campground with tents and trailer/RV sites (no hookups). Bathroom with showers, hiking trails with ocean views, and within walking distance of downtown Monterey.

Dog Friendly Beaches

Pfeiffer Beach may be smaller than some, but it's big in scenic beauty. At low tide you and Rover can romp for about 0.5 mile on a firmly packed, spectacular white sand beach framed by steep cliffs and a photogenic wave-sculpted rock arch. The beach is 2 miles down winding, one-lane, paved Sycamore Canyon Road off of CA 1 in Big Sur, just 0.5 mile past the Big Sur Station on the east side of the highway. There's good news and bad news. The good news is that this hidden jewel is on dog friendly Los Padres National Forest land, which is a rare find in Big Sur, where restrictive state parks and beaches abound. National forests often allow dogs the freedom of voice control, but the bad news is that on this patch of national forest territory, Rover will have to be content just enjoying the spindrift brushing his coat, salty air on his nose, and sand between his paws on leash. Los Padres National Forest, www.fs.usda.gov/lpnf; campgrounds, (805) 434-1996, campone.com

Carmel River State Beach, at the south end of Carmel-by-the-Sea, is postcard perfect with the Carmel River lagoon and the Carmel Valley hills as a backdrop, enhanced by the Point Lobos cypress and rock finger in the foreground. The white sand beach is inviting for picnics and walks with dogs on leash and connects to the Carmel Meadows trail (see hike 5). But the steep drop-off into the marine canyon and the smashing swells of frothy waves that assault the shore are forces to be

Carmel City Beach is an idyllic playground for dogs and their owners.

respected from a distance. At high tide the volume and force of the waves frequently washes over the beach into the lagoon, making the south end of the beach impassable and treacherous. During the winter a more tumultuous storm-stirred surf and the Carmel River's robust flow combine to slice a channel where the freshwater pours out of the lagoon to swirl with the incoming surge from the Pacific, cutting off passage to the Carmel Meadows trail for several weeks to a few months at a time. Having your dog on leash protects the birdlife in the lagoon and keeps your dog safe from being swallowed by this shore's unforgiving force. The beach is accessed from a parking lot at 26591 Carmelo St. at the intersection of Scenic Road in Carmel-by-the-Sea. California State Parks, (831) 649-2836, parks.ca.gov

Carmel City Beach is a voice-control pooch paradise that dogs would dream of if there were a beach at the end of Rainbow Bridge. This is a 1-mile stretch of firm-packed white sand with a gentle slope and generally gentle to moderate surf conditions. This beach is below the Carmel Bluffs trail (see hike 6). The shoreline is perfect for dogs that like to splash, spring, and pounce in the water as well as dogs that get high on hurling themselves into the surf to swim for floating toys. It's a great beach for Bowsers that like to take their humans for a jog. The beach is accessed from the parking lot at the bottom of Ocean Avenue or from several stairways along Scenic Road south of Ocean Avenue in Carmel-by-the-Sea. City of Carmel-by-the-Sea, (831) 620-2000

Asilomar State Beach at its longest uninterrupted sandy stretch is a lovely 0.5-mile-long strand at the foot of the boardwalk trailhead for the Asilomar to Bird Rock trail (see hike #7) tracing the Links at Spanish Bay golf resort. Dogs are welcome on leash. The beach is accessed from Sunset Drive at Pico Avenue in Pacific Grove. California State Parks, (831) 646-6440, parks.ca.gov

Del Monte Beach's flat, wide strand of light sand beach seems to go on forever, stretching north from Municipal Wharf #2. It's one of the more gentle shores on Monterey Bay and very popular with kayakers. Dogs on leash can take their owners for a 2-mile stroll or jog north as far as the Monterey Tides Resort, the only dog friendly lodging on Del Monte Beach. The hotel has a lobby canteen to enjoy lunch and dinner with your bowwow, or order "to go" for the patio. The beach is best accessed from the parking area at Municipal Wharf #2 on Del Monte Avenue. The beach overlaps the city and the state beach but is managed by the City of Monterey, (831) 646-3860.

Moss Landing City Beach is in the quaint commercial fishing harbor named after Charles Moss, the wealthy Texan who settled on this coast in 1866 and built a 200-foot wharf that would become a bustling pier for water traffic and the seed for fishing-related industries. This beach is the only sand-and-surf spot for several miles where you can enjoy the coast with Fido on leash. This stretch of sand also has the interesting distinction of being behind two major landmarks and local institutions of a different kind: Phil's Fish Market and Eatery, a no-frills favorite with locals and tourists for over 30 years, and the Monterey Bay Aquarium Research Institute

(MBARI), founded by David Packard in 1987 to conduct a variety of oceanographic research projects. The beach can be accessed at 7600 Sandholdt Rd. in Moss Landing near Phil's. City of Moss Landing, (831) 633-4501

Coastal Attractions

Partington Cove, at the north end of Julia Pfeiffer Burns State Park, in a bend in the road 10 miles south of Pfeiffer Big Sur State Park, is a hidden trace of history. During the 1880s a man named John Partington purchased land on the east side of what is now CA 1 to log and export tan oak trees. The high concentration of tannic acid was used to cure leather until the advent of synthetics in the 1930s. Partington Cove is a natural secluded harbor easily imagined as a perfect pirate or smuggler's hideaway. A short, steep hike from CA 1 takes you to the cove via a tunnel that was originally cut through rock to get Partington's wagons to the ships' loading platform. You can still see some remnants of the operation in the iron-bolt-embedded rock and wooden booms.

Andrew Molera State Park, 45500 CA 1, Big Sur 93920; (831) 667-2315; parks.ca.gov. This coastal state park offers a scenic bluff trail accessed from the parking lot on a seasonal bridge across the Big Sur River. The trail climbs to the bluffs and drops back to the beach for a loop. This hike was intended as one of the featured coastal trails in this book, but unfortunately state parks in Big Sur were closed during the summer into the fall of 2016 as a result of the devastating Soberanes Fire that threatened many areas of Big Sur. Andrew Molera State Park is named after one of the early settlers. His ranch house in the park is now a museum open to the public on weekends when volunteer caretakers are present. In addition, the park is home to the California Condor Discovery Center operated by the Ventana Wildlife Society and open on weekends. Another way to experience the coast in the state park is on horseback with the Molera Horseback Tours, (831) 625-5486.

Point Sur Lighthouse, 19 miles south of Carmel at the intersection of Rio Road and CA 1, Big Sur; (831) 625-4419; pointsur.org. The first light keepers began service at this lighthouse in 1889. The light was automated in the 1970s, and the original Fresnel lens is on display at the Monterey Maritime Museum, 5 Custom House Plaza, across from the Old Fisherman's Wharf. Walking tours of the light station are available weekly on a seasonal schedule.

Palo Corona Regional Park, part of the Monterey Peninsula Regional Park District, is over 4,000 acres of spectacular open space and ecosystems on the east side of CA 1. Inspiration Point is a moderate climb on an old ranch road to a bluff overlooking Carmel Bay. This scenic 1-mile excursion rewards hikers with fabulous views of the Carmel coast cradled between Point Lobos and Pebble Beach. The bench and table make a sweet picnic spot. Parking is limited to the shoulder on CA 1, and park access is by permit only. Visit mprpd.org for additional information and permit application.

Point Pinos Lighthouse
in Pacific Grove

Point Pinos Lighthouse, 80 Asilomar Blvd., Pacific Grove 93950; (831) 648-3176; pointpinoslighthouse.org. This is the oldest continuously operating lighthouse on the West Coast since 1855. Open for tours Thurs through Mon from 1 to 4 p.m.

Fort Ord Dunes State Park, Beach Range Rd., Marina 93933; (831) 649-2836; parks.ca.gov. Opened in 2004, this low-key day-use park has 4 miles of beach and a short boardwalk with a viewing platform. Military history buffs will appreciate the interpretive panels and historical photos depicting the history of this former military post. The paved roads within the park are open to bicycles and hikers with dogs on leash.

Pezzini Farms, 460 Nashua Rd., Castroville 95012; (831) 757-7434; pezzini farms.com. The retail store in the heart of the "Artichoke Capital of the World" is the place to indulge or discover your love of these coastal fog-nurtured thistle delicacies with tender flower buds. Pezzini Farms has been growing heirloom Green Globe artichokes for over 80 years. The small farm stand and retail store filled with fresh artichokes, an array of artichoke products, and other pantry goods stands alone and is visible on the east side of CA 1.

Monterey Bay Kayaks, 693 Del Monte Ave., Monterey 93940; (831) 373-5357; montereybaykayaks.com. The Monterey Peninsula's coastline is a primo kayaking spot, and Monterey Bay Kayaks' rentals offer the opportunity to enjoy a front-row seat to observe the wildlife residents of this scenic bay and national marine sanctuary. Monterey Bay Kayaks also has a rental location at 2390 CA 1, Moss Landing, for paddling the Elkhorn Slough National Estuarine Reserve's tidal wetlands. Four-legged kayakers are welcome as long as their enthusiasm doesn't disturb the marine residents. Kayakers are responsible for respecting the rules and liable for any fines. Make sure you pack Rover's life jacket.

BEST COASTAL FARMERS' MARKETS

Carmel-by-the-Sea Certified Farmers' Market is a happening spot in the heart of this 1-square-mile oceanfront town known for its village vibe, high-end shops, and fairy-tale cottages. The market vendors set up by the park at 6th and Mission Streets on Thurs from 10 a.m. to 2 p.m.

Old Monterey Marketplace is an expansive, bustling pedestrian venue lined with myriad vendors including produce, flowers, baked goods, and crafts. Locals and tourists flock to sample the fresh products, hot foods to go, and live music on downtown Alvarado Street every Tues from 4 to 8 p.m. May through Sept and 4 to 7 p.m. Oct through Apr.

Monterey Peninsula College Certified Farmers' Market is a local favorite for organic produce, grass-fed meats, sustainable fish, local olive oil, and a wide array of flowers, potted plants, seedlings, and herbs. The market operates on the college campus year-round at 980 Fremont St., Monterey, on Fri from 10 a.m. to 2 p.m.

Seafood samples at Fisherman's Wharf

SANTA CRUZ COUNTY

World-class surfing, funky to charming beach resort communities, a historic oceanfront amusement park, and one of the most liberal hang-loose communities in California are all images associated with the **COUNTY OF SANTA CRUZ.** The county's seat and largest city of the same name is also known as a super-hip university town with an outer-edge liberal attitude. Mountains draped in redwood forests taper west to agricultural terraces fertile with lettuce, artichokes, and brussels sprouts. But the real nutritional treats for coastal visitors are the berry farms along CA 1. What coastal trail hike isn't sweeter with a stash of precious olallieberries in your pack? Cliffs edge much of the coastline, and coastal trails typically thread the bluff tops, flanked by the Pacific and hidden white sand coves on one side and farmland on the other.

Thanks to the establishment of the Monterey Bay National Marine Sanctuary—the largest marine sanctuary in the country, established in 1992 to protect almost 300 miles of shoreline (San Luis Obispo County north to Marin County) and over 6,000 square miles of ocean embracing the Monterey Bay—no oil rig will ever blemish the pristine views on coastal trails along this stretch of coastline. The National Oceanic and Atmospheric Administration (NOAA) manages the country's thirteen national marine sanctuaries, four of which are in California.

Note: See map on page 20.

9. WEST CLIFF TRAIL

WHY GO?

Santa Cruz is synonymous with surfing. This is a stretch of the California Coastal Trail at the northern boundary of Monterey Bay along an urban multiuse coastal trail in Northern California's surfing mecca. It's wheelchair accessible and offers the best vantage point for front-row surfer watching along one of the last open headlands in a California urban area.

THE RUNDOWN

Distance: 6.0 miles out and back

Start: Santa Cruz wharf

Nearest town: Santa Cruz

Hiking time: About 3 hours

Fees and permits: None

Conveniences: Restrooms, outdoor showers, water, trash and recycling containers

Beach access: Yes; dogs allowed on some beaches on leash and under voice control at Mitchell Cove Beach at certain times of day

Trail users: Hikers, cyclists, and dogs on leash

Trailhead elevation: 16 feet

Highest point: 46 feet

Trail surface: Paved

Difficulty: Moderate

Seasonal highlights: Whale migration in the spring and fall

Managing agency: City of Santa Cruz, 323 Church St., Santa Cruz 95060; (831) 420-5270; cityofsantacruz.com

FINDING THE TRAILHEAD

From Santa Cruz on CA 1 and Bay Street, turn south on Bay Street and drive 1 mile to Beach Street. Turn left on Beach Street and drive 100 yards to the wharf. There is parking on nearby streets. **GPS:** N36 57.75' / W122 01.41'

WHAT TO SEE

The West Cliff Trail begins at the Santa Cruz Wharf at the north end of the famous Santa Cruz Beach Boardwalk, a National Historic Landmark. It traces the bluffs above the Pacific and several stretches of beach on the west side as it parallels West Cliff Drive and the cliff-top residential neighborhood on the east side. Although it's far from a serene nature experience, the views across Monterey Bay and overlooking the isolated coves and beaches in the shadow of the cliffs go a long way toward

Surfers with the wharf and historic Santa Cruz
Beach Boardwalk in the background

making this a special hike. As you walk along, you can't help but notice how many coves are dotted with wet-suited surfing enthusiasts sitting, paddling, bobbing, and standing on their boards, ready for that next perfect set of waves. You quickly understand why Santa Cruz was designated a World Surfing Reserve in 2012. It is one of only two locations in the United States to have this unique status and one of only four around the world, joining Malibu in Southern California, Ericeira in Portugal, and Manly Beach in Australia in the exclusive club of World Surfing Reserves.

The start of the hike at the wharf, so close to the popular Santa Cruz Boardwalk and the main beaches in the heart of the tourist hub, is a bit jolting. But you quickly leave the throbbing center to walk uphill and continue along the cliffs. Looking back from the cliffs, you will have unobstructed views of Santa Cruz and its south-facing beaches and boardwalk. The rest of the hike offers sweeping views across Monterey Bay and the marine sanctuary. There are benches along the way on the ocean side and a couple of restrooms along a few stretches of parkland on the east side. For the most part, West Cliff Drive is lined with residences on the east side all the way to Natural Bridges State Beach.

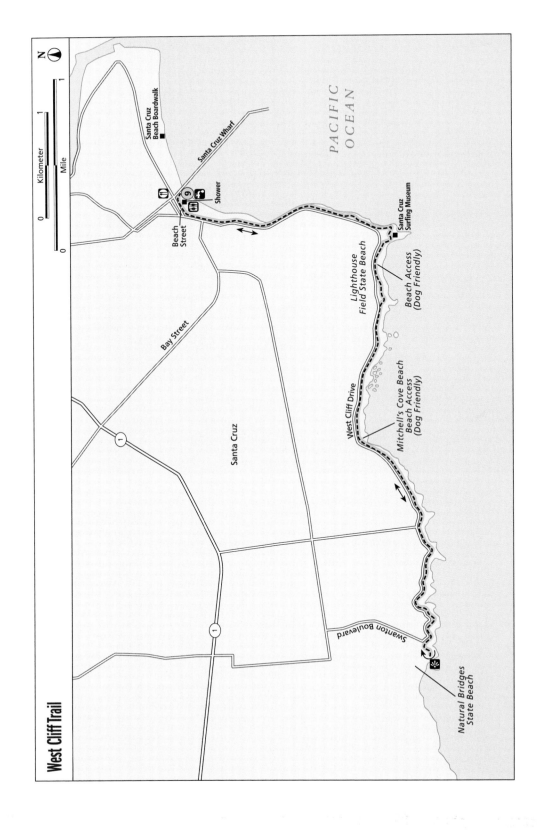

It is interesting to note that Santa Cruz has passed a city ordinance declaring all parks a "no smoking" environment, thus minimizing cigarette butt litter that often ends down the storm drains and into the ocean. Smokers can dispose of their cigarettes in the specially designed cigarette butt disposal containers strategically placed in parking areas around public trails.

At 0.7 mile you come to a sculpture of a surfer with a surfboard dedicated to all surfers. The next landmark is the Surfing Museum at 1.0 mile. The museum is housed in the iconic Mark Abbott Memorial Lighthouse on Lighthouse Point. This area attracts wintering monarch butterflies as well as surfers and tourists. The lighthouse and the solid-beam light are owned and maintained by the City of Santa Cruz's Parks and Recreation Department. The museum point has a viewing scope as well as a plaque describing how Hawaiian royalty introduced surfing to California's coast in 1885.

At 1.1 miles you come to a set of stairs down to Lighthouse Field State Beach, where dogs are allowed on leash. The area across the street is part of the state beach, and there is parking on the inland side of the street. The next dog friendly beach is Mitchell Cove Beach, almost 1 mile farther up the coast, where dogs can gallivant under voice control at certain times of the day.

The trail ends at 3.0 miles at the entrance parking for Natural Bridges State Beach. Besides the natural rock bridges and archways off the coast, this day-use state beach and park boasts the Monarch Butterfly Natural Preserve in the eucalyptus groves. Up to 100,000 butterflies roost in the trees during the winter.

It's about a 0.3-mile walk from the end of the trail at the park entrance to the park visitor center, where there are picnic tables, grills, restrooms, water, and trash and recycling containers. There is no fee for walking into the park.

MILES AND DIRECTIONS

0.0 Start at the Santa Cruz Wharf and walk uphill from the wharf map board.

1.0 Arrive at the Santa Cruz Surfing Museum.

1.1 Come to stairs down to dog friendly (on leash) Lighthouse Field State Beach.

1.9 Come to stairs down to dog friendly (voice control) Mitchell's Cove Beach.

3.0 Arrive at the Natural Bridges State Beach entrance and a viewpoint parking lot above the state beach. Go back to the trailhead the way you came.

6.0 Arrive back at the trailhead.

Looking north toward Lighthouse Point

Watching surfers from a trail bluff

BAKERIES, BREWERIES, EATS, AND SLEEPS

Good Companion Bakeshop, 2341 Mission St., Santa Cruz 95060; (831) 252-2253; companionbakeshop.com. Try their signature seasonal berry pies. The peanut butter cookies are divine.

Kelly's French Bakery, 402 Ingalis St., Santa Cruz 95060; (831) 423-9059; kellysfrenchbakery.com. An assortment of baked goodies to go. Kelly's also serves breakfast, lunch, and dinner.

Santa Cruz Mountain Brewery, 402 Ingalis St., Santa Cruz 95060; (831) 425-4900; scmbrew.com. Burgers, sandwiches, and brews. Dog friendly on leash.

The Picnic Basket, 125 Beach St., Santa Cruz 95060; (831) 427-9946; the picnicbasket.com. Farm-to-table menu for eating in or to go. Dog friendly patio.

Adobe on Green Street Bed and Breakfast, 103 Green St., Santa Cruz 95060; (831) 469-9866; adobeongreen.com. Quiet location.

West Cliff Inn Bed and Breakfast, 174 W. Cliff Dr., Santa Cruz 95060; (800) 979-0901; e-mail: westcliffinn@foursisters.com. A 1877 grande dame that is dog friendly.

Darling House B&B, 314 W. Cliff Dr., Santa Cruz 95060; (831) 458-1958; darlinghouse.com. Historic landmark with Spanish-style architecture and elegant interiors boasting West Cliff's ocean views.

CAMPING

Santa Cruz Harbor RV Camping, Brommer St. and 7th St., Santa Cruz 95060; (831) 475-3279; santacruzharbor.com. Waterfront location with hookups.

New Brighton State Beach, 1500 Park Ave., off of CA 1, Capitola 95010; (831) 464-6330; parks.ca.gov. Trailers and RVs (max 36 feet) with some hookups and tents.

10. **COVE-BLUFF TRAIL**

WHY GO?

Wilder Ranch State Park pleases hikers, mountain bikers, and equestrians with bluffs, beaches, and redwood ridges. The flat exposed trail along the scalloped coastal bluffs is a 360-degree panoramic treat of blue Pacific, rich farmland, and tree-studded hilltops.

THE RUNDOWN

Distance: 12.0 miles out and back

Start: Old Cove Landing Trailhead

Nearest town: Santa Cruz

Hiking time: About 5 hours

Fees and permits: Day-use parking fee

Conveniences: Flush toilets, drinking fountain, outdoor sink, trash and recycling containers, and map board in parking area; picnic tables behind historic dairy and ranch buildings at visitor center

Beach access: Yes

Trail users: Hikers and mountain bikers

Trailhead elevation: 71 feet

Highest point: 71 feet

Trail surface: Dirt

Difficulty: Moderate

Seasonal highlights: Migrating whales and dolphins offshore; wildflowers in the spring

Managing agency: Wilder Ranch State Park, 1401 Old Coast Rd., Santa Cruz 95060; (831) 423-9703 or (831) 426-0505; parks.ca.gov

FINDING THE TRAILHEAD

From Santa Cruz at CA 1 and CA 17, drive 5 miles north on CA 1 to the Wilder Ranch State Park entrance on the left (west side of CA 1). Follow the signs for day-use parking. **GPS:** N36 57.61' / W122 05.12'

WHAT TO SEE

Like most of California, the history begins with native people. The Ohlone Indians thrived on these coastal prairies until the Spanish explorers arrived and the Franciscan padres established the mission system. Over time the land became part of the Mexican land grants known as "ranchos." Ranchos were further divided and acquired by new settlers when California became a republic independent of both Spain and Mexico. Following statehood, several entrepreneurs left their imprint on

Information panel above
Old Cove Landing

the former Rancho del Refugio now part of Wilder Ranch State Park. Cattle grazing, sawmills, creameries, and dairy farms are all part of the property's history.

In the 1970s the land was saved from development and protected as open space
by vote of the citizens of Santa Cruz County. California State Parks acquired the
property in 1974. The park protects the watershed that flows into the Monterey
Bay National Marine Sanctuary and the cultural history connected to the preserved
buildings making up the dairy complex at the visitor center. There are maps for a
self-guided walking tour of the historic dairy site and the various buildings. Follow
the paved path and the signs to the historic site.

The hike begins along the Old Cove Landing Trail across meadows bordered by
farmland, much of which is artichoke fields. Looking to the east of CA 1, the coastal
prairie rises to chaparral-covered hills and oak woodlands in the distance, rimmed
with pines and some redwoods. This hike is exposed all the way except for a very
short stretch of cypress trees acting as a momentary windbreak on some of the more
blustery days. There's an old railroad track running along the far west end of the
park, and you will cross it for the first time just 0.1 mile from the trailhead.

At 0.7 mile you come to a viewpoint and interpretive panel overlooking the
beach at the Old Cove Landing. The trail continues along the bluff and meanders
inland, tracing several coves and gullies carved by seasonal creeks and erosion. Except
for a couple of unmarked junctions at the railroad track, the trail is fairly straight-
forward since you are generally along the coast or following the natural contours
of the land. You will pass several unmarked short spurs heading closer to the cliffs,
but heed the warnings on the signs about the sheer cliffs and stay on the main trail.
Except for 4 Mile Beach at your turnaround, the stunning beaches along the way
are mostly inaccessible.

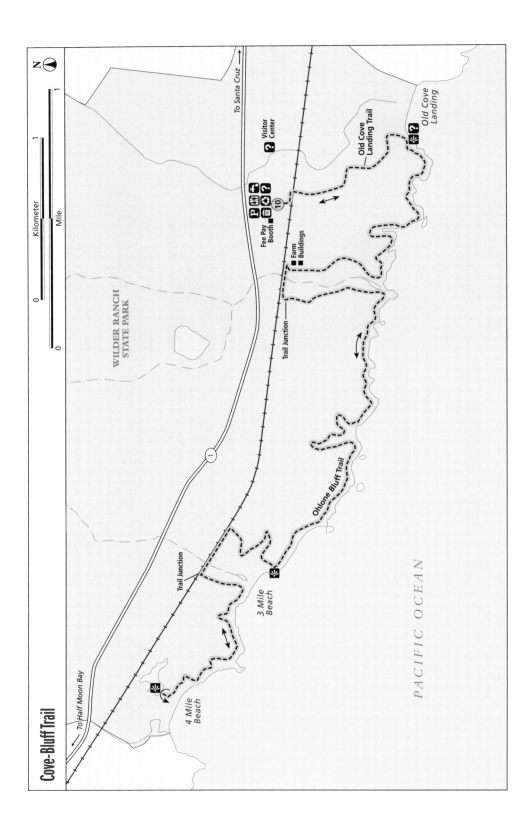

Cove-Bluff Trail

N

Kilometer

Mile

To Half Moon Bay

To Santa Cruz

1

WILDER RANCH STATE PARK

Visitor Center

Fee Pay Booth

Farm Buildings

Old Cove Landing Trail

Old Cove Landing

Trail Junction

Trail Junction

Ohlone Bluff Trail

3 Mile Beach

4 Mile Beach

PACIFIC OCEAN

10

You will see your first and only mention of the Ohlone Bluff Trail on a sign at about 1.4 miles above unmarked Sand Plant Beach. The trail sign on one side of the post reads "Old Cove Landing Trail 1.25," with an arrow pointing back the way you came. The other side of the post reads "Ohlone Bluff Trail 2.5," with an arrow pointing down to the beach. Ignore the arrow and continue walking on the bluff trail away from the beach toward a cluster of farm buildings and CA 1.

At 2.0 miles you come to the weathered farm buildings. Continue walking past the farmhouse to the railroad track. If you want a shorter hike, less than 3 miles, walk across the railroad track just a few yards up the dirt road and turn right. The path will take you back to the park entrance and parking lot.

To continue on the longer hike described here, turn left at the railroad track. Do not cross the track. Follow the path on the west side of the track for about 0.2 mile and turn left on the unmarked spur trail. The trail is narrow and parallels farmland back to the bluffs.

You come to a beach overlook at 4.3 miles. At 4.8 miles the trail meets the railroad track. Turn left and stay on the west side of the track. You come to another unmarked trail junction 0.2 mile ahead. Turn left and walk back toward the ocean. Walk another mile along the bluff and come to the unmarked 4 Mile overlook and a small grove of windswept cypress trees. This is your turnaround point. There is a primitive trail going down to the beach if you would like to linger for a picnic before going back the way you came.

Your next opportunity for a shortcut on this hike if you do not want to go all the way back on the Old Cove Landing Trail will be back at the farmhouse and railroad track, with the shortcut described above at 2.0 miles. This is where you can turn left across the track and follow the road toward the park entrance and parking lot.

MILES AND DIRECTIONS

0.0 Start at the map board and Old Cove Landing Trailhead in the day-use parking lot.

0.1 Walk across the railroad track.

0.7 Come to a viewpoint overlooking the beach at the Old Cove Landing.

2.0 Arrive at the farmhouse and turn left at the railroad track ahead.

2.2 Come to an unmarked spur trail and turn left.

4.3 Arrive at a beach overlook.

4.8 Come to the railroad track and turn left on the west side of the track.

5.0 Come to an unmarked trail junction and turn left toward the ocean.

6.0 Come to the unmarked 4 Mile Beach overlook and your turnaround point. Go back to the trailhead the way you came.

12.0 Arrive back at the trailhead.

BAKERIES, BREWERIES, EATS, AND SLEEPS

Whale City Bakery Bar and Grill, 490 Coast Rd., Davenport 95017; (831) 423-9009; whalecitybakery.com. Breakfast, lunch, and dinner. Delicious olallieberry croissants.

Good Companion Bakeshop, 2341 Mission St., Santa Cruz 95060; (831) 252-2253; companionbakeshop.com. Try their signature seasonal berry pies. The peanut butter cookies are divine.

Santa Cruz Mountain Brewery, 402 Ingalis St., Santa Cruz 95060; (831) 425-4900; scmbrew.com. Burgers, sandwiches, and brews. Dog friendly on leash.

Adobe on Green Street Bed and Breakfast, 103 Green St., Santa Cruz 95060; (831) 469-9866; adobeongreen.com. Quiet location.

West Cliff Inn Bed and Breakfast, 174 West Cliff Dr., Santa Cruz 95060; (800) 979-0901; e-mail: westcliffinn@foursisters.com. A 1877 grande dame that is dog friendly.

CAMPING

Costanoa Resort and KOA Campground, 2001 Rossi Rd. at CA 1, Pescadero 95060; (650) 879-1100 for lodge; (800) 562-9867 for KOA campground; costanoa .com. The resort has a spa and a range of accommodations, along with a restaurant and general store. The campground (RV and tent) is clean and classy, with "comfort stations" that have shower and sauna facilities as well as an outdoor fireplace.

Coastal winds help seagulls and hats fly.

Dogs enjoy Mitchell's Cove Beach.

Dog Friendly Beaches

Lighthouse Field State Beach, at the foot of the cliff below Lighthouse Point, is a good spot to walk your dog on leash while scanning for surfers riding the waves in famous Steamer Lane. The beach is accessed down a staircase at 701 West Cliff Dr. along the West Cliff Trail (see hike 9), just beyond the Mark Abbott Memorial Lighthouse and Santa Cruz Surfing Museum. Santa Cruz Department of Parks and Recreation, (831) 429-2850

Mitchell's Cove Beach is a south-facing beach below the bluff along the West Cliff Trail (see hike 9). This beach may not be one of the longest or widest, but size doesn't matter to dogs when their paws land on a spot where they can pounce and spin in and out of the surf under voice control, even if it's only before 10 a.m. and after 4 p.m. They must be on leash outside of those windows of free-spirit times. City of Santa Cruz, (831) 420-5270

Coastal Attractions

Santa Cruz Lighthouse, part of Lighthouse Field State Beach, 701 West Cliff Dr., Santa Cruz 95060; (831) 420-6289; parks.ca.gov. The Santa Cruz Lighthouse was established in 1869 and moved back from the eroding cliffs twice. The original light keeper's daughter, Laura Heacox, assumed the responsibilities as light keeper for several decades after her father's death. The lighthouse was deconstructed after the light was automated. In 1967 a brick light tower was built as a memorial to Mark Abbott, a teenager who drowned in a surfing accident. It became home to the Santa Cruz Surfing Museum in 1986, and a solid beam replaced the blinking light in a dedication ceremony in 2013. The museum houses 100 years of surfing history depicted in photographs and memorabilia. Call ahead for seasonal hours of operation.

Capitola Village by the Sea, off of CA 1 south of Santa Cruz; capitolavillage .com. This quaint seaside community was founded in 1869 and is the oldest resort town in California. Walk the Esplanade and sample the shops and restaurants, or stroll along Capitola Beach.

Davenport Bluffs and Davenport Beach, off of CA 1 at Ocean Street in Davenport north of Santa Cruz, is a scenic spot with free parking. The bluff trails and the beach are dog friendly on leash.

Swanton Berry Farm, 25 Swanton Rd., Davenport 95017; swantonberryfarm .com. This is the place to pick your own medley of seasonal berries including strawberries, olallieberries, and blackberries on the different ranch parcels. The indoor farm stand sells jams, fresh pies, and other comfort treats. Swanton strawberry jam is the real deal.

BEST COASTAL FARMERS' MARKETS

Santa Cruz Farmers' Market downtown is colorful Santa Cruz's oldest and largest farmers' market. You'll find farm products, artisan delicacies, a cafe seating area, and live music. It's 1 block off of Pacific Avenue between Cedar and Lincoln Streets. Open Wed from 1:30 to 6:30 p.m. spring/summer and 1:30 to 5:30 p.m. fall/winter.

SAN MATEO COUNTY

The third-smallest county by land area in California feels like a hybrid of Santa Cruz's more rural and open-space landscape and San Francisco's more densely populated urban communities. You have to look at the historical county boundaries to understand San Mateo's conflicted image. **SAN MATEO COUNTY** was created in 1857 by splitting San Francisco County along the tip of the San Francisco Peninsula and along the Bay, and everything south of the line became the new San Mateo County. A decade later, San Mateo County annexed parts of northern Santa Cruz County, which includes the Santa Cruz Mountains for the entire length of the county.

Wharf pilings decorated with kelp and barnacles

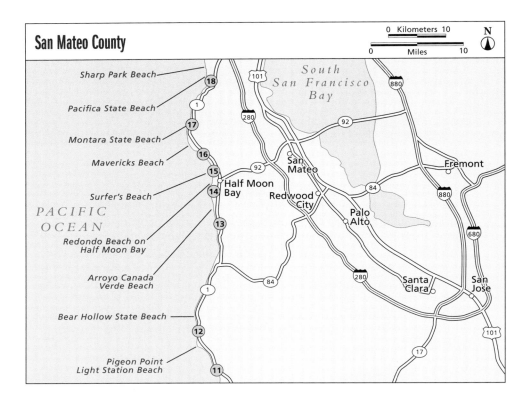

These days, San Mateo County's most prominent cultural landmarks are San Francisco International Airport to the north and Silicon Valley to the south. Although not a large county as defined by geographic boundaries, 40 percent of San Mateo's landmass is water frontage, including some San Francisco Bay and Pacific Ocean coastline, along with shoreline estuaries for prime coastal trail settings. Thanks to the establishment of the Monterey Bay National Marine Sanctuary—the largest marine sanctuary in the country, established in 1992 to protect almost 300 miles of shoreline (San Luis Obispo County north to Marin County) and over 6,000 square miles of ocean embracing the Monterey Bay—no oil rig will ever blemish the pristine views on coastal trails along this stretch of coastline. The National Oceanic and Atmospheric Administration (NOAA) manages the country's thirteen national marine sanctuaries, four of which are in California.

11. FRANKLIN POINT

WHY GO?

This is a superb hike on one of Ano Nuevo State Preserve's less-traveled coastal trails. Set on a coastal prairie, the eighth-rarest ecosystem in the United States, the trail hugs the coast on grassy bluffs and across pristine wind-sculpted sand dunes.

THE RUNDOWN

Distance: 5.6 miles out and back

Start: Cascade Creek Trailhead

Nearest town: Santa Cruz

Hiking time: About 3 hours

Fees and permits: None

Conveniences: Small parking area off of CA 1

Beach access: Yes

Trail users: Hikers only

Trailhead elevation: 83 feet

Highest point: 83 feet

Trail surface: Grass and sand

Difficulty: Easy

Seasonal highlights: Wildflowers in the spring

Managing agency: Ano Nuevo State Park, CA 1 at New Years Creek Road, Pescadero 94060; (650) 879-2025

FINDING THE TRAILHEAD

 From Santa Cruz at CA 1 and CA 17, drive 25 miles north on CA 1 to Cascade Creek Trailhead, discreetly marked on the west side of CA 1 in Ano Nuevo State Park. This trailhead is 3 miles north of the main entrance to the park. **GPS:** N37 08.72' / W122 20.17'

WHAT TO SEE

Ano Nuevo State Park is best known for its natural preserve where elephant seals come annually to the beaches to breed, give birth, and molt their skin. It is one of the largest mainland breeding colonies in the world for the northern elephant seal, and the preserve was established to further protect the seals. This area of the park is accessible from the main entrance at the north end, and visitors must obtain a self-guided permit or be on a docent-led tour to access the viewing area.

Quiroste Indians were a prominent tribe in the region when they welcomed the Spanish overland expedition of 1769 on its way to Monterey Bay. European disease eventually decimated the tribe, and the land became a prime grazing area for Mission

View south over Whitehouse
Creek meeting the Pacific

Santa Cruz livestock. Ano Nuevo became a private ranch in 1842 during the Mexican era. Cattle grazing continued along with the planting of various crops. The land subsequently passed through many American hands for cattle ranching, dairy farming, and row-crop farming. The State of California acquired the property in 1971 and began the slow process of restoring the land and erasing the scars of agriculture.

The Atkinson Bluff Trail to Franklin Point north of the preserve's main entrance and visitor center does not have the popular appeal of the prime elephant seal viewing area at Ano Nuevo Point. The trade-off is an opportunity for more solitude and to experience a sense of the wild and the beauty of a coastal terrace prairie with all its diversity of native grasses, wildflowers, and habitats, including California oat grass and blue sky lupine.

The hike begins at the interpretive panel and map behind the yellow gate at the Cascade Creek Trailhead. The first 0.5 mile of grassy path leads across the meadow to the bluffs and a trail junction for Cascade Creek Beach to the left and Whitehouse Creek to the right. Turn left to the Cascade Creek Beach overlook on a short lollipop detour before coming back to the trail junction to continue to Whitehouse Creek.

Overlooking Smuggler's Cove

You will cross a seasonal creek on a wooden footbridge at 1.4 miles and continue 0.2 mile to the stairs at the south end of Whitehouse Creek Beach. Walk across the beach to seasonal Whitehouse Creek. Be aware that in the winter and spring after rainfall, the creek may run more vigorously. Carry sandals in your pack if you don't want to finish the hike with soggy shoes. Once across the creek, walk along the sandstone wall and up a narrow trail to rejoin the Atkinson Bluff Trail to Franklin Point at the top. Turn left to Franklin Point at the marked trail junction. There's a wooden bench just ahead on the bluff. This is a great spot for a snack break and soaking up the coastal views, watching the changing hues of the ocean synchronized with the light and skies. One moment it can be blue and turquoise, and the next the moss green of the prairie grasses.

The sandy trail narrows and overlooks a rocky beach as you approach Smuggler's Cove at 2.0 miles. Bear left at the next trail junction just ahead and continue to Franklin Point. The trail transitions from grass to sand among healthy coastal dunes, where poison oak shrubs seem to thrive. At 2.6 miles bear left at the trail junction partially obscured by shifting sand, and continue along the sandy corridor sculpted

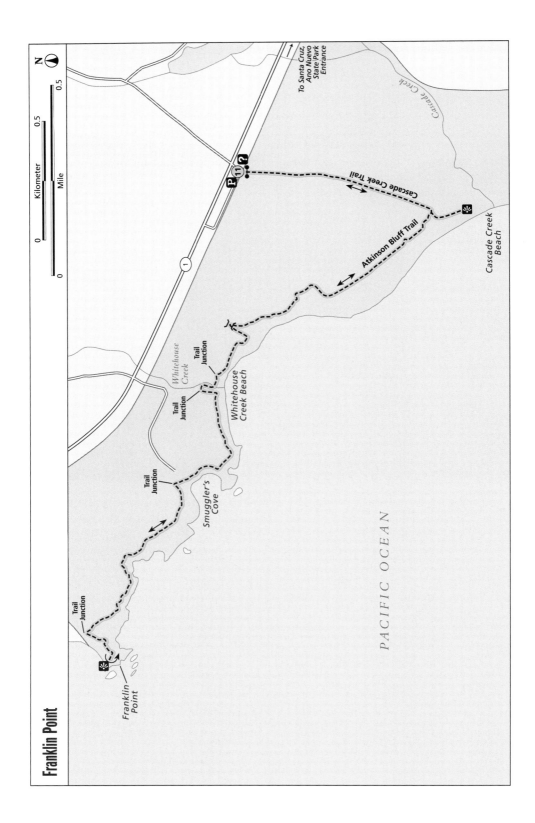

Franklin Point

Franklin Point

Trail Junction

Trail Junction

Smuggler's Cove

Trail Junction

Trail Junction

Whitehouse Creek Beach

Whitehouse Creek

Atkinson Bluff Trail

Cascade Creek Trail

Cascade Creek Beach

Cascade Creek

PACIFIC OCEAN

To Santa Cruz,
Ano Nuevo
State Park
Entrance

P

N

0   0.5   Kilometer   0.5

0   Mile   0.5

by wind and rain. The boardwalk leads you to a viewing deck with a bench on Franklin Point. Franklin Point was named after the *Sir John Franklin* clipper ship that wrecked in the fog off the coast in 1865. On a clear day Pigeon Point Lighthouse towers on the point to the north and Ano Nuevo Island Lighthouse is visible to the south. Both of these lighthouses were built partly as a result of the Franklin Point tragedy. This viewing deck is a unique and scenic spot for a picnic lunch before going back to the trailhead the way you came.

MILES AND DIRECTIONS

0.0 Start at the yellow gate and Cascade Creek Trailhead.

0.5 Come to a trail junction with signs for Cascade Creek Beach to the left and Whitehouse Creek to the right. Turn left to Cascade Beach.

0.6 Come to the Cascade Beach overlook. Go back to the trail junction to continue to Whitehouse Creek.

1.4 Walk across the wooden footbridge.

1.6 Walk down the wooden steps to Whitehouse Beach and across Whitehouse Creek at the north end of the beach.

1.7 Come to a trail junction and bear left to Franklin Point.

2.0 Arrive at the Smuggler's Cove overlook.

2.1 Come to a trail junction and bear left to Franklin Point.

2.6 Come to a trail junction and bear left to Franklin Point.

2.8 Arrive at Franklin Point and the viewing platform. Go back to the trailhead the way you came.

5.6 Arrive back at the trailhead.

BAKERIES, BREWERIES, EATS, AND SLEEPS

Whale City Bakery Bar and Grill, 490 Coast Rd., Davenport 95017; (831) 423-9009; whalecitybakery.com. Breakfast, lunch, and dinner. Delicious olallieberry croissants.

Arcangeli/Norm's Market, 287 Stage Rd., Pescadero 94060; (650) 879-0147; normsmarket.com. Family run since 1929, the market's artichoke garlic bread is a taste bud sensation. The fresh baked pies and seasonal jams are extra treats. Wines from the family vineyard.

Highway 1 Brewing Company, 5720 CA 1/Cabrillo Hwy., Pescadero 94060; (650) 879-9243; highway1brewery.com. Grass-fed locally grown beef and organic chicken. Beer garden is dog friendly when open.

Duarte's Tavern, 202 Stage Rd., Pescadero 94060; (650) 879-0464; duartes tavern.com. This is a casual comfort food station dating back to the late 1890s. Save room for their olallieberry pie.

Boardwalk leads out to Franklin Point.

Pescadero Creek Inn, 393 Stage Rd., Pescadero 94060; (650) 879-1898; pescaderocreekinn.com. Relax in the comforts of the renovated 100-year-old farmhouse in historic Pescadero, just 2 miles inland from the coast.

HI Pigeon Point Lighthouse Hostel, 210 Pigeon Point Rd., Pescadero 94060; (650) 879-0633; hiusa.org. Dorms, rooms, and common-area amenities in a uniquely scenic location.

CAMPING

Costanoa Resort and KOA Campground, 2001 Rossi Rd. at CA 1, Pescadero 95060; (650) 879-1100 for lodge; (800) 562-9867 for KOA campground; costanoa .com. The resort has a spa and a range of accommodations, along with a restaurant and general store. The campground (RV and tent) is clean and classy, with "comfort stations" that have shower and sauna facilities as well as an outdoor fireplace.

12. **BEAN HOLLOW**

WHY GO?
The whole family, including the four-legged furry ones (on leash), can enjoy this short, flat, pleasant hike. The trail hugs the coast just below CA 1 between two splendid state beaches with picnic spots at each end.

THE RUNDOWN

Distance: 2.0 miles out and back

Start: South end of parking lot at north Bean Hollow State Beach (Pebble Beach)

Nearest towns: Pescadero and Half Moon Bay

Hiking time: About 1 hour

Fees and permits: None

Conveniences: Vault toilets at both ends of the trail in the beach parking lot, picnic tables, and trash and recycling containers at turnaround, but no water at either end

Beach access: Yes; dogs allowed on leash

Trail users: Hikers and dogs on leash on the trail and beaches

Trailhead elevation: 21 feet

Highest point: 38 feet

Trail surface: Dirt and sand

Difficulty: Easy

Seasonal highlights: Wildflowers in the spring

Managing agency: California State Parks, San Mateo Coast Sector Office, 95 Kelly Ave. off of CA 1, Half Moon Bay 94019; (650) 726-8819 or (650) 879-2170; parks.ca .gov

FINDING THE TRAILHEAD

From Half Moon Bay at CA 1 and CA 92, drive 17 miles south on CA 1 and turn right (ocean side) into the Bean Hollow State Beach (Pebble Beach entrance) parking lot. **GPS:** N37 14.15' / W122 24.96'

WHAT TO SEE
Bean Hollow State Beach was part of a Mexican rancho in the late 1830s, and the beach was originally known as Arroyo de los Frijoles. Today the state beach protects a unique area of native coastal plants. Although the hike is short, the trail's meandering route sprinkled with interpretive panels and dotted with multiple wooden footbridges highlighted by myriad wildflowers makes it an especially picturesque

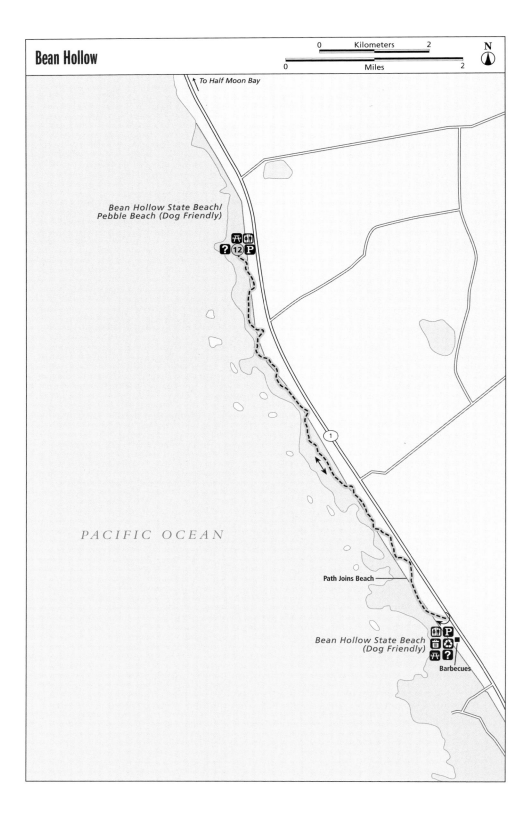

Bean Hollow

0 Kilometers 2
0 Miles 2

N

↑ To Half Moon Bay

Bean Hollow State Beach/
Pebble Beach (Dog Friendly)

PACIFIC OCEAN

1

Path Joins Beach

Bean Hollow State Beach
(Dog Friendly)

Barbecues

Spring brings green to the coastal trails.

jaunt. The path is the meeting of a native garden with extensive tidepools anchored by sheltered beaches at each end. Watch for shorebirds and harbor seals.

You begin in the parking lot at the north Bean Hollow State Beach (Pebble Beach), where the parking is more ample than at south Bean Hollow State Beach. Having said that, you can choose to park in either parking lot and hike the trail in either direction.

Take time to explore the tidepools, ponder on a bench overlooking the ocean, or snap the perfect shot of a spring poppy as you thread the coast on the narrow trail. Take advantage of the picnic tables at both ends of the trail and bring a snack. If you are hiking with your furry family member, spend some time walking the beach before going back to the trailhead the way you came.

MILES AND DIRECTIONS

0.0 Start at the south end of dog friendly (on leash) north Bean Hollow State Beach (Pebble Beach).

0.8 Come to dog friendly (on leash) south Bean Hollow State Beach and walk on the beach up to the parking lot and end of trail.

1.0 Come to the south Bean Hollow State Beach parking lot and your turn-around point. Go back to the trailhead the way you came.

2.0 Arrive back at the trailhead.

Nonnative ice plant decorates the trail.

BAKERIES, BREWERIES, EATS, AND SLEEPS

Arcangeli/Norm's Market, 287 Stage Rd., Pescadero 94060; (650) 879-0147; normsmarket.com. Family run since 1929, their artichoke garlic bread is a taste bud sensation. The fresh baked pies and seasonal jams are extra treats. Wines from the family vineyard.

Highway 1 Brewing Company, 5720 CA 1/Cabrillo Hwy., Pescadero 94060; (650) 879-9243; highway1brewery.com. Grass-fed locally grown beef and organic chicken. Beer garden is dog friendly when open.

Duarte's Tavern, 202 Stage Rd., Pescadero 94060; (650) 879-0464; duartes tavern.com. This is a casual comfort food station dating back to the late 1890s. Save room for their olallieberry pie.

Pescadero Creek Inn, 393 Stage Rd., Pescadero 94060; (650) 879-1898; pescaderocreekinn.com. Relax in the comforts of the renovated 100-year-old farm-house in historic Pescadero, just 2 miles inland from the coast.

Bridges allow access across seasonal creeks.

CAMPING

Half Moon Bay State Beach, 95 Kelly Ave. off of CA 1, Half Moon Bay 94019; (650) 726-8819 or (650) (726-8820); parks.ca.gov. Tent and RV spaces (no hookups).

    Costanoa Resort and KOA Campground, 2001 Rossi Rd. at CA 1, Pescadero 95060; (650) 879-1100 for lodge; (800) 562-9867 for KOA campground; costanoa .com. The resort has a spa and a range of accommodations, along with a restaurant and general store. The campground (RV and tent) is clean and classy, with "comfort stations" that have shower and sauna facilities as well as an outdoor fireplace.

13. COWELL-PURISIMA TRAIL

WHY GO?

This is a sweet stretch of the California Coastal Trail tucked between the Pacific and land farmed for over 150 years. Except for an unexpectedly short and picturesque dip through a lush coastal scrub canyon, the hike traces the bluffs along a wide flat trail with unobstructed coastal views.

THE RUNDOWN

Distance: 6.8 miles out and back

Start: Cowell-Purisima Trail sign to the right of restrooms

Nearest town: Half Moon Bay

Hiking time: About 3.5 hours

Fees and permits: None

Conveniences: Restrooms with vault toilets and trash container at trailhead; portable toilet at turnaround point

Beach access: Yes

Trail users: Hikers and mountain bikers

Trailhead elevation: 172 feet

Highest point: 172 feet

Trail surface: Compacted soil and dirt

Difficulty: Moderate

Seasonal highlights: Wildflowers in the spring

Managing agency: California State Parks, San Mateo Coast Sector Office, 95 Kelly Ave., off of CA 1, Half Moon Bay 94019; (650) 726-8819; www.parks.ca.gov. Peninsula Open Space Trust, 222 High St., Palo Alto 94301; (650) 854-7696; openspacetrust.org.

FINDING THE TRAILHEAD

From Half Moon Bay at CA 1 and CA 92, drive 5 miles south to the Cowell-Purisima Coastal Trail parking lot on the right. **GPS:** N37 23.77' / W122 24.96'

WHAT TO SEE

The trail was established with the cooperation of private landowners, land trusts, and the State Coastal Conservancy, resulting in an easement at the west end of agricultural land between Cowell Ranch and Purisima Farms. The deal protects open space, adds another link to the ambitious California Coastal Trail project, and preserves wildlife habitat and over 1,700 acres of farmland. California grows 99 percent of the

Looking north at pocket beaches

The trail threads along small agricultural plots.

brussels sprouts consumed by Americans, much of which are grown in the region and generate millions of dollars at harvest.

The hike begins just off CA 1 at the trail gate and information panel. The ADA-accessible trail follows a corridor between fenced farmland for the first 0.3 mile. At the T junction the trail on the left goes to the scenic overlook. You can turn left for the overlook and return to the junction to follow the trail to Cowell Ranch State Beach. The route described here has you turning right on the bluff to Cowell Ranch State Beach and going to the scenic overlook on the way back to the trailhead.

The next 0.7 mile is a pleasant, flat journey with a panorama of ocean, cliffs, and hidden beaches on the left and meticulously cultivated land on the right against a backdrop of coastal prairies rolling against tree-studded hills across CA 1. There are several interpretive panels along the way describing the cultural history, the land and marine wildlife habitat, and the vegetation.

At 1.0 mile you come to a gate and the end of the ADA-accessible trail. Walk through the open gate to continue the hike along a narrower curving trail dipping into a lush ravine. You cross a footbridge over Purisima Creek just 0.2 mile ahead and follow the trail out of the ravine. You then crest and continue walking along the bluff.

At 2.4 miles you cross a footbridge over a gully and continue walking along the bluff on the wide trail, with more farmland and grazing cattle on the right. On a clear day you can see a giant white golf-ball-looking installation on a cliff to the north. That's the Air Force Station at Pillar Point above Half Moon Bay.

At 3.0 miles you come to a three-way trail junction and a gate. There is a portable toilet at the junction. Walk through the open gate and turn left to the overlook and bench past the stairs to Cowell Ranch State Beach on the right. The trail to the right goes back to CA 1 and a parking area. That parking area is the designated trailhead for Cowell Ranch State Beach. The narrow dirt trail straight ahead going north along the bluff goes to the Ritz-Carlton and connects to another trail network that is part of the California Coastal Trail.

Theoretically you could keep walking approximately 9 miles to the north and end up at Half Moon Bay Harbor. On this hike, you get to enjoy the views and a snack at the overlook or on the beach before going back the way you came.

If you did not turn left for the scenic overlook at the first trail junction at the beginning of the hike, you can continue to the overlook on the way back and back-track to the junction to return to the trailhead.

MILES AND DIRECTIONS

0.0   Start at the gate and sign for the Cowell-Purisima Trail.

0.3   Come to a trail junction for the scenic overlook to the left and Cowell Ranch State Beach to the right. Turn right to Cowell Ranch State Beach.

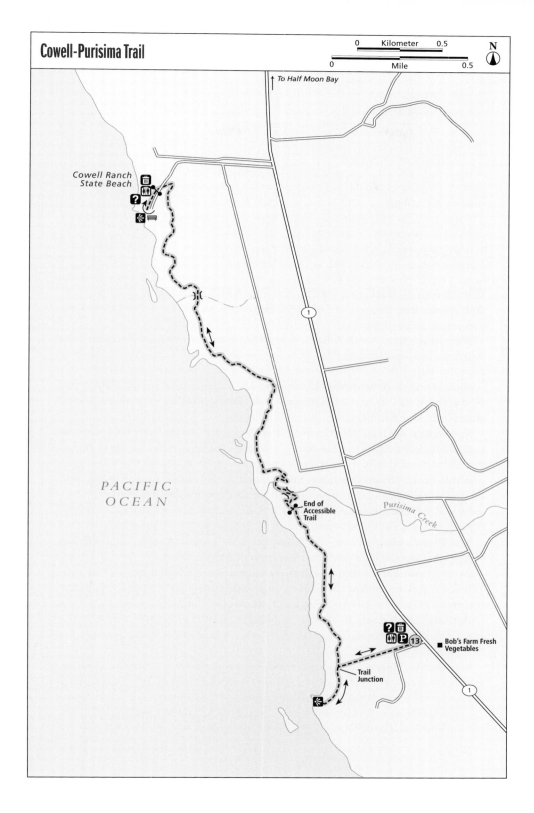

Cowell-Purisima Trail

Kilometer

N

Mile

To Half Moon Bay

Cowell Ranch
State Beach

PACIFIC
OCEAN

End of
Accessible
Trail

Purisima Creek

Trail
Junction

Bob's Farm Fresh
Vegetables

1.0   Walk through the open gate.

1.2   Walk across Purisima Creek on a footbridge.

2.4   Walk across the gully on a footbridge.

3.0   Walk through the open gate and come to a trail junction. Turn left to the overlook and bench.

3.1   Arrive at the overlook. Go back the way you came past the first trail junction at 0.3 mile to continue to the scenic overlook at the south end of the trail.

6.2   Arrive at the scenic overlook. Go back to the trail junction and turn right to return to the trailhead.

6.8   Arrive back at the trailhead.

BAKERIES, BREWERIES, EATS, AND SLEEPS

Half Moon Bay Bakery, 514 Main St., Half Moon Bay 94019; (650) 726-484. An assortment of baked goodies.

Moonside Bakery and Cafe, 604 Main St., Half Moon Bay 94019; (650) 726-9070; moonsidebakery.com. Breakfast and lunch in addition to mouthwatering cakes and tarts.

Half Moon Bay Brewing Company, 390 Capistrano Rd., Half Moon Bay 94019; (650) 728-2739; hmbbrewingco.com. Food prepared with seasonal local ingredients. Dog friendly patio

San Benito House, 356 Main St., Half Moon Bay 94019; (650) 726-3425; san benitohouse.com. The loud bar of this 100-year-old inn serves craft beers on tap that are updated weekly.

Bob's Farm Fresh Vegetable Stand, on Cabrillo Hwy. S./CA 1 across from Cowell-Purisima trailhead. The locally grown English peas are a sweet treat.

New Leaf Community Market, 150 San Mateo Rd., Half Moon Bay 94019; (650) 726-3110. The chain prides itself in its "hippie roots and foodie palates."

San Benito House Deli, 356 Main St., Half Moon Bay; (650) 726-3425; san benitohouse.com. Hearty sandwiches, cookies, and other treats.

Pasta Moon Ristorante and Bar, 315 Main St., Half Moon Bay 94019; (650) 726-5125; pastamoon.com. Succulent house-made pasta and a pizza Margherita worthy of its Italian roots. One dog friendly table.

Barbara's Fish Trap & To Go, 281 Capistrano Rd., Half Moon Bay 94019; (650) 728-7049; barbarasfishtrap.com. Fun harbor setting and outdoor table for food to go if pooch is tagging along.

San Benito House, 356 Main St., Half Moon Bay 94019; (650) 726-3425; san benitohouse.com. This 100-year-old inn has small, charming upstairs rooms (some private baths and some shared baths); no phone or TV in rooms.

Comfort Inn, 2930 Cabrillo Hwy./CA 1, Half Moon Bay 94019; (650) 712-1999; choicehotels.com. Quiet, dog friendly comfort.

Wandering south across the headlands

Cowell-Purisima is a bike-friendly trail.

Ritz-Carlton Resort, Miramontes Point Rd., Half Moon Bay 94019; (650) 712-7000; ritzcarlton.com. The epitome of post-hike luxury for you and your furry four-legged pal.

HI Pigeon Point Lighthouse Hostel, 210 Pigeon Point Rd., Pescadero 94060; (650) 879-0633; hiusa.org. Dorms, rooms, and common-area amenities in a uniquely scenic location.

CAMPING

Half Moon Bay State Beach, 95 Kelly Ave. off of CA 1, Half Moon Bay 94019; (650) 726-8819 or (650) 726-8820; www.parks.ca.gov. Tent and RV spaces (no hookups).

Pelican Point RV Park, 1001 Miramontes Rd., Half Moon Bay 94019; (650) 726-9100; pelicanpointrv.com.

Pillar Point RV Park, 4000 Cabrillo Hwy./CA 1, Half Moon Bay 94019; (650) 712-9277; pillarpointrvparklive.com. Oceanfront with hookups; free Wi-Fi and cable. No reservations, but website updates daily availability.

Costanoa Resort and KOA Campground, 2001 Rossi Rd. at CA 1, Pescadero 95060; (650) 879-1100 for lodge; (800) 562-9867 for KOA campground; costanoa .com. The resort has a spa and a range of accommodations, along with a restaurant and general store. The campground (RV and tent) is clean and classy, with "comfort stations" that have shower and sauna facilities as well as an outdoor fireplace.

Wildflowers color the coastal trail.

14. HALF MOON BAY STATE BEACH TO RITZ-CARLTON

WHY GO?

This is a primo stitch of the California Coastal Trail, partly paved multiuse and partly dirt. This southern segment begins in a nicely developed state park campground and ends on the golf course by an exclusive bluff-top resort.

THE RUNDOWN

Distance: 8.6 miles out and back

Start: Ocean side of Half Moon Bay State Beach entrance

Nearest town: Half Moon Bay

Hiking time: About 4 hours

Fees and permits: Parking fee

Conveniences: Restrooms with flush toilets, outdoor shower, picnic tables, grills, trash and recycling containers, campground

Beach access: Yes; dogs allowed on beaches south of the state park (parts voice control, parts on leash)

Trail users: Hikers, mountain bikers, golfers in carts on golfcourse section, and dogs (on leash on some sections)

Trailhead elevation: 40 feet

Highest point: 95 feet

Trail surface: Pavement and dirt

Difficulty: Moderate

Seasonal highlights: Wildflowers in the spring

Managing agency: California State Parks, San Mateo Coast Sector Office, 95 Kelly Ave. off of CA 1, Half Moon Bay 94019; (650) 726-8819; www.parks.ca.gov

FINDING THE TRAILHEAD

From Half Moon Bay at CA 1 and CA 92, drive 0.3 mile south to Kelly Avenue. Turn right and drive 0.5 mile on Kelly Avenue to the end of the street and turn right into the Half Moon Bay State Beach parking lot. **GPS:** N37 27.92'/W122 26.68'

WHAT TO SEE

Thanks to Half Moon Bay State Park's Coastside Trail, this hike runs along an extensive stretch of the California Coastal Trail (CCT) on bluffs overlooking wide strips of white sand beaches and across coastal prairies. What makes this coastal trail unique

Moody morning along
Redondo Beach

is that the oceanfront golf cart path at the resort also happens to double as a multi-use trail, where golfers, hikers, and bikers share the trail. How often do you see the CCT's blue wave logo alongside signs for the next golf hole? This takes the term "multiuse" to a new level.

You set off walking south along the paved trail to wide-open views of the Pacific and the coastline. In the spring, blooming ice plant colors the trailside in pinks and yellows. At 0.8 mile there's a portable toilet and bicycle tool and pump station at the edge of the parking lot for the Poplar Street staging area. Oceanfront benches are sprinkled along the first mile of paved trail until you cross the Seymour wooden footbridge at 1.0 mile. The trail becomes dirt on the other side of the bridge, and a sign on the right announces that you are entering the Bird Trail at Wavecrest for about 0.3 mile. The next couple of miles meander around eroded inlets on the bluffs of coastal scrub protected as Wavecrest Open Space. Stay on the main trail as it laces the bluff top, and respect the warning signs about staying away from the eroding cliff edge.

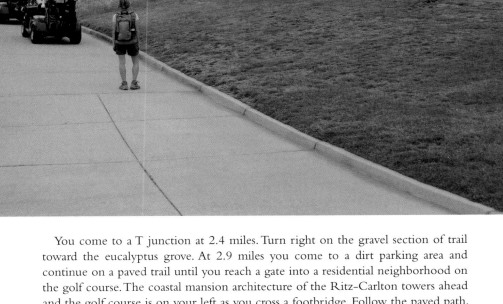

The California Coastal Trail shares the golf cart path south of the Ritz-Carlton.

You come to a T junction at 2.4 miles. Turn right on the gravel section of trail toward the eucalyptus grove. At 2.9 miles you come to a dirt parking area and continue on a paved trail until you reach a gate into a residential neighborhood on the golf course. The coastal mansion architecture of the Ritz–Carlton towers ahead and the golf course is on your left as you cross a footbridge. Follow the paved path, which becomes a golf path at 3.6 miles, with the lodge on your left as you climb the hill to the crest. You are now officially on the golf course, sharing the path with golf carts, hotel guests on a stroll, and cyclists. Be respectful of the golfers and refrain from talking or making noise when passing a golfer preparing to swing. If your four-legged pal is hiking with you, use your best golf trail etiquette and keep him on a short leash when passing golf carts.

You come to a beach access stairway on the right at 3.8 miles. The picnic table at the top of the stairs is an idyllic spot for a snack break. If time permits on the return, walk down the stairs to enjoy beautiful, dog friendly Arroyo Canada Verde Beach/Pelican Point Beach below the sheer cliffs. Continue on the path along the fence and turn right over a footbridge to continue along the CCT. You come to the

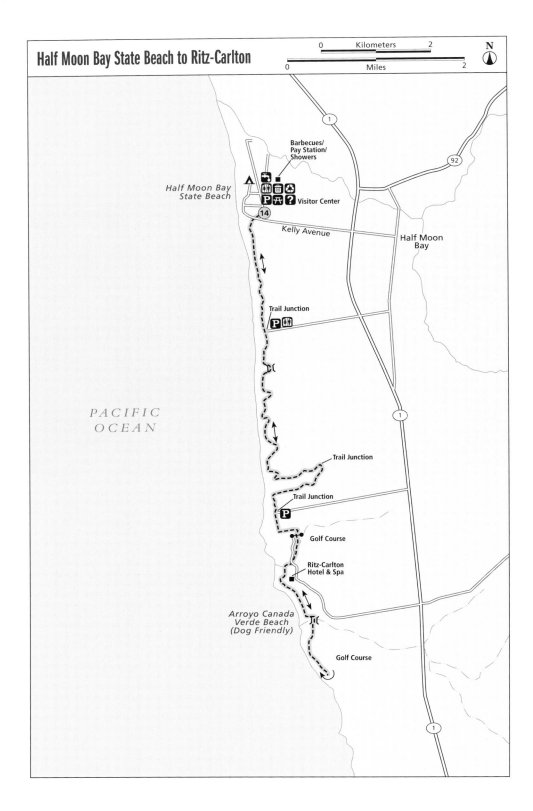

Half Moon Bay State Beach to Ritz-Carlton

0   Kilometers   2

0   Miles   2

N

Barbecues/
Pay Station/
Showers

Half Moon Bay
State Beach

Visitor Center

14

Kelly Avenue

Half Moon
Bay

Trail Junction

PACIFIC
OCEAN

Trail Junction

Trail Junction

Golf Course

Ritz-Carlton
Hotel & Spa

Arroyo Canada
Verde Beach
(Dog Friendly)

Golf Course

1

92

1

1

end of the trail at 4.3 miles. The bench at the fence is another convenient spot for a snack while savoring the sweeping views of the coastline. Go back to the trailhead the way you came.

MILES AND DIRECTIONS

0.0 Start on the ocean side of the Half Moon Bay State Beach entrance.

0.8 Walk across unmarked Poplar Road.

1.0 Walk across the Seymour footbridge.

2.4 Come to a T junction and turn right.

2.9 Walk across the dirt parking lot to the paved trail.

3.2 Walk through a gate and across a footbridge.

3.6 Walk on the golf path and uphill past the hotel to the crest.

3.8 Come to the dog friendly (voice control) Arroyo Canada Verde beach access stairs on the right and turn right over the wooden footbridge.

4.3 Arrive at the fence and bench and the trail end. Go back to the trailhead the way you came.

8.6 Arrive back at the trailhead.

BAKERIES, BREWERIES, EATS, AND SLEEPS

Half Moon Bay Bakery, 514 Main St., Half Moon Bay 94019; (650) 726-484. An assortment of baked goodies.

Moonside Bakery and Cafe, 604 Main St., Half Moon Bay 94019; (650) 726-9070; moonsidebakery.com. Breakfast and lunch in addition to mouthwatering cakes and tarts.

Half Moon Bay Brewing Company, 390 Capistrano Rd., Half Moon Bay 94019; (650) 728-2739; hmbbrewingco.com. Food prepared with seasonal local ingredients. Dog friendly patio.

San Benito House Deli, 356 Main St., Half Moon Bay; (650) 726-3425; san benitohouse.com. The loud bar of this 100-year-old inn serves craft beers on tap that are updated weekly.

New Leaf Community Market, 150 San Mateo Rd., Half Moon Bay 94019; (650) 726-3110. The chain prides itself in its "hippie roots and foodie palates."

Barbara's Fish Trap & To Go, 281 Capistrano Rd., Half Moon Bay 94019; (650) 728-7049; barbarasfishtrap.com. Fun harbor setting and outdoor table for food to go if pooch is tagging along.

Pasta Moon Ristorante and Bar, 315 Main St., Half Moon Bay 94019; (650) 726-5125; pastamoon.com. Succulent house-made pasta and a pizza Margherita worthy of its Italian roots. One dog friendly table.

Launching from a coastal bluff

Comfort Inn, 2930 Cabrillo Hwy./CA 1, Half Moon Bay 94019; (650) 712-1999; choicehotels.com. Quiet, dog friendly comfort.

San Benito House, 356 Main St., Half Moon Bay 94019; (650) 726-3425; san benitohouse.com. This 100-year-old inn has small, charming upstairs rooms (some private baths and some shared baths); no phone or TV in rooms.

Ritz-Carlton Resort, Miramontes Point Rd., Half Moon Bay 94019; (650) 712-7000; ritzcarlton.com. The epitome of post-hike luxury for you and your furry four-legged pal.

CAMPING

Half Moon Bay State Beach, 95 Kelly Ave. off of CA 1, Half Moon Bay 94019; (650) 726-8819 or (650) 726-8820; parks.ca.gov. Tent and RV spaces (no hookups).

Pelican Point RV Park, 1001 Miramontes Rd., Half Moon Bay 94019; (650) 726-9100; pelicanpointrv.com.

Pillar Point RV Park, 4000 Cabrillo Hwy./CA 1, Half Moon Bay 94019; (650) 712-9277; pillarpointrvparklive.com. Oceanfront with hookups; free Wi-Fi and cable. No reservations, but website updates daily availability.

Costanoa Resort and KOA Campground, 2001 Rossi Rd. at CA 1, Pescadero 95060; (650) 879-1100 for lodge; (800) 562-9867 for KOA campground; costanoa .com. The resort has a spa and a range of accommodations, along with a restaurant and general store. The campground (RV and tent) is clean and classy, with "comfort stations" that have shower and sauna facilities as well as an outdoor fireplace.

15. HALF MOON BAY STATE BEACH TO PILLAR POINT HARBOR

WHY GO?

Half Moon Bay's Coastside Trail provides almost 9 miles of developed multiuse trail as part of the California Coastal Trail. This northern segment from the state beach is on a paved surface all the way to the picturesque harbor. The trail connects pristine coastal scrub habitat with residential and commercial neighborhoods. This trail is also ideal for exploring on two wheels so you can savor the most pristine sections if you have limited time.

THE RUNDOWN

Distance: 7.8 miles out and back

Start: East side of Half Moon Bay State Beach entrance

Nearest towns: Half Moon Bay and Princeton-by-the-Sea

Hiking time: About 4 hours

Fees and permits: Parking fee

Conveniences: Restrooms with flush toilets, outdoor shower, picnic tables, grills, trash and recycling containers, campground

Beach access: Yes; dogs on leash on Surfer's Beach/El Granada Beach and Mavericks Beach (see map)

Trail users: Hikers, cyclists, and dogs on leash

Trailhead elevation: 40 feet

Highest point: 40 feet

Trail surface: Paved

Difficulty: Moderate

Seasonal highlights: Wildflowers in the spring

Managing agency: California State Parks, San Mateo Coast Sector Office, 95 Kelly Ave. off of CA 1, Half Moon Bay 94019; (650) 726-8819; parks.ca.gov. San Mateo County Parks, (650) 355-8289 or (650) 363-4020, smcoparks.org.

FINDING THE TRAILHEAD

From Half Moon Bay at CA 1 and CA 92, drive 0.3 mile south to Kelly Avenue. Turn right and drive 0.5 mile on Kelly Avenue to the end of the street, then turn right into the Half Moon Bay State Beach parking lot.

GPS: N37 28.00' / W122 26.67'

WHAT TO SEE

The northern segment of Half Moon Bay's Coastside Trail starting at the state beach entrance greets cyclists with a stunning umbrella of cypress trees. The trail threads along the strand of state beaches over four footbridges and across a couple of roads. The first couple of miles are the most serene, with picnic areas on the ocean side and meadows of coastal scrub as a buffer between the Pacific and CA 1. There are restrooms at each of the beach parking lots. In the springtime the scrub bursts with yellow lupine, pale mauve wild radish, fields of bright mustard, and splashes of golden poppies. Interpretive panels along the trail describe the ecology, habitats, and marine life.

The last couple of miles brush up against more residential development on the east side, and the paved path merges with Mirada Road past a couple of inns and restaurants before you turn left to continue on the last section of paved trail through Mirada Surf County Park. There are restrooms and an information panel at this trailhead.

The trail is closely tucked between the water and CA 1 for a short distance before arriving at Pillar Point Harbor and the map board that marks the end of the multiuse trail next to the kayak rental shop at Johnson Pier. Pillar Point Harbor is known for its commercial and sport fishing facilities and its rescue operations.

You can stroll around the harbor and the quaint harbor-front community of Princeton-by-the-Sea before going back to the trailhead the way you came.

Option: This route makes for a great bicycle ride. Follow the same directions in about an hour on a bike.

MILES AND DIRECTIONS

0.0 Start on the east side of the Half Moon Bay State Beach entrance and proceed north.

0.5 Cross Pilarcitos Creek on the footbridge.

1.0 Pass Venice Beach across the road.

1.2 Cross the footbridge.

1.6 Cross the road past Dunes and Roosevelt Beaches.

2.3 Cross another footbridge and continue along Mirada Road.

2.6 Turn left onto the paved path at Mirada Surf County Park and cross the footbridge.

3.6 Come to Pillar Point Harbor. Take the crosswalk across the road. The trail continues on the west side.

3.9 Arrive at the end of the trail on the west side of the road at the map board. Retrace your steps back to the trailhead.

7.8 Arrive back at the trailhead.

Half Moon Bay State Beach to Pillar Point Harbor

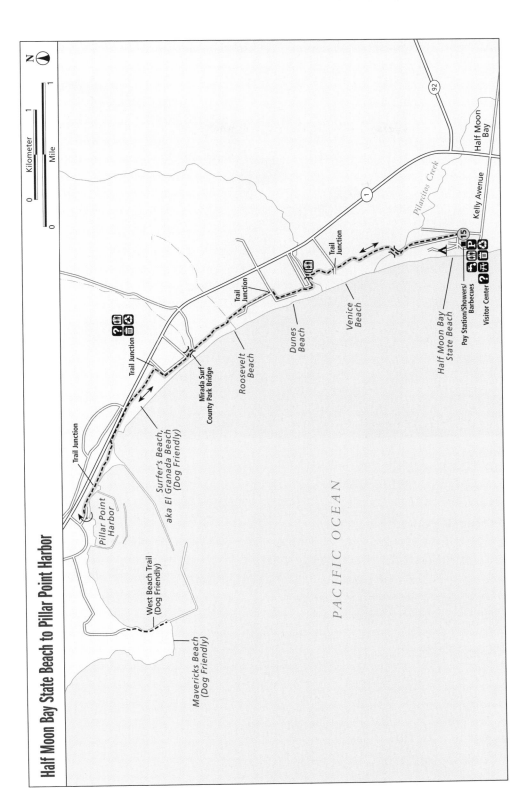

Taking a break to study the California Coastal Trail map

Looking south along Surfer's Beach

BAKERIES, BREWERIES, EATS, AND SLEEPS

Half Moon Bay Bakery, 514 Main St., Half Moon Bay 94019; (650) 726-484. An assortment of baked goodies.

Moonside Bakery and Cafe, 604 Main St., Half Moon Bay 94019; (650) 726-9070; moonsidebakery.com. Breakfast and lunch in addition to mouthwatering cakes and tarts.

Half Moon Bay Brewing Company, 390 Capistrano Rd., Half Moon Bay 94019; (650) 728-2739; hmbbrewingco.com. Food prepared with seasonal local ingredients. Dog friendly patio

San Benito House Deli, 356 Main St., Half Moon Bay; (650) 726-3425; sanbenitohouse.com. Hearty sandwiches, cookies, and other treats.

Barbara's Fish Trap & To Go, 281 Capistrano Rd., Half Moon Bay 94019; (650) 728-7049; barbarasfishtrap.com. Fun harbor setting and outdoor table for food to go if pooch is tagging along.

Princeton Seafood Company Market and Restaurant, 9 Johnson Pier, Half Moon Bay 94019; (650) 726-2722. Family owned for over 30 years. The clam chowder is a family recipe. Great spot to eat or order crab in season.

The Inn at Mavericks, 346 Princeton Ave., Half Moon Bay 94019; (650) 728-1572; innatmavericks.com. Quaint location and dog friendly.

Comfort Inn, 2930 Cabrillo Hwy./CA 1, Half Moon Bay 94019; (650) 712-1999; choicehotels.com. Quiet, dog friendly comfort.

HI Point Montara Lighthouse Hostel, 8800 Cabrillo Hwy./CA 1, Montara 94037; (650) 728-7177; hiusa.org. Dorm or private rooms in a nineteenth-century light station with common-area amenities.

CAMPING

Half Moon Bay State Beach, 95 Kelly Ave. off of CA 1, Half Moon Bay 94019; (650) 726-8819 or (650) 726-8820; parks.ca.gov. Tent and RV spaces (no hookups).

Pillar Point RV Park, 4000 Cabrillo Hwy./CA 1, Half Moon Bay 94019; (650) 712-9277; pillarpointrvparklive.com. Oceanfront with hookups; free Wi-Fi and cable. No reservations, but website updates daily availability.

Costanoa Resort and KOA Campground, 2001 Rossi Rd. at CA 1, Pescadero 95060; (650) 879-1100 for lodge; (800) 562-9867 for KOA campground; costanoa.com. The resort has a spa and a range of accommodations, along with a restaurant and general store. The campground (RV and tent) is clean and classy, with "comfort stations" that have shower and sauna facilities as well as an outdoor fireplace.

16. PILLAR POINT BLUFF

WHY GO?

A little local knowledge goes a long way to getting to the trailhead, even with a landmark that looks like a giant golf ball. This short, isolated stretch of the California Coastal Trail on a bluff laced with spur trails delivers phenomenal views topped with a dash of iconic California surfing culture.

THE RUNDOWN

Distance: 2.4-mile circuit

Start: Pillar Point Bluff at yellow gate across from West Shoreline Access parking lot

Nearest towns: Princeton and Half Moon Bay

Hiking time: About 1 hour

Fees and permits: None

Conveniences: Portable toilets, trash and recycling container and information panel at south end of parking lot across the road from trailhead

Beach access: No from the trail, but yes from the West Shoreline Access parking lot along West Beach Trail. Dogs on leash on West Beach Trail to Mavericks Beach (see map).

Trail users: Hikers, mountain bikers, equestrians, and dogs on leash

Trailhead elevation: 29 feet

Highest point: 191 feet

Trail surface: Pavement and dirt

Difficulty: Easy

Seasonal highlights: Be awed by winter's high surf and giant waves; wildflowers in the spring.

Managing agency: San Mateo County Parks, (650) 355-8289 or (650) 363-4020, smcoparks.org

FINDING THE TRAILHEAD

From CA 1 at CA 92, drive 3.7 miles north on CA 1 to Avenue Granada, which turns into Capistrano, and turn left along the harbor. Drive 0.3 mile on Prospect Avenue and turn left on Broadway Avenue, which becomes Princeton Avenue. Turn left on West Point at the T junction and hug the coast toward the giant golf ball structure (Pillar Point Air Force Station) on the bluff. Turn left into the parking lot for West Shoreline Access at the foot of the hill. The trailhead is across the road from the parking lot at the yellow gate. **GPS:** N37 30.12' / W122 29.82'

WHAT TO SEE

San Mateo County acquired the bluff land in 2011 with a grant. The open space provides habitat for wildlife and has added another stitch to the California Coastal Trail. The bluffs are part of the rare "coastal prairie" ecosystem. Tilling, development, and invasive plant species are some of the culprits in the loss of coastal prairies; only 5 to 10 percent remain intact in California. California blackberry, coffeeberry, and coyote bush thrive on the bluff, and yellow mustard blooms in the spring.

The bluffs are laced with trails, some very close to the eroding cliffs. Respect the signs warning hikers to stay back from the dangerous cliffs. The paved service road is the easiest and safest way to approach the bluffs and return to the trailhead. The dirt trails described in this hike are close enough to the cliffs to reward you with grand views while staying at a safe distance from the eroded sections.

Part of this hike is along the Jean Lauer Trail. The first mile of the trail is on the eastern edge of the bluffs overlooking the airport and revealing views of Montara Mountain at the northern end of the Santa Cruz Mountains.

The second half of the circuit is about the dramatic, panoramic coastal views and the stunning beach at the foot of the cliffs. Pillar Point Bluffs are famous for looking out toward the Mavericks, the legendary massive winter waves that draws twenty-four of the world's best big-wave surfers and enthusiastic spectators for the Titans of Mavericks surfing contest. Some scenes from the movie *Chasing Mavericks,* based on

Reefs off Pillar Point

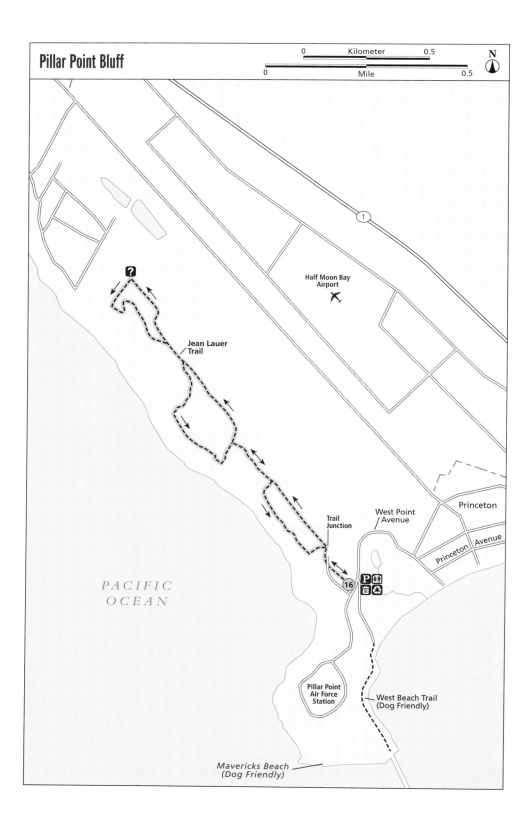

Pillar Point Bluff

Kilometer

0   0.5

Mile

0   0.5

N

Half Moon Bay
Airport

Jean Lauer
Trail

PACIFIC
OCEAN

Trail
Junction

West Point
Avenue

Princeton

Princeton Avenue

16

Pillar Point
Air Force
Station

West Beach Trail
(Dog Friendly)

Mavericks Beach
(Dog Friendly)

1

the life of Jay Moriarty, who first surfed Mavericks at the age of 16, were filmed at Half Moon Bay. The famous break caused by an unusually shaped underwater rock formation was supposedly named after a surfer's dog named Maverick, who would often try to follow him into the water.

Even if you're not a surfer, it's a pretty cool spot to experience and a dazzling hike you can share with Fido.

MILES AND DIRECTIONS

0.0 Start at the yellow gate across from the Shoreline Access parking lot and walk up the paved service road.

0.1 Come to the end of the paved road, with the radio tower on the right. Continue on the dirt trail.

0.5 Come to an unmarked trail junction and wide dirt trail. Turn right.

0.8 Come to a fork and bear right.

1.0 Arrive at an interpretive panel, "Land's End Scrub and Habitat," at the edge of a residential development. Turn left to loop back.

1.2 Come to an unmarked trail junction and turn left to walk on the main trail.

1.4 Merge onto the main trail and close a loop. Bear right after the bench ahead to walk on the main bluff trail.

1.9 Come to a T junction and bear right through the pine grove.

2.0 Turn right at the fork to continue on the bluffs, or walk straight to the radio tower and paved service road.

2.4 Arrive back at the trailhead.

BAKERIES, BREWERIES, EATS, AND SLEEPS

Half Moon Bay Bakery, 514 Main St., Half Moon Bay 94019; (650) 726-484. An assortment of baked goodies.

Moonside Bakery and Cafe, 604 Main St., Half Moon Bay 94019; (650) 726-9070; moonsidebakery.com. Breakfast and lunch in addition to mouthwatering cakes and tarts.

Half Moon Bay Brewing Company, 390 Capistrano Rd., Half Moon Bay 94019; (650) 728-2739; hmbbrewingco.com. Food prepared with seasonal local ingredients. Dog friendly patio

San Benito House Deli, 356 Main St., Half Moon Bay; (650) 726-3425; sanbenitohouse.com. Hearty sandwiches, cookies, and other treats.

Barbara's Fish Trap & To Go, 281 Capistrano Rd., Half Moon Bay 94019; (650) 728-7049; barbarasfishtrap.com. Fun harbor setting and outdoor table for food to go if pooch is tagging along.

View of Pillar Point
Air Force Station

Princeton Seafood Company Market and Restaurant, 9 Johnson Pier, Half Moon Bay 94019; (650) 726-2722. Family owned for over 30 years. The clam chowder is a family recipe. Great spot to eat or order crab in season.

The Inn at Mavericks, 346 Princeton Ave., Half Moon Bay 94019; (650) 728-1572; innatmavericks.com. Quaint location and dog friendly.

Comfort Inn, 2930 Cabrillo Hwy./CA 1, Half Moon Bay 94019; (650) 712-1999; choicehotels.com. Quiet, dog friendly comfort.

HI Point Montara Lighthouse Hostel, 8800 Cabrillo Hwy./CA 1, Montara 94037; (650) 728-7177; hiusa.org. Dorm or private rooms in a nineteenth-century light station with common-area amenities.

CAMPING

Half Moon Bay State Beach, 95 Kelly Ave. off of CA 1, Half Moon Bay 94019; (650) 726-8819 or (650) 726-8820; parks.ca.gov. Tent and RV spaces (no hookups).

Pillar Point RV Park, 4000 Cabrillo Hwy./CA 1, Half Moon Bay 94019; (650) 712-9277; pillarpointrvparklive.com. Oceanfront with hookups; free Wi-Fi and cable. No reservations, but website updates daily availability.

Costanoa Resort and KOA Campground, 2001 Rossi Rd. at CA 1, Pescadero 95060; (650) 879-1100 for lodge; (800) 562-9867 for KOA campground; costanoa.com. The resort has a spa and a range of accommodations, along with a restaurant and general store. The campground (RV and tent) is clean and classy, with "comfort stations" that have shower and sauna facilities as well as an outdoor fireplace.

17. DEVIL'S SLIDE

WHY GO?

This is what 1 mile of abandoned highway looks like when it is reinvented as a spectacular stretch of paved California Coastal Trail enjoyed by hikers and bikers. It's a rare hike that heaps so many historical, geological, natural, and scenic rewards on such a short jaunt.

THE RUNDOWN

Distance: 2.4 miles out and back

Start: Devil's Slide Trail south trailhead

Nearest towns: Pacifica and Half Moon Bay

Hiking time: About 1 hour

Fees and permits: None

Conveniences: Brochures, map boards, vault toilets, drinking fountains, trash and recycling containers, benches, and interpretive panels at both the north and south trailheads

Beach access: No

Trail users: Hikers, cyclists, and dogs on leash

Trailhead elevation: 257 feet

Highest point: 472 feet

Trail surface: Pavement

Difficulty: Easy

Seasonal highlights: Migrating whales in the spring and fall

Managing agency: San Mateo County Parks, (650) 355-8289 or (650) 363-4020, smcoparks.org

FINDING THE TRAILHEAD

 From Half Moon Bay at CA 1 and CA 92, drive 9 miles north and turn left at the signal just before entering the tunnel. The parking lot and south trailhead to Devil's Slide are immediately off of CA 1. From the south, you must use the southern parking lot and trailhead.

From Pacifica at Linda Mar Boulevard, drive 3 miles south on CA 1 and turn right into the parking lot before the bridge and tunnel for the north trailhead to Devil's Slide. If you want to hike the trail from the southern parking lot and trailhead, continue over the bridge and through the tunnel. The parking lot for the south trailhead is on the right just as you exit the tunnel. The hike described here begins from the south trailhead. **GPS:** N37 34.35' / W122 30.99'

WHAT TO SEE

The route to connect Pacifica with Montara dates back to the late 1800s, when travel over the mountain was far more treacherous. A railroad tunnel was carved and tracks were laid just in time for the Great San Francisco Earthquake to cause damage and delay progress. The construction of California State Route 1, known as Highway 1 (CA 1), in 1937 was a vast safety improvement for vehicles traveling along this stretch of coastline. But Mother Nature never made it easy. A landslide closed CA 1 at Devil's Slide for the first time in 1940, marking the beginning of a problematic stretch of road that would continue to suffer landslides and increased erosion.

By the 1960s it became evident that an alternate route was necessary. The California Department of Transportation drew plans to bypass Devil's Slide and build a six-lane freeway over Montara Mountain. The California Coastal Act of 1976, which mandated the protection of coastal resources, saved the mountain. Highway 1 at Montara and other designated areas would remain a scenic two-lane road.

Dedicated activism over three decades resulted in a ballot initiative for the construction of a tunnel to bypass Devil's Slide. Voters made their voices heard loud and clear in favor of the tunnel over the freeway plan. The engineering feat was several years in the planning and 7 years of construction. The Tom Lantos Tunnels opened to traffic in 2013, and the conversion of the old highway segment to a multiuse trail was completed in 2014. This is a short but vital stitch in the 1,200-mile California Coastal Trail that will extend from the Mexican border to Oregon.

You can hike or bike the trail from either the south or north trailhead and parking lot. Both trailheads have been developed with ample parking, restroom facilities, water, and interpretive panels. This hike starts from the south trailhead on the old highway. You immediately leave civilization behind as if a curtain were dropped as you step out of the parking lot and begin walking up the converted highway. The trail rises moderately as you walk past the Devil's Slide face of the mountain to where the trail crests before the mellow descent to the north end and parking lot. There are several benches to sit and enjoy the front-row seat as the Pacific drama unfolds before you. The scopes invite you to scan the surf for spouting whales, dancing dolphins, and soaring birds. The interpretive panels along the way take you on the region's natural and cultural historical journey.

At 0.5 mile you come to the actual "slide" area and the interpretive panel that explains the geology responsible for the ongoing movement of the rock on the cliffs. You can make the crest your destination at 0.9 mile before going back to the trailhead the way you came, or continue down 0.3 mile more to the north trailhead and parking lot for the full Devil's Slide Trail experience before going back to the trailhead the way you came.

South trailhead to
Devil's Slide

DEVIL'S SLIDE COASTAL TRAIL

Funding for this project was provided by the following agencies.

Caltrans   Coastal Conservancy   natural resources

Devil's Slide Coastal Trail is operated and maintained by San Mateo County Parks.

Enjoying views north along the
highway-to-trail conversion

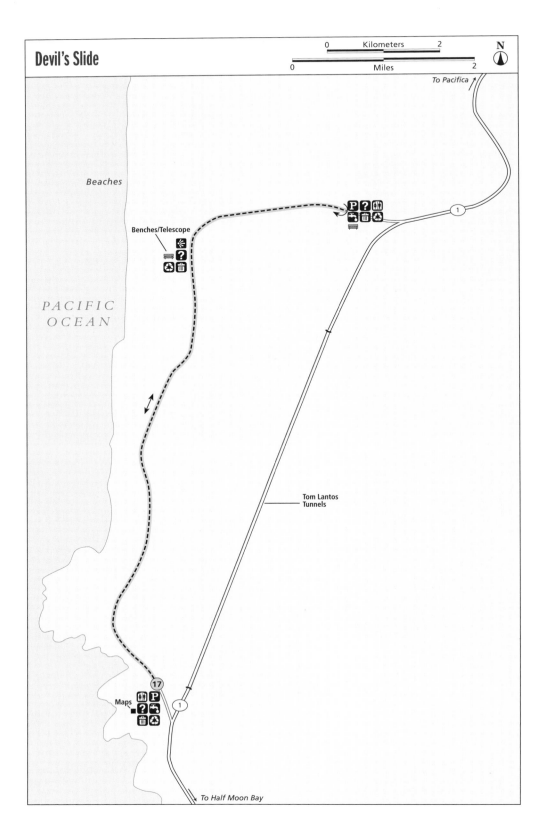

Devil's Slide

0 Kilometers 2

0 Miles 2

N

To Pacifica

Beaches

Benches/Telescope

PACIFIC OCEAN

1

Tom Lantos Tunnels

17

Maps

1

To Half Moon Bay

MILES AND DIRECTIONS

0.0 Start at the Devil's Slide Trail south trailhead.

0.9 Come to the crest and viewpoint.

1.2 Arrive at the north trailhead and parking lot. Go back to the south trailhead the way you came.

2.4 Arrive back at the trailhead.

BAKERIES, BREWERIES, EATS, AND SLEEPS

Mazzetti's Bakery, 101 Manor Dr., Pacifica 94044; (650) 355-1007; mazzettis bakery.com. Baking pastries, pies, and cakes for over 40 years.

Devil's Canyon Taproom, 5560 CA 1, Pacifica 94044; (650) 898-8855; devils slidetaproom.com. Craft beers on tap and good bar bites.

Gorilla Barbeque, 2145 CA 1, Pacifica 94044; (650) 359-7427; gorillabbq.com. A local success since 2006. Even vegetarians can make a tasty meal from the long list of sides with barbecue sauce.

Puerto-27, 525 Crespi Dr., Pacifica 94044; (650) 733-7343; puerto27.com. A Peruvian lunch and dinner menu and a Pisco Bar.

Nick's Restaurant, 100 Rockaway Beach Ave., Pacifica 94044; (650) 359-3900; nicksrestaurant.net. The story started in the Macedonia region of Greece in 1887, when Nick the Greek made his way to America and the West. Nick began to serve diners at this oceanfront location in 1927, and the family continues the tradition with breakfast, lunch, and dinner. The bar and lounge have music and dancing on the weekends.

Seabreeze Motel, 100 Rockaway Beach Ave., Pacifica 94044; (650) 359-3903; nicksrestaurant.net. No-frills motel rooms.

Pacifica Beach Hotel, 525 Crespi Dr., Pacifica 94044; (650) 355-9999; pacifica beachhotel.com. Jacuzzi tubs in every room.

Best Western Plus Lighthouse Hotel, 105 Rockaway Beach Ave., Pacifica 94044; (650) 355-6300; bestwestern.com. Rooms have a small fridge. Dog friendly for a max of 2 dogs per room with pet fee.

HI Point Montara Lighthouse Hostel, 8800 Cabrillo Hwy./CA 1, Montara 94037; (650) 728-7177; hiusa.org. Dorm or private rooms in a nineteenth-century light station with common-area amenities.

CAMPING

Half Moon Bay State Beach, 95 Kelly Ave. off of CA 1, Half Moon Bay 94019; (650) 726-8819 or (650) 726-8820; parks.ca.gov. Tent and RV spaces (no hookups).

18. PACIFICA STATE BEACH TO PIER

WHY GO?

This trail is a significant link in the California Coastal Trail. It has the distinction of passing through Mori Point, one of the more recent additions to the Golden Gate National Recreation Area. The hike is a cornucopia of vast views and a scenic adventure as you thread the bluffs along beaches and climb ridges.

THE RUNDOWN

Distance: 7.0 miles out and back

Start: California Coastal Trail at information board and start of paved multiuse path in north parking lot

Nearest town: Pacifica

Hiking time: About 3.5 hours

Fees and permits: Parking fee

Conveniences: Restrooms with flush toilets, outdoor shower, trash and recycling containers

Beach access: Yes; dogs allowed on leash on Pacifica State Beach, Rockaway Beach, and Sharp Park Beach (see map)

Trail users: Hikers, cyclists on paved sections, and dogs on leash

Trailhead elevation: 16 feet

Highest point: 341 feet

Trail surface: Pavement, dirt, and sand

Difficulty: Strenuous

Seasonal highlights: Wildflowers in the spring

Managing agency: Pacifica State Beach, California State Parks, Dept. of Parks and Recreation, (650) 738-7381, parks.ca.gov. Golden Gate National Recreation Area, Fort Mason, Building 201, San Francisco 94123; (415) 556-0560; nps.gov/goga. Mori Point, (415) 561-4323.

FINDING THE TRAILHEAD

From Pacifica at CA 1 and Linda Mar Boulevard, turn west into the Pacifica State Beach parking lot. **GPS:** N37 35.89' / W122 30.13'

WHAT TO SEE

This trail passes through various agency jurisdictions including state, federal, city, and county, but one of the most influential players is the National Park Conservancy.

The trail passes through a bluff-top meadow.

Mori Point's 110 acres are at the heart of this hike. Native Americans and Spanish explorers touched this land before the Mori family settled here to farm in the 1880s.

In recent times the oceanfront parcel attracted lots of commercial attention as a prime spot for various developments, and the land sat neglected and scarred as it awaited its fate. Luckily Pacifica citizens, environmental groups, and land trusts including the California Coastal Conservancy had a different vision. The Trust for Public Land purchased Mori Point in 2000 and transferred it to the National Park Service in 2002. The promontory and surrounding marshes were rehabilitated with designated trails for recreation and protected areas to restore balance for the endangered, colorful San Francisco garter snake and the red-legged frog. A multiuse trail was established to connect Pacifica State Beach to the Pacifica Pier.

The hike described here combines the paved multiuse trail with some of the more challenging and primitive dirt trails that lace the bluffs and cliffs between the south end of Pacifica State Beach and the Pacifica Pier 3 miles north.

The first 0.3 mile is easy and flat along the paved trail until you turn left and climb up the side of the hill on the dirt trail. Be aware that this cross-country hike uphill and down-swale on the bluffs will be challenging, and some trail sections are intimidating. But if you can handle a little thrill, the views are worth it. Otherwise, you can get to the pier by staying on the multiuse trail. The downside to the multiuse trail is that parts of it run along busy CA 1, and apart from suffering the traffic noise, you will miss out on 360-degree views.

The dirt trail is a huff-and-puff rewarded by sweeping views of the coastline. At the top you cross the paved trail before continuing down the other side on a narrow, more primitive trail. You rejoin the paved trail near the bottom and come to the Rockaway Beach parking lot. There are restrooms and an outdoor shower on your right as you walk across the parking lot and over a seasonal creek on a footbridge at 1.1 miles. Turn left after the bridge to continue walking on a narrow dirt trail. The creek and beach are on your left. Continue hugging the coast as you walk across the parking lot between Rockaway Beach and a few restaurants and motels.

At 1.4 miles you come to a seasonal creek. Depending on the flow, expect to get your feet wet if the water is higher than the rocks laid down as a footbridge. Once across the creek, you climb up the next hill along a steep, narrow dirt trail.

At 1.7 miles you have the choice of turning left downhill on the bluff to Mori Point or right uphill along the ridge for another dose of views before going down to the point. The trail described here takes you right and up to the ridge. You will see a sign for Mori Point at 1.8 miles on your way up to the ridge. You reach the summit

Rocky trail across seasonal creek

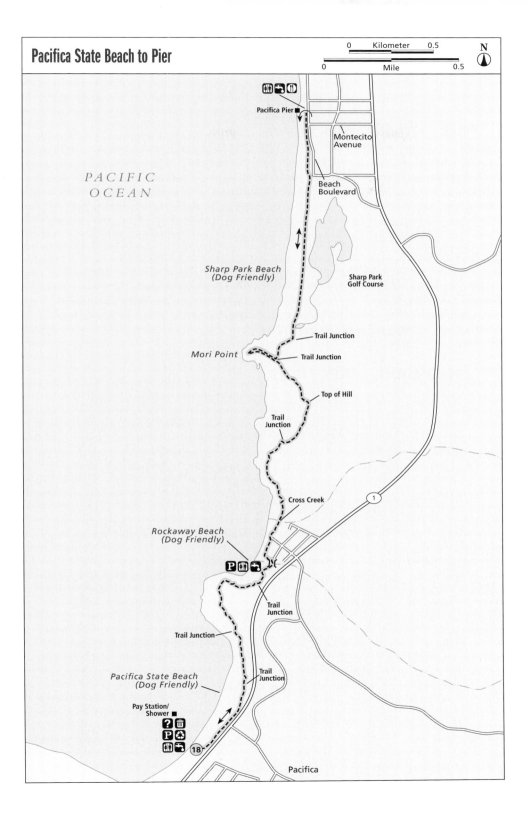

Pacifica State Beach to Pier

PACIFIC
OCEAN

Pacifica Pier ■

Montecito
Avenue

Beach
Boulevard

Sharp Park Beach
(Dog Friendly)

Sharp Park
Golf Course

Trail Junction

Mori Point   Trail Junction

Top of Hill

Trail
Junction

Cross Creek

1

Rockaway Beach
(Dog Friendly)

P

Trail
Junction

Trail Junction

Pacifica State Beach
(Dog Friendly)

Trail
Junction

Pay Station/
Shower ■

P

18

Pacifica

at 2.0 miles, and the views are spectacular. But what gets this far up must go down. Turn left and begin the steep descent to Mori Point. Hiking sticks and footwear with good traction will ease the stiff grade.

At 2.3 miles you reach Mori Point past several trail signs and a bench on the left. If you are here in the spring, your eyes will feast on the cascading blooms of yellow tidytips and goldfields. The pier is in sight up the coast on your right. Walk back up 0.2 mile to the California Coastal Trail sign for Bootlegger's Steps on the left. Turn left down the 200 steps and then left again at the interpretive panel to the pier and seawall. Sharp Park Beach will be on your left and Sharp Park Golf Course and wetlands on your right. There are picnic tables on your right just before the pier.

You arrive at the pier at 3.5 miles. There are restrooms, a drinking fountain, and the Chitchat Cafe at the entrance to the concrete pier. Dogs are not allowed on the pier. Take time to walk down the pier, where there are always anglers fishing for ocean salmon, striped bass, and Dungeness crab. Go back to the trailhead the way you came or along the multiuse trail.

MILES AND DIRECTIONS

0.0   Start on the multiuse trail at the north end of the dog friendly (on leash) Pacifica State Beach parking lot.

0.3   Turn left on the unmarked dirt trail and up the hill.

0.6   Walk across the paved trail.

1.0   Join the paved trail and walk downhill to the Rockaway Beach parking lot.

1.1   Walk across the creek on the footbridge and make a sharp left on the dirt trail. Continue hugging the coast.

1.4   Walk across the seasonal creek and continue walking uphill on the dirt trail.

1.7   Turn right and walk up the trail along the ridge.

2.0   Arrive on the summit and turn left down the steep trail toward Mori Point.

2.3   Arrive at Mori Point. Soak up the views and walk back to the trail junction on the left.

2.5   Come to a trail junction for the California Coastal Trail and Bootlegger's Steps to Old Mori Road on the left. Walk down the steps.

2.6   Turn left to the pier and seawall.

3.5   Arrive at the Pacifica Pier. Go back to the trailhead the way you came, or follow the multiuse trail back to the trailhead.

7.0   Arrive back at the trailhead.

Steep descent toward Sharp Park Beach and the Pacifica Pier

BAKERIES, BREWERIES, EATS, AND SLEEPS

Mazzetti's Bakery, 101 Manor Dr., Pacifica 94044; (650) 355-1007; mazzettis bakery.com. Baking pastries, pies, and cakes for over 40 years.

Devil's Canyon Taproom, 5560 CA 1, Pacifica 94044; (650) 898-8855; devils slidetaproom.com. Craft beers on tap and good bar bites.

Gorilla Barbeque, 2145 CA 1, Pacifica 94044; (650) 359-7427; gorillabbq.com. A local success since 2006. Even vegetarians can make a tasty meal from the long list of sides with barbecue sauce.

Puerto-27, 525 Crespi Dr., Pacifica 94044; (650) 733-7343; puerto27.com. A Peruvian lunch and dinner menu and a Pisco Bar.

Nick's Restaurant, 100 Rockaway Beach Ave., Pacifica 94044; (650) 359-3900; nicksrestaurant.net. The story started in the Macedonia region of Greece in 1887, when Nick the Greek made his way to America and the West. Nick began to serve diners at this oceanfront location in 1927, and the family continues the tradition with breakfast, lunch, and dinner. The bar and lounge have music and dancing on the weekends.

Chitchat Cafe, 5 W. Manor Dr., Pacifica 94044; (650) 738-2380.

Seabreeze Motel, 100 Rockaway Beach Ave., Pacifica 94044; (650) 359-3903; nicksrestaurant.net. No-frills motel rooms.

Pacifica Beach Hotel, 525 Crespi Dr., Pacifica 94044; (650) 355-9999; pacifica beachhotel.com. Jacuzzi tubs in every room.

Best Western Plus Lighthouse Hotel, 105 Rockaway Beach Ave., Pacifica 94044; (650) 355-6300; bestwestern.com. Rooms have a small fridge. Dog friendly for a max of 2 dogs per room with pet fee.

HI Point Montara Lighthouse Hostel, 8800 Cabrillo Hwy./CA 1, Montara 94037; (650) 728-7177; hiusa.org. Dorm or private rooms in a nineteenth-century light station with common-area amenities.

CAMPING

Half Moon Bay State Beach, 95 Kelly Ave. off of CA 1, Half Moon Bay 94019; (650) 726-8819 or (650) 726-8820; parks.ca.gov. Tent and RV spaces (no hookups).

Dog Friendly Beaches

Pigeon Point Light Station Beach is a convenient stretch of sandy beach to stop for a stretch with your dog on leash or explore tidepools at low tide. The beach is accessed just a short walk north of the Pigeon Point Light Station and Hostel. Pigeon Point Light Station SHP, 210 Pigeon Point Rd., Pescadero; (650) 879-2120; parks.ca.gov

Bean Hollow State Beach is actually made up of two separate beaches that anchor the north and south ends of the Bean Hollow trail (see hike 12). Both beaches allow dogs on leash and have picnic tables at the edge of the parking lots. Beachcombing is a popular activity at this spot. The beaches are easily accessed right off of CA 1 at 11000 Cabrillo Hwy., 3 miles south of Pescadero. California State Parks, (650) 726-8819, parks.ca.gov

Enjoying a refreshing romp at a dog friendly beach

Arroyo Canada Verde Beach (aka Pelican Point Beach) is a sweeping sand beach at the south end of the Half Moon Bay Links golf course and the multiuse segment of the California Coastal Trail (see hike 14). Dogs can gallivant under voice control and hobnob with some of the Ritz canine guests. There are some nice tidepools at low tide. The beach is accessed from a long stairway at the foot of the Ritz-Carlton bluffs, 1001 Miramontes Point Rd., Half Moon Bay. City of Half Moon Bay, (650) 726-8297

Redondo Beach is north of Arroyo Canada Verde Beach, and at low tide you can walk almost 2 miles south to the south end of Canada Verde Beach and the Half Moon Bay tidepools. Dogs are welcome on leash on Redondo Beach. The beach is accessed from a parking lot at the end of Redondo Beach Road off CA 1 in Half Moon Bay. Choose your path down to the beach carefully, since erosion has made some access points precarious. Coastside Land Trust, 788 Main St., Half Moon Bay 94019; (650) 726-5056

Mavericks Beach is named after a local dog that insisted on swimming out with his surfer-dude human. This beach is a surfing hot spot, and dogs are welcome to hang out here on leash. Fido can go home with tales of how he set his paws and sniffed around the site of the world-renowned annual big-wave surfing competition. The beach is accessed from CA 1 through Princeton-by-the-Sea on West Point Avenue by walking right past the harbor on a trail past the jetty. San Mateo County Harbor District, 1 Johnson Pier, Half Moon Bay 94019; (650) 726-4382

Montara State Beach's photogenic mile-long stretch of sand against sandstone cliffs is worth a stroll with dogs on leash. The beach is accessed 8 miles north of Half Moon Bay at 1st Street in Montara off of CA 1. California State Parks, (650) 726-8819, parks.ca.gov

Pacifica State Beach (aka Linda Mar Beach) is almost 1 mile of firm-packed sand for beachcombing with dogs on leash (see hike 18). The beach is accessed at 5000 Pacific Coast Hwy., Pacifica. City of Pacifica, (650) 738-7381

Sharp Park Beach offers 1 mile of on-leash strolling with pooch at low tide. South of the pier near Sharp Park Golf Course, the brown sand beach is wider (see hike 18). The beach is accessed from the parking lot on Montecito Avenue just south of the Pacifica Pier. City of Pacifica, (650) 738-7381

Coastal Attractions

Pie Ranch, 2080 Cabrillo Hwy./CA 1, Pescadero 94060; (650) 879-9281; pieranch.org. This working farm offers culinary classes and a farm stand with organic produce and seasonal pies baked fresh daily.

Pescadero Marsh Natural Preserve, off of CA 1 at New Years Creek Road, Pescadero 94960; (650) 593-3281; coastsidestateparks.org. This is almost 250 acres of wintering habitat for waterfowl on the Pacific Flyway on the east side of CA 1. The breathtaking marshland is a tapestry of habitats that can be sampled on the scenic nature walk along salt marshes and Pescadero Creek with a loop back to Pescadero Beach.

A sea of Calla Lilies along the coast

Princeton-by-the-Sea, off of CA 1 at West Shoreline Access at the north end of Half Moon Bay, has a quaint fishing village vibe. From here you can follow a 0.5-mile trail to Mavericks Beach.

Titans of Mavericks surfing competition. The opening ceremony for this international surfing competition is typically in October, but the one-day event is dependent on the precise surf conditions and can occur any time between November and March. Go to titansofmarvericks.com for details on signing up for the "alert" call and best viewing locations.

Pescadero is a small historic town 2 miles inland from CA 1 and Pescadero Beach. Stroll the main street, where stagecoaches dropped off weekend San Franciscans, and prepare to be charmed by this unexpected pocket that time forgot.

BEST COASTAL FARMERS' MARKETS

Coastside Farmers' Market (coastsidefarmersmarkets.org) prides itself in supporting young farmers as well as established family farms. The market is open at the Shoreline Station off CA 1 in Half Moon Bay every Sat from 9 a.m. to 1 p.m. The market is also at Rockaway Beach off CA 1 in Pacifica on Wed from 2:30 to 6:30 p.m.

San Francisco and Marin Counties

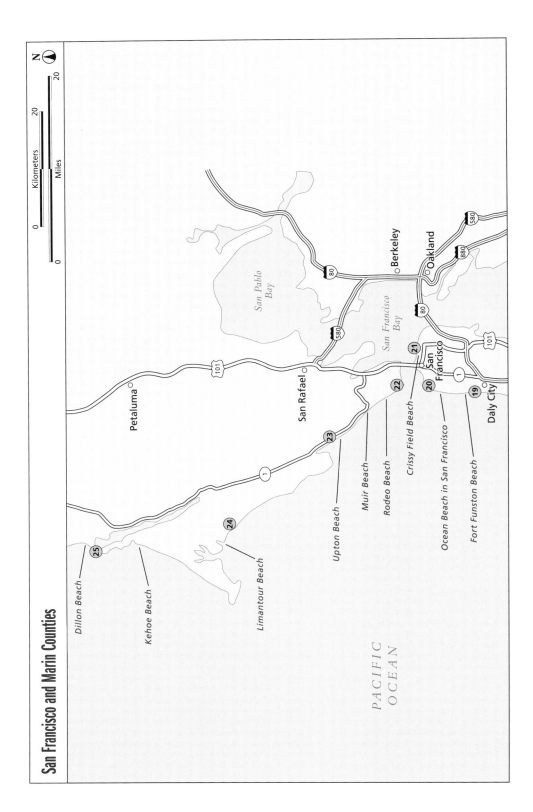

SAN FRANCISCO COUNTY

SAN FRANCISCO COUNTY is the only consolidated city-county in California, and has been since 1856. It is the state's smallest county, with a larger-than-life world-scale appeal for skyline esthetics, dynamic topography, historical and cultural attractions, and palate pleasers. Whether it's Alcatraz Island, the Golden Gate Bridge, Pier 39, Ghirardelli Square, Golden Gate Park, or the Presidio, these iconic landmarks are never far from view along a coastal trek. The San Francisco Peninsula's setting, cradled by the Pacific and the Bay with portals into nature through the Golden Gate National Recreation Area's ridges and beaches, is the ultimate in coastal access for wanderings on foot as well as on two wheels. You won't be the first to leave your heart in San Francisco.

Coastal bloom in springtime

19. FORT FUNSTON

WHY GO?

There are three good reasons to hike the trail on the former military complex at the southwestern corner of San Francisco, now part of the Golden Gate National Recreation Area. The coastal views north across to the Marin Headlands are stunning. The trail is a stitch in the California Coastal Trail. Best of all, Fort Funston is canine central for hikers with four-legged trail pals.

THE RUNDOWN

Distance: 2.2 miles out and back

Start: Ocean Beach at south end of parking lot

Nearest town: San Francisco

Hiking time: About 1 hour

Fees and permits: None

Conveniences: Water, portable toilets, and trash containers

Beach access: Yes; dogs under voice control at Fort Funston Beach

Trail users: Hikers, equestrians, and dogs under voice control

Trailhead elevation: 184 feet

Highest point: 184 feet

Trail surface: Pavement and sand

Difficulty: Easy

Seasonal highlights: Migrating whales in the spring and fall

Managing agency: Golden Gate National Recreation Area, Fort Mason, Building 201, San Francisco 94123; (415) 556-0560; nps.gov/goga. Fort Funston, (415) 556-8642. Call or check the website for current dog policy.

FINDING THE TRAILHEAD

From CA 35/Skyline Boulevard at John Muir Drive, drive 0.25 mile south and turn right into Fort Funston. Follow the signs for parking. **GPS:** N37 42.88' / W122 30.16'

WHAT TO SEE

Lake Merced Military Reservation was established in 1900 as a defense post for San Francisco Bay. The base was renamed for General Frederick Funston in 1917, and the fort was a Nike missile launch site during the Cold War. The compound was deactivated in the 1960s and eventually absorbed into the Golden Gate National Recreation Area.

Fort Funston is a dog walker's heaven.

The sandstone cliffs are steep, and erosion has made them unstable in various places. Signs are posted reminding hikers to keep away from the cliff edge. The 200-foot-high bluffs on the western edge are popular with hang gliders. There is a wheelchair-accessible viewing deck and launch area at the southwest end of the parking lot. If you enjoy the mesmerizing effect of watching hang gliders, Fort Funston's 200-foot-high cliffs are a premier hand-glider viewing location. The fort also provides an opportunity to experience Mother Nature's tenacity, where the surf is eroding the cliffs and sand dunes are gradually gobbling some of the old military base's web of paved roads.

For you who hike with your dog or if you just enjoy a friendly canine, Fort Funston is known as a mecca for dogs. Dog owners have always felt welcome in San Francisco, and when it was established, the Golden Gate National Recreational Area (not Golden Gate National Park) was guaranteed as an "urban" park where all family members would always have access to open space to romp. In the case of four-legged furry children, they would continue to enjoy leash-free playgrounds

The trail crosses shifting sand dunes.

and beaches even with the change of management structure. In the last decade, dogs on leash and leash free in the Golden Gate National Recreation Area have become a topic of great controversy, with a very active pro-dog community pushing back against the National Park Service's attempts to limit bowwow access and institute what some call "draconian" changes. For now, it's still party time for canines. Saying that the trails are popular with dog owners is an understatement. Doggie nannies from around the Bay Area and local dog owners gather at Fort Funston daily. It is not uncommon to see as many as one hundred dogs of all shapes and breed varieties romping and bounding in the dunes and walking on the trails with their humans for their morning outing.

The first hint that dogs rule at Fort Funston is the water fountain at the trailhead. There's a water fountain for humans and a lower one for pooches.

You set off from the Ocean Beach trailhead on a paved path, which was wheelchair accessible until drifting sand covered sections of the trail. One of the most amazing phenomena at Fort Funston is how much of the paved trails and former paved roads have been covered by the shifting sand dunes.

Returning after a play day at Fort Funston Beach

At 0.3 mile you come to a trail junction with a water fountain for humans as well as a Fido-height fountain. There were so many dogs at this junction when we hiked the trail that they almost had to take a number and stand in line for their turn to lap up the wet stuff. Fortunately all were well behaved and gregarious as they stood at the community water cooler. The view opens up toward Merced Lake on the right across Skyline Boulevard. The trail forks ahead, and both spurs head downhill to meet up on the main trail 0.2 mile ahead. Bear right on the trail going down and consider coming back up on the other trail on your return.

At 0.5 mile you come to another trail junction. Turn left at the sign for Funston Beach Trail. Please note that Fort Funston Beach is no longer accessible from this point. Continue walking north. Several patches of windswept sand interrupt the pavement as you continue forward, and metal barriers on the left guide you along as you walk toward the views of the headlands across the bay. At 0.6 mile there's something surreal about seeing benches buried by sand drifts and paths erased.

At 0.9 mile the pavement ends abruptly at a trail junction. The horse trail is on the right, heading back to the parking lot. Bear left of the trees and continue on

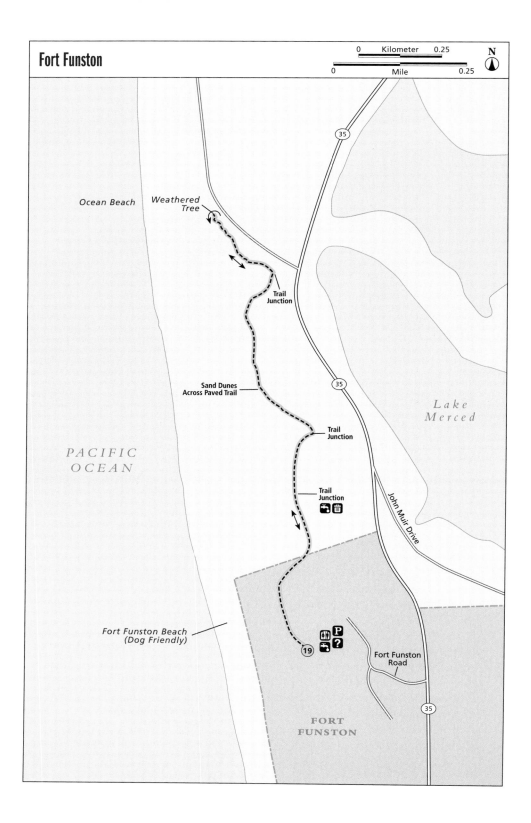

Fort Funston

Ocean Beach

Weathered
Tree

Trail
Junction

Sand Dunes
Across Paved Trail

PACIFIC
OCEAN

Trail
Junction

Trail
Junction

Fort Funston Beach
(Dog Friendly)

19

FORT
FUNSTON

Lake
Merced

John Muir Drive

Fort Funston
Road

35

35

35

N

Kilometer
0   0.25
0   0.25
Mile

a narrow sand trail around the post. The narrow trail meanders over the swales of dunes above Skyline Boulevard. At 1.1 miles you come to an ailing cypress tree perched on the left above Ocean Beach. This is your turnaround.

MILES AND DIRECTIONS

0.0 Start at the Ocean Beach trailhead.

0.3 Come to a trail junction and bear right.

0.5 Come to a trail junction and turn left at the sign for Funston Beach Trail.

0.6 The sand takes over parts of the trail as you walk north.

0.9 Come to a trail junction for the horse trail on the right. Pavement ends. Bear left around the post onto a narrow trail.

1.1 Come to a wind-battered cypress tree on the dunes above Ocean Beach. Go back to the trailhead the way you came.

2.2 Arrive back at the trailhead.

BAKERIES, BREWERIES, EATS, AND SLEEPS

Boudin Bakery and Cafe, 3251 20th Ave., San Francisco 94132; (415) 564-1849. Dog friendly patio.

Beach Chalet Brewery & Restaurant, 1000 Great Hwy., San Francisco 94121; (415) 386-8439; beachchalet.com.

Sunset Reservoir Brewing Company, 1735 Noriega St., San Francisco 94122; (415) 571-8452; sunsetbeerssf.com.

Original Joe's, 11 Glenwood Ave., Daly City 94015; (650) 755-7400. Neighborhood Italian favorite since 1956.

Seal Rock Inn Restaurant, 545 Point Lobos Ave., San Francisco 94121; (415) 752-8000. The restaurant on the ground floor of the Seal Rock Inn serves a breakfast and lunch menu all day.

Seal Rock Inn, 545 Point Lobos Ave., San Francisco 94121; (415) 752-8000; sealrockinn.com. This very convenient hotel on the doorstep of beaches and coastal trails has been a popular rest stop since 1959. Some rooms have fireplaces.

Alpine Inn and Suites, 560 Carter St., Daly City 94014; (415) 586-4237; alpine motorinn.com. Continental breakfast included. Fridge and microwave in room.

Ocean Park Motel, 2690 46th Ave., San Francisco 94116; (415) 566-7020; oceanparkmotel.com. It was the first motel in San Francisco in 1937 and is dog friendly.

20. LANDS END

WHY GO?

This scenic, popular trail to Eagles Point, part of the California Coastal Trail along the historic Cliff House Railway route, is both the land's end and the gateway to San Francisco Bay. This hike is a showcase of shady cypress groves, rocky beaches, panoramic viewpoints, and interpretive panels about San Francisco Bay's natural and cultural history.

THE RUNDOWN

Distance: 2.8 miles out and back

Start: North end of Lands End Lookout Visitor Center parking lot

Nearest town: San Francisco

Hiking time: About 1.5 hours

Fees and permits: None

Conveniences: Bicycle rack, drinking fountain, benches, trash and recycling containers; gift shop, bookstore, deli, and restrooms at visitor center

Beach access: Yes; dogs on leash to Mile Rock Beach (see map)

Trail users: Hikers, cyclists on the first half, and dogs on leash

Trailhead elevation: 155 feet

Highest point: 284 feet

Trail surface: Compacted granite for wheelchair-accessible section, dirt, and wooden steps

Difficulty: Moderate

Seasonal highlights: Great spot for watching winter Pacific storms

Managing agency: Golden Gate National Recreation Area, 201 Fort Mason, San Francisco 94123-0022; (415) 561-4700 or (415) 426-5240; nps.gov/goga

FINDING THE TRAILHEAD

From the intersection of Fulton Street and Great Highway at the northwest corner of Golden Gate Park, drive approximately 1 mile, past the Cliff House on the west side where Great Highway becomes Point Lobos Avenue. Drive 0.1 mile up Point Lobos Avenue to the Lands End Lookout Visitor Center on the left. Turn left into the parking lot. **GPS:** N37 46.85' / W122 30.71'

WHAT TO SEE

Easy access from the city and nearby residential neighborhoods, its proximity to the historic Cliff House, ample parking, and well-developed facilities at the Lands End

View of Marin Headlands and
Golden Gate Bridge

Lookout Visitor Center make this trail a very popular family outing with locals and tourists. But somehow, even on a busy weekend, this rugged stretch of coastline with inspiring views up the headlands to the north remains an enchanting place with a sense of wildness.

You begin the hike at the north end of the parking lot just beyond the Lands End Lookout Visitor Center and follow the signs for Eagle's Point. The first approximate 0.5 mile is wheelchair accessible. The rest of the trail is dirt and can be muddy following winter rains. You pass several interpretive panels and viewing scopes along the way, including a lookout over the Sutro Bath ruins. In the late 1880s, seven swimming pools were once part of several seaside attractions developed by Adolph Sutro. The spur trails on the right lead up to El Camino del Mar.

At 0.7 mile you come to a junction on the left with a set of wooden stairs—256 steps heading down to rocky Mile Rock Beach down the Mile Rock Lookout Trail. There is usually a sign marking this junction, but unfortunately on occasion someone decides to take a sign rather than a postcard or a photo as a memento. A fork partway down the stairs leads to Lands End Point to the right. There is a very

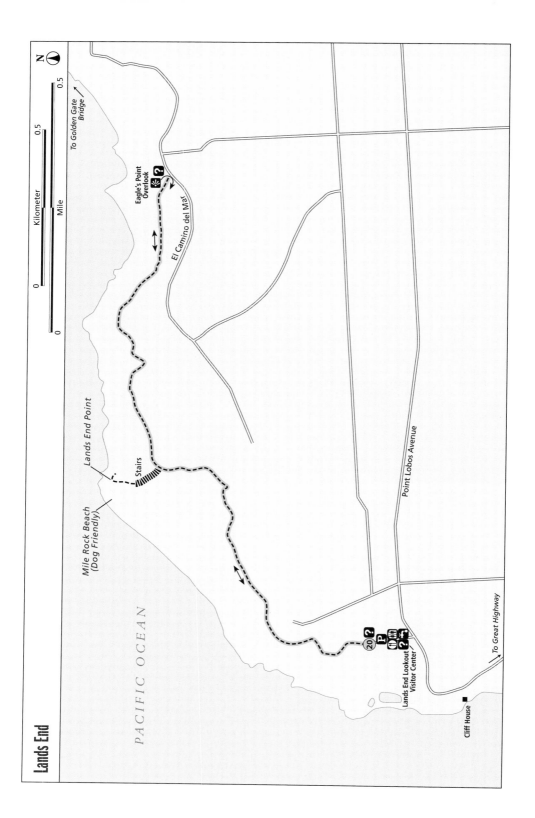

Lands End

To Golden Gate Bridge

Eagle's Point
Overlook

El Camino del Mar

Lands End Point

Stairs

Mile Rock Beach
(Dog Friendly)

PACIFIC OCEAN

Point Lobos Avenue

Lands End Lookout
Visitor Center

Cliff House

To Great Highway

N

Kilometer

Mile

0   0.5

0   0.5

narrow primitive trail to the point and an equally primitive trail that loops down to Mile Rock Beach from the point. What goes down must come up, and those 256 steps are quite the thigh pumpers on the way up. If time and energy permit, you can do this side trip to the beach and point on your return from Eagle's Point Overlook.

Just short of 1 mile, you come to another set of wooden stairs straight ahead. Walk up the 139 steps over this rise and prepare to walk down more steps as the trail continues to wind along the bluff toward Eagle's Point. The views across to the headlands are quite dramatic, and on a clear day you can see the sea stacks of the Farallon Islands 27 miles west off the coast in the Gulf of the Farallones National Marine Sanctuary. The islands, a designated wilderness area and national wildlife refuge, are crucial to a large seabird colony and migrating marine species including orcas, humpbacks, gray and blue whales, several species of seals, and the great white shark. The islands are often referred to as the "Galapagos of Central California."

At 1.4 miles you arrive at the end of the trail at El Camino del Mar just past Eagle's Point Overlook. A terrace has replaced the wooden deck at the overlook, and Eagle's Point rewards hikers with a stunning view of the Golden Gate Bridge and an excellent vantage point for postcard–perfect photos. Wisps of fog often give the bridge a very moody, mystical feel.

MILES AND DIRECTIONS

0.0 Start at the California Coastal Trail sign at the north end of the Lands End Lookout Visitor Center parking lot.

0.7 Come to a wooden staircase heading down on the left.

1.4 Arrive at Eagle's Point and the end of the trail at El Camino del Mar. Return the way you came.

2.8 Arrive back at the trailhead.

BAKERIES, BREWERIES, EATS, AND SLEEPS

Butter Love Bakeshop, 94122 Balboa St., San Francisco 94121; (415) 602-3988; butterlovebakeshop.com. If you love pie, this is the spot.

Boudin Bakery & Cafe, 160 Jefferson St., San Francisco 94121; (415) 928-1849; boudinbakery.com. A French family and wild yeast in the bay's air became the winning recipe for the famous San Francisco sourdough French bread, which has been tingling taste buds since 1849. Don't miss the flagship location complete with bistro, gifts, museum, and 30-foot window on the bakers at work. Dog friendly patio.

Beach Chalet Brewery & Restaurant, 1000 Great Hwy., San Francisco 94121; (415) 386-8439; beachchalet.com.

The Bistro and Sutro's at the Cliff House, 1090 Point Lobos Ave., San Francisco 94121; (415) 386-3330; cliffhouse.com. The Cliff House building site is a piece of history that has endured various incarnations since 1858. It is now part of

Viewpoint over Mile Rock Beach

the Golden Gate Recreation Area and houses two restaurants to savor a meal and soak in the views.

Seal Rock Inn Restaurant, 545 Point Lobos Ave., San Francisco 94121; (415) 752-8000. The restaurant on the ground floor of the Seal Rock Inn serves a break-fast and lunch menu all day.

Seal Rock Inn, 545 Point Lobos Ave., San Francisco 94121; (415) 752-8000; sealrockinn.com. This very convenient hotel on the doorstep of beaches and coastal trails has been a popular rest stop since 1959. Some rooms have fireplaces.

Inn at the Presidio, 42 Moraga Ave., San Francisco 94129; (415) 800-7356; innatthepresidio.com. It's a boutique hotel and National Historic Landmark at a former US Army post. Some dog friendly rooms.

21. FISHERMAN'S WHARF TO GOLDEN GATE BRIDGE

WHY GO?

It would be unthinkable to hike the California coast and ignore one of the most picturesque ocean bays in the world. This San Francisco Bay waterfront trail is a brilliant example of thoughtful redevelopment that blends conservation, preservation, and recreation.

THE RUNDOWN

Distance: 7.6 miles out and back

Start: San Francisco Maritime National Historical Park at west end of Jefferson Street in front of Dolphin Club

Nearest town: San Francisco

Hiking time: About 4 hours

Fees and permits: None

Conveniences: Public restrooms on second floor of Maritime Museum and along the trail; benches and trash and recycling containers along the waterfront trail

Beach access: Yes; dogs under voice control on Crissy Field Beach

Trail users: Hikers, cyclists, in-line skaters, and dogs on leash

Trailhead elevation: 5 feet

Highest point: 139 feet

Trail surface: Pavement and dirt

Difficulty: Moderate

Seasonal highlights: Blue lupine bushes in the spring on parts of the trail

Managing agency: Golden Gate National Recreation Area, 201 Fort Mason, San Francisco 94123-0022; (415) 561-4700 or (415) 426-5240; nps.gov/goga

FINDING THE TRAILHEAD

In San Francisco, drive to the west end of Fisherman's Wharf on Jefferson Street to Hyde Street and the Maritime National Historical Park below Ghirardelli Square. You will have to find parking on the side streets.
GPS: N37 48.45' / W122 25.32'

WHAT TO SEE

The San Francisco Bay Trail is one aspect of the phenomenal Golden Gate National Recreation Area created out of land and facilities formerly owned by the US military. Grassroots groups under the banner of People for a Golden Gate National

Alcatraz Island behind the old sailing ship *Balclutha* in Aquatic Park

Recreation Area, supported by visionary politicians of the 1960s, campaigned for the federal government to purchase the land to protect it from development and preserve the ecological and scenic wealth of the landscape as well as the cultural heritage and historical landmarks. The Golden Gate National Recreation Area (GGNRA) protects over 80,000 acres.

This hike begins at the foot of Ghirardelli Square, named after the third–oldest chocolate company in the United States. The California gold rush was responsible for spawning several new enterprises in the state and in blossoming San Francisco. Domenico Ghirardelli was lured from Peru to California by dreams of a rich strike before eventually turning to the importation of Peruvian cocoa beans for the Ghirardelli Chocolate Company incorporated in 1852. Ghirardelli Square is an official San Francisco City Landmark. It's difficult to imagine this famous tourist destination bustling with family entertainment as part of the seedy, raucous, and notoriously lawless district once known as the Barbary Coast, the name given to it by sailors. Watch for the brass Barbary Coast Trail medallions embedded in the sidewalk at the beginning of the trail.

Continue walking west past the aquatic park beach on your right, and you will come to the Municipal Pier on your right at 0.4 mile. A sign on the left marks the beginning of Fort Mason. Walk straight uphill and follow the paved path to the top, overlooking the Fort Mason buildings converted into small commercial spaces, primarily art- and food-related businesses. Bear right on the path and downhill on the grassy slope. There's a paved bike trail on the left, but you can stay on the dirt trail if you bear right.

At 0.8 mile come to the Fort Mason Gate on the right. Walk across the parking lot to Yacht Harbor and hug the waterfront. There are benches and a parcourse on the left. The Marina District treats you to unobstructed views of Alcatraz Island and Angel Island State Park. Alcatraz Island preserves the intriguing lore of Alcatraz Federal Penitentiary in the restored buildings and museum, whereas Angel Island is popular with hikers, cyclists, and weekend sailors.

At 1.5 miles turn left around the marina, then turn right to leave the marina about 0.3 mile ahead. Notice the restrooms just across the road. You will walk across Yacht Road to the water at 1.9 miles. There are picnic tables and restrooms on the left of the field. Leave the paved path and begin on the dirt trail across Crissy Field along the Golden Gate Promenade. The views of the Golden Gate Bridge and the Marin Headlands just keep getting more impressive as you parallel the historic landing field and Crissy Field Beach, which is the city pooches' favorite playground. It's not uncommon to see San Franciscan doggie nannies with four to six canines at the ends of leashes or romping on the beach and greenbelts.

At 2.3 miles you cross the estuary on a footbridge. The Greater Farallones National Marine Sanctuary Visitor Center is on your right about 0.7 mile ahead.

Lifting fog reveals the Golden Gate Bridge.

Fisherman's Wharf to Golden Gate Bridge

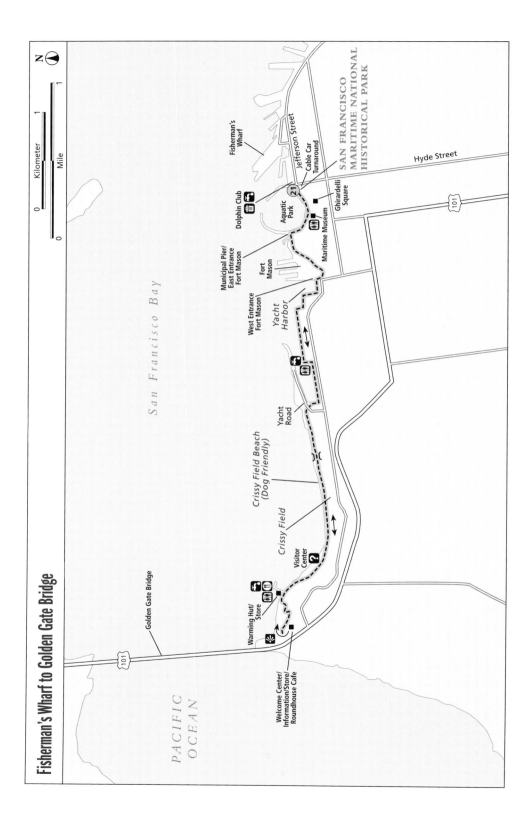

At 3.4 miles the Warming Hut and Park Store is a convenient stop to get a bite in the cafe and use the restrooms before turning left in the crosswalk and continuing up the stairs to the Golden Gate Bridge. If time permits, you can continue to the right to Fort Point. Follow the signs to the Golden Gate Bridge and bear right at the top of the stairs. There's a bike trail on the left. Walk through the tunnel and arrive at the viewing terrace at 3.8 miles. This hike ends here, where you can get close-up photos of the bridge and use the scope to look across the bay to Fort Baker and the old officers' residences converted into the luxurious Cavallo Point Lodge. There's a welcome center for information and gifts along with the Roundhouse Café and outdoor tables to the left above the terrace across the bike trail. If you want to walk across the Golden Gate Bridge, continue up the path. Expect to share the panorama with herds of tourists driving, busing, and biking if you hike this trail on weekends and holidays. Go back to the trailhead the way you came.

MILES AND DIRECTIONS

- **0.0**   Start in front of the Dolphin Club and the San Francisco Maritime National Historical Park.
- **0.4**   Come to the Municipal Pier on the right and enter Fort Mason straight ahead.
- **0.8**   Bear right at the Fort Mason Gate.
- **1.5**   Come to a junction. Turn left around the marina.
- **1.9**   Walk across Yacht Road to the waterfront and continue on the dirt trail along Crissy Field on the Golden Gate Promenade above dog friendly Crissy Field Beach.
- **2.3**   Walk across the estuary on a footbridge.
- **3.0**   Come to the Greater Farallones National Marine Sanctuary Visitor Center on the right.
- **3.4**   Come to the Warming Hut Park Store & Cafe. Turn left past the buildings and cross the street to continue up the stairs, following the signs for the Golden Gate Bridge.
- **3.8**   Arrive at the viewing terrace and the turnaround point. Go back to the trailhead the way you came.
- **7.6**   Arrive back at the trailhead.

BAKERIES, BREWERIES, EATS, AND SLEEPS

Boudin Bakery & Cafe, 160 Jefferson St., San Francisco 94121; (415) 928-1849; boudinbakery.com. A French family and wild yeast in the bay's air became the winning recipe for the famous San Francisco sourdough French bread, which has been tingling taste buds since 1849. Don't miss the flagship location complete with bistro, gifts, museum, and 30-foot window on the bakers at work. Dog friendly patio.

Viewing terrace above Fort Point
and Golden Gate Bridge

Greens, Fort Mason Center, Building A, 2 Marina Blvd., San Francisco 94123; (415) 771-6222. Originally part of the San Francisco Zen Center, Greens opened in 1979 and has been at the forefront of fresh organic vegetarian cuisine. Morning pastries, snacks, and light meals are also packaged to go.

Goody Cafe, Fort Mason Center, Building C, San Francisco 94123; (510) 918-4026; fortmason.org. Tucked in a used books store; enjoy a panini and something for your sweet tooth.

Beer 39, Pier 39, Beach St., San Francisco 94133; (415) 421-2699; beerthirty nine.com. Local craft beers and beer tasting.

Inn at the Presidio, 42 Moraga Ave., San Francisco 94129; (415) 800-7356; innatthepresidio.com. Boutique hotel and National Historic Landmark at a historic US Army post. Some dog friendly rooms.

Argonaut Hotel, 495 Jefferson St., San Francisco 94109; (415) 563-0800; argonauthotel.com. Boutique hotel with mariner flavor in a 1907 brick building at the edge of Fisherman's Wharf. Some dog friendly rooms.

Dog Friendly Beaches

Fort Funston Beach (see hike 19) is at the foot of the bluff trails, where hang gliders love to soar. This sandy and often windy beach is a great voice-control playground. But what goes down must come up, so be aware that it is a long, strenuous trek back up to the parking lot. The beach is also popular with horseback riders, so if your dog is not horse friendly, keep him on leash. The beach is accessed from a sandy trail south of the parking lot off Skyline Boulevard at John Muir Drive in Fort Funston, San Francisco. Golden Gate National Recreation Area, Building 201, Fort Mason, San Francisco 94123; (415) 561-4700

   Ocean Beach is the mother of all beaches as far as scope, running from the Cliff House south to Sloat Boulevard along the Great Highway. Dogs can romp under voice control on this frequently windy stretch of firm-packed sand. If your dog is gaga for water, watch him carefully, as the water is cold and the currents strong. When in doubt, protect pooch from himself with a leash. The beach is accessed from the parking lot at Sloat Boulevard off the Great Highway, San Francisco. Golden Gate National Recreation Area, Building 201, Fort Mason, San Francisco 94123; (415) 561-4700

   Crissy Field Beach along the Golden Gate Promenade (see hike 21) is one of the most popular pooch playgrounds for dog owners as well as the city's many dog

Dogs love to romp at
Crissy Field Beach.

nannies. The sandy beach is perfect for spinning and bouncing with tail-wagging friends, and the gentle shoreline and calm water make it a safe place for swimming and splashing around off leash. The stunning views of the Golden Gate Bridge and the Marin Headlands north and across the bay to Alcatraz and Angel Island are extra perks for the human tagging along for the jaunt. The beach is accessed at 1199 East Beach at the east end of Crissy Field Park in the old Presidio area in San Francisco. Golden Gate National Recreation Area, Building 201, Fort Mason, San Francisco 94123; (415) 561-4700

Coastal Attractions

From Pier 39 to Ghirardelli Square, San Francisco's waterfront is well known for its fanfare of street performers, hot chowder stands, a famous chocolatier, arcades, tourist merchandise, and streetcar nostalgia—all part of this grande dame's charm and mystique. Beyond the brushstroke of what visitors love most about the celebrated City by the Bay are other layers of coastal attractions.

Golden Gate Bridge Pavilion at Bridge Plaza on US 101 at the south end of the bridge is the ideal visitor center to enjoy exhibits, merchandise, and striking photography viewpoints. You can get up close and personal with the bridge and walk across the bay on the 1.7-mile stretch of sidewalk on the east side to the Vista Point at the north end of the bridge. Bicycles are allowed on the east and west sidewalks with some restrictions. Among the many bike rental businesses in San Francisco, the following three concessionaires have the most locations: Blazing Saddles (blazingsaddles.com), Bike and Roll (bikethegoldengate.com), and Bay City Bikes (baycitybike.com). Go to goldengatebridge.org for information on public transit options to the bridge as well as the rules and seasonal schedule for sidewalk traffic.

Sightseeing around San Francisco Bay by ferry is a perfect complement to exploring the coastal trails on foot and bike. The Blue and Gold Fleet (blueandgold fleet.com) runs ferries to the bay's most interesting, picturesque, and fun locations, including Angel Island State Park, Jack London Square in Oakland on the east side of the bay, Sausalito, and Tiburon.

Alcatraz Island National Park is a cultural and natural history tour covering the establishment of the first lighthouse and US-built fort on the West Coast, a close-up look at the infamous penitentiary with tales about the legendary Rock's notorious inmates, Alcatraz's role in the Native American rights movement of the 1960s, and the importance of the island as a seabird sanctuary. The only way to access the island is with Alcatraz Cruise Company, the concessionaire under contract with the National Park Service. For tickets and reservations, call (415) 981-7625; alcatrazcruises.com.

San Francisco Ferry Building, at the Embarcadero and Market Street in San Francisco, was completed in 1898 with a clock tower modeled on a twelfth-century bell tower in Seville, Spain. Until the construction of the Bay and Golden Gate

Bridges, which carried railroad traffic, the Ferry Building was the second-busiest transit terminal in the world after London's Charring Cross Station. The building suffered neglect over the decades, and the construction of the Embarcadero Freeway in the 1950s further distracted from this prominent waterfront landmark. The 1989 Loma Prieta earthquake devastated parts of the city, including the controversial Embarcadero Freeway. But out of the rubble came the opportunity for San Franciscans to weigh in on the future of the Embarcadero. The freeway idea was rejected, and a boulevard reconnected the city to its waterfront. The Ferry Building's classic character was revived in 2003 and injected with new purpose to enhance its water and rail transit function serving commuters and visitors. The Ferry Building is a San Francisco landmark on the National Register of Historic Places, housing a vibrant marketplace pulsating with locals and tourists and hosting the city's popular farmers' market on the terminal grounds three days a week year-round. The Marketplace's Euro influence is reflected in the array of outlets offering artisan cheeses, breads, sweets, and fresh local food products as well as other culinary shops. The cafes and restaurants are gathering places for local cuisine. Walking tours of the Ferry Building led by City Guides volunteers are offered on certain days of the week; see ferrybuildingmarketplace.com.

Boudin Bakery & Cafe, 160 Jefferson St., San Francisco 94121; (415) 928-1849; boudinbakery.com. If I only have time for one stop off the coastal trail, I choose Boudin every time. A French family and wild yeast in the bay's air became the winning recipe for the famous San Francisco sourdough French bread, which has been tinglesing the taste buds since 1849. The waterfront's carnival atmosphere is the perfect location for the flagship store. You can watch the bakers' craft through the 30-foot street-front window; browse the shop's assortment of edible, practical, and whimsical gifts; brush up on the bakery's history in the museum; and cap the visit with fresh bread to go or a quick bite from the casual cafe and counter service. Better yet, relax in traditional San Francisco style in the upstairs bistro for a sumptuous meal with a view of the bay.

BEST COASTAL FARMERS' MARKETS

Ferry Plaza Farmers' Market (415-291-3276; cuesa.org) has a phenomenal location and is nothing short of a happening, with a bounty of fresh produce, artisan goods for true foodies, and a seasonal schedule of cooking demos. The market is located on the Ferry Terminal grounds, 1 Ferry Building, at the Embarcadero and Market Street and operates three days a week year-round: Sat 8 a.m. to 2 p.m. and Tues and Thurs 10 a.m. to 2 p.m.

MARIN COUNTY

Just a wave away from San Francisco across the Golden Gate Bridge, **MARIN COUNTY**'s location with hilly open space hemmed in by the bay and the Pacific is synonymous with outdoor recreation. It is not a surprise that it was the cradle of two popular sports: cross-country running and mountain biking. Marin annually hosts the Dipsea Race, the oldest cross-country running event in the country. Mount Tamalpais is popular for mountain biking, which was invented on its slopes. It is an affluent eco-minded county, boasting two coastal jewels under federal protection for preservation and recreation: the magnificent Marin Headlands within the Golden Gate National Recreation Area and the spectacular Point Reyes National Seashore. Point Reyes's historic dairies, ranches, and rich soil have catapulted its small hamlets to the forefront of the food movement associated with organic, sustainable, and artisan quality. If hiking a coastal trail on one of Marin County's biodiverse public lands isn't ecologically impressive enough, Marin claims three of the nation's thirteen national marine sanctuaries—Greater Farallones, Monterey Bay, and the Cordell Bank National Marine Sanctuaries—parts of which are in the United Nation's Golden Gate Biosphere Reserve. Add popular and secluded strands of sandy beaches, and Marin County offers a stellar northern coastal experience.

Note: See map on page 142.

22. GOLDEN GATE BRIDGE TO MARIN HEADLANDS VISITOR CENTER

WHY GO?

This hardy hike spends more time hemmed in by coastal chaparral than the headlands' surf-battered shores. But the highlights that make this a standout hike include historic battery sites with unique vantage points to appreciate the iconic Golden Gate Bridge, hiking the California Coastal Trail and the Bay Area Ridge Trail, and a worthwhile descent to stunning Black Sands Beach. If you intend to hike with your four-legged pal, shorten the distance by hiking the trail one way and arranging to be picked up at the visitor center for the return to the trailhead. This also allows more time to linger at Black Sands Beach and the viewpoints.

THE RUNDOWN

Distance: 14.4 miles out and back

Start: Bay Trail at west end of parking lot

Nearest towns: Sausalito and San Francisco

Hiking time: About 7 hours

Fees and permits: None

Conveniences: Portable toilets at trailhead; restrooms with flush toilets, drinking fountain, picnic tables, and trash and recycling containers at visitor center

Beach access: Yes

Trail users: Hikers, bikers, equestrians, and dogs on leash

Trailhead elevation: 16 feet

Highest point: 817 feet

Trail surface: Pavement and dirt

Difficulty: Strenuous

Seasonal highlights: Wildflowers in the spring

Managing agency: Golden Gate National Recreation Area, 201 Fort Mason, San Francisco 94123-0022; (415) 561-4700 or (415) 426-5240; nps.gov/goga

FINDING THE TRAILHEAD

From US 101 at the south end of Sausalito, take the Alexander Avenue exit and drive north 0.2 mile to Danes Drive and turn left. Drive 0.1 mile on Danes Drive and make a sharp right onto East Bunker Road. Drive 0.5 mile on East Bunker Road to Murray Circle, which becomes Moore Road, and turn right. Drive 0.1 mile on Moore Road to Sommerville Road and turn left into the parking lot across from the Coast Guard Station. **GPS:** N37 50.01' / W122 28.67'

WHAT TO SEE

The Golden Gate National Recreation Area was created out of land and facilities formerly owned by the US military. Grassroots groups under the banner of People for a Golden Gate National Recreation Area, supported by visionary politicians of the 1960s, campaigned for the federal government to purchase the land to protect it from development and preserve the ecological and scenic wealth of the landscape as well as the cultural heritage and historical landmarks. The Golden Gate National Recreation Area (GGNRA) protects over 80,000 acres.

The Marin Headlands hills and estuaries were the lands of plenty for the Native American Miwok tribe before being settled by Spanish and Mexican ranchers followed by dairy farmers said to have emigrated from the Portuguese Azores. From the 1890s through World War I, World War II, and the Cold War, the Marin Headlands were a strategic site for defense. The headlands' military history is visible on many of the ridges where fortifications including missile sites, bunkers, gun batteries, and observation sites were installed. Some have been preserved as part of the area's historic legacy, and many nonprofit organizations operate from some of the military buildings maintained for their historic significance. The Marin Headlands Hostel at Fort Barry, Marine Mammal Center, Headland Center for the Arts, and Marin Headlands Visitor Center are examples of military buildings being put to public use.

The Golden Gate National Recreation Area was established in 1972, and a combination of flukes, zoning controversies, timely protests by conservation activists, public awareness, and lawsuits resulted in the Marin Headlands land being rescued from development as the Marincello planned community. The 2,000-acre chunk was purchased from the Gulf Oil Corporation by The Nature Conservancy and transferred to the newly created Golden Gate National Recreation Area. Three of the people at the forefront of the battle to halt the development of the headlands became the founders of the Trust for Public Lands, which operates across the United States.

The Marin Headlands is in the Golden Gate National Recreation Area, which is recognized as the Golden Gate Biosphere Reserve by the United Nations. The headlands' ridges and valleys provide excellent habitat for deer, mountain lions, foxes, coyotes, wild turkeys, rabbits, raccoons, and skunks.

The hike begins on the Bay Trail at the base of the Golden Gate Bridge on the north side of San Francisco Bay, where you are dwarfed by the colossal engineering infrastructure above you. This trailhead is an opportunity to see the complex and massive skeleton of this grande dame of bridges and enjoy a unique perspective from below the bridge and along the scenic bay. Walk on the shoulder paralleling the paved service road and continue up the paved service road passing under the Golden Gate Bridge to a parking area and the trail sign for Rodeo Beach, Bay Area Ridge

Trail sign before reaching Golden Gate Bridge

Trail, and California Coastal Trail (CCT). You will see the CCT's blue-and-white wave logo on the trail post.

You leave the paved road and parking area and begin on the narrow dirt trail under a cypress canopy on uphill switchbacks through the coastal chaparral of wild grape, poison oak, yellow sticky monkey, and purple lupine. In the spring and early summer, the tangle of coyote brush is enhanced by pink blooms. This stretch of the trail treats you to breathtaking views of the bay across to Angel Island, Alcatraz Island, and San Francisco's seductive skyline behind the north tower of the Golden Gate Bridge. If you're wondering how this radiant orange-painted bridge got its golden name, it's not because it's golden in color. It was named after the narrows between the Pacific Ocean and San Francisco Bay. The narrows were named the Golden Gate Strait by explorer and US Army officer John C. Frémont in 1846, two years prior to the gold rush.

At 0.9 mile you come to a crosswalk at Conzelman Road. Turn left on the dirt trail paralleling the road on this side of the crosswalk and walk 0.4 mile up to Battery Spencer for fabulous views of the Golden Gate Bridge, the bay, and the Marin

View of San Francisco beyond
the Golden Gate Bridge

Headlands coastline. This is a great photo perch. Walk back down to the crosswalk and across the road to continue on the CCT. Follow the signs for Rodeo Beach up more switchbacks.

At 2.4 miles the double tunnels through the mountain come into view. These tunnels were nicknamed the Rainbow Tunnels in the early 1970s when a retiring director of the San Francisco District of California Highways decided to have the portals of the tunnels painted with a rainbow. Although his superiors did not appreciate the director's creativity, the public reaction was so positive that the rainbow remained. Urban legend quickly spread giving creative credit to the local hippies, who, of course, could never have completed such a paint job overnight undetected.

You continue walking, following the sign for the CCT at the 2.7-mile T junction. Be prepared for blustery winds on foggy days along this ridge. At 3.0 miles you have the option of going up a left spur for 0.2 mile to Slacker Ridge for more bay views. This hike continues straight downhill past the Slacker Ridge junction to McCollough Road. Continue to the other side of the road in the crosswalk past a parking area and restroom with a vault toilet. The only views for the next 0.5 mile or so are of the headland hills and Rodeo Valley to the north. At 3.8 miles you will get a glimpse of the ocean in the V-shaped head of Rodeo Valley.

Trail down to Black
Sands Beach

At 4.6 miles you come to the junction for the Upper Fisherman's Trail. Turn left and at the next junction you will come to a sign for the CCT and visitor center to the right and Upper Fisherman's Trail and Black Sands Beach straight. Continue straight on this spur to Black Sands Beach. Black Sands Beach is a stiff 0.3-mile descent on a dirt trail and wooden steps. You have the option of only going as far as the trail takes you overlooking the beach if you are hiking with your four-legged pal (dogs are not allowed on Black Sands Beach) or continuing down to the beach. It's a picturesque stretch of beach worth the huff back up. The overlook or the beach itself can make a very pleasant shorter destination and turnaround point.

You arrive at Black Sands Beach at 5.2 miles. When you come back to the junction, turn left to continue on the CCT, undulating through the chaparral hills for almost 1.0 mile to the stables. Bear right along the stables to the road. Continue in the crosswalk to the other side of the road, then bear left to a set of wooden steps back to the road and to the other side of the road in the crosswalk just before the parking area. Follow the sign for the visitor center and walk uphill. At 6.5 miles the distant view opens toward the lagoon and the ocean to the west. You will see white houses to the right below the trail. Those former military residences are the Marin Headlands Hostel.

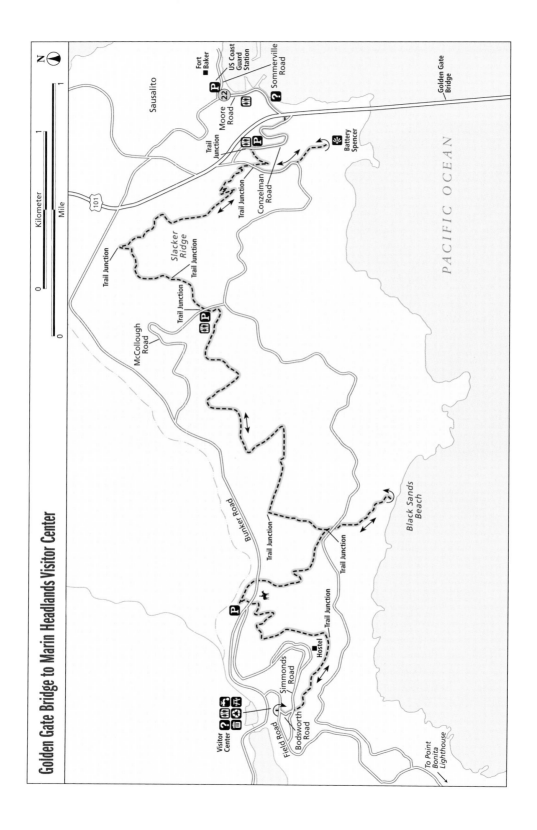

Golden Gate Bridge to Marin Headlands Visitor Center

Sausalito

Fort Baker

US Coast Guard Station

Sommerville Road

Moore Road

Trail Junction

Conzelman Road

Battery Spencer

Golden Gate Bridge

PACIFIC OCEAN

Trail Junction

Slacker Ridge

Trail Junction

Trail Junction

McCollough Road

Trail Junction

Bunker Road

Trail Junction

Trail Junction

Black Sands Beach

Visitor Center

Field Road

Simmonds Road

Bodsworth Road

Hostel

Trail Junction

To Point Bonita Lighthouse

N

Kilometer

Mile

0   1

0   1

At 6.8 miles you come to a trail junction for the hostel to the right and the visitor center straight. The Marin Headlands Visitor Center is 0.4 mile ahead across the road from where Bodsworth, Simmonds, and Field Roads converge. The visitor center has an extensive display of exhibits as well as a good inventory of books for sale. Enjoy a snack break at the picnic table, and if you have the time and energy, you can continue down to Rodeo Beach along the lagoon less than 1.0 mile ahead.

MILES AND DIRECTIONS

0.0 Start at the Bay Trail sign at the west end of the parking lot and follow the paved road uphill, passing under the Golden Gate Bridge

0.7 Come to a parking lot on the right and the trail sign for Rodeo Beach, Bay Area Ridge Trail, and California Coastal Trail (CCT) on the left. Turn left and walk uphill on the dirt trail.

0.9 Come to Conzelman Road and crosswalk. Turn left before the crosswalk and walk parallel to the road uphill to Spencer Battery and the viewpoint.

1.3 Arrive at Spencer Battery. Go back to the crosswalk and walk across Conzelman Road toward Rodeo Beach.

2.7 Come to a T junction. Turn left on the CCT.

3.0 Come to a trail junction for Slacker Ridge on the left. Continue straight downhill on the CCT.

3.2 Arrive at the McCollough Road crosswalk. Continue across the road on the CCT past a parking area and restroom with a vault toilet.

4.6 Come to a trail junction for the CCT and Upper Fisherman's Trail. Turn left.

4.9 Come to a trail junction for the CCT and visitor center to the right and Upper Fisherman's Trail straight. Continue straight on the Upper Fisherman's Trail and walk down the steps to Black Sands Beach.

5.2 Arrive at Blacks Sands Beach. Go back to the trail junction and turn left on the CCT to the visitor center.

6.0 Bear right at the stables.

6.1 Come to Bunker Road and continue across the road in the crosswalk and bear left.

6.2 Arrive at a parking area and walk up the wooden steps on the left. Walk across Bunker Road in the crosswalk. Walk uphill and continue to the visitor center.

6.8 Come to the trail junction for the hostel to the right. Continue walking straight to the visitor center.

7.2 Come to Bodsworth/Simmonds/Field Roads. Walk across the roads and arrive at the visitor center. Take the time to enjoy the exhibits inside the visitor center and refuel with a snack before going back the way you came.

14.4 Arrive back at the trailhead.

BAKERIES, BREWERIES, EATS, AND SLEEPS

Sausalito Bakery and Cafe, 571 Bridgeway, Sausalito 94965; (415) 331-9552. Patrons keep coming back for the banana bread pudding and blueberry cream cheese strudel.

Marin Brewing Company, 1809 Larkspur Landing Circle, Larkspur 94939; (415) 461-4677; marinbrewing.com. It's all about award-winning classic brews with local landmark names and regular innovative flavors to pair with grass-fed burgers and wood-fired pizzas. The menu includes soups, salads, sandwiches, favorite pub fare, and mouthwatering baked desserts.

Farley Bar at Cavallo Point Lodge, 601 Murray Circle, Sausalito 94965; (415) 339-4700; cavallopoint.com. The lounge's leather furnishings, warm wood, and fireplace say San Francisco sophisticated relaxation. The bar menu ranges from comfort food staples like burgers and brews to splurges with bubbles and small bites like Dom Perignon champagne with house truffle fries.

Murray Circle Restaurant, 601 Murray Circle, Sausalito 94965; (415) 339-4700; cavallopoint.com. It's elegance for breakfast, lunch, brunch, and dinner. The breakfast menu is extensive and divine, and the house-made granola is a hit. Lunch has a bite for every palate, whereas dinner is limited, with more exotic and wild flavors.

The Trident, 558 Bridgeway, Sausalito 94965; (415) 331-3232; www.thetrident .net. Whether you crave lunch, brunch, or dinner, the extensive menu and atmosphere of this historic waterfront landmark will hit the spot.

Inn Above Tide, 30 El Portal, Sausalito 94965; (415) 332-9535; innabovetide .com. Sausalito is a charming, picturesque town with a vibrant artist colony. It is conveniently and quietly set across the Golden Gate Bridge from San Francisco near the Marin Headlands. The inn is boutique luxury with views.

Hotel Sausalito, 161 El Portal, Sausalito 94965; (415) 332-0700; hotelsausalito .com. This luxurious boutique hotel exudes Mediterranean charm with a colorful history quilted by tales of bordello brawls and guests ranging from gangsters to sailors to bohemians. The 1915 landmark was renovated in 1996 to welcome a new generation of travelers.

Cavallo Point Lodge, 601 Murray Circle, Sausalito 94965; (415) 339-4700; cavallopoint.com. Honored with awards from the National Trust for Historic Preservation and the US Green Council, the lodge nestled at the edge of the 75,000-acre Golden Gate National Recreational Area is also dog friendly for lodging as well as dining on the restaurants' (Farley Bar and Murray Circle) covered porch overlooking San Francisco and the Golden Gate Bridge. You can walk from Cavallo to the trailhead. Fort Baker's historic officers' quarters have been meticulously restored and refurbished with modern amenities that meld in perfect harmony with the Colonial Revival architectural style of the early 1900s. The newer contemporary guest rooms tucked against the hillside boast expansive bay views.

Descending to visitor center and turnaround point

HI Marin Headlands Hostel, 941 Rosenstock Rd., Golden Gate National Recreation Area, Sausalito 94965; (415) 331-2777; hiusa.org. This turn-of-the-twentieth-century military post converted into unique lodging is a portal to great coastal access.

23. STINSON BEACH TO BOLINAS LAGOON

WHY GO?

This is one of the most picturesque coastal hikes you can enjoy with or without a canine companion in the Golden Gate National Recreation Area.

THE RUNDOWN

Distance: 4.6 miles out and back

Start: Stinson Beach Park north parking lot

Nearest town: Stinson Beach

Hiking time: About 2.5 hours

Fees and permits: None

Conveniences: Restrooms with flush toilets, water, changing rooms, trash and recycling containers, picnic tables, and grills

Beach access: Yes; sections OK for dogs on leash (see map)

Trail users: Hikers and dogs on leash on part of the beach

Trailhead elevation: 15 feet

Highest point: 15 feet

Trail surface: Sand

Difficulty: Easy

Seasonal highlights: Whale migration in the spring and fall; solitude in the winter

Managing agency: Golden Gate National Recreation Area, 201 Fort Mason, San Francisco 94123-0022; (415) 561-4700 or (415) 426-5240; nps.gov/goga. Marin County Civic Center, 3501 Civic Center Dr., Ste. 260, San Rafael 94903; (415) 473-6387.

FINDING THE TRAILHEAD

From Stinson Beach at CA 1, turn west into the Stinson Beach Park/Golden Gate National Recreation Area parking lot. **GPS:** N37 53.88' / W122 38.55'

WHAT TO SEE

The little funky hamlet of Stinson Beach feels like it's been plunked on this isolated and dreamy stretch of CA 1. Although just an arm's length from San Francisco's hustle and bustle, the Stinson Beach hike envelops you in solitude within a few yards of stepping out of Stinson Beach Park onto the sand.

The Pacific on the west side hugs the wide, firm sand beach and dune-front homes on the east side. The weatherworn houses as you first start the hike scream of

Striding along Stinson Beach

View across Bolinas Lagoon
at turnaround point

classic California beach town. But the real estate gets spiffier very quickly, and the architectural flair tells you Stinson Beach has been discovered.

The green forested hills make an idyllic backdrop to the east as you approach the spit where the tidal lagoon flares inland, feeding a spectacular marshland. At the tip of the spit, Bolinas sits frustratingly close across the narrows of the estuary. Bolinas is a tiny community exuding incredible charm in a "time forgot" sort of way. But that's just the way the locals like it, and urban legend has it that every time the county puts up a directional sign to Bolinas at the CA 1 intersection, it quickly disappears.

If you are hiking with your furry family member, be forewarned that if he likes seafood, he'll think he's landed at a buffet with all the tiny sand crabs scattered along the way.

Depending on the tide, once you arrive at the point of the spit, it's possible to follow the edge of the lagoon on the right for a while before going back the way you came.

MILES AND DIRECTIONS

0.0 Start at the north parking lot to the right of the restrooms and turn right, walking north along the beach.

2.3 Arrive at the mouth of the Bolinas Lagoon at the tip of the spit. Go back to the trailhead the way you came.

4.6 Arrive back at the trailhead.

BAKERIES, BREWERIES, EATS, AND SLEEPS:

The Parkside compound is a one-stop shop to satiate your appetite and thirst. It houses a bakery, snack bar, cafe restaurant, market, and coffee cart. Although there are no breweries in Stinson Beach, the Parkside Cafe serves Marin County's Iron Springs Brewery beer on tap.

Parkside Bakery, 43 Arenal Ave., Stinson Beach 94970; (415) 868-1272; park sidecafe.com. Part of the Parkside compound, the bakery serves pastries and hand-shaped organic flour artisan bread.

Parkside Snack Bar, 43 Arenal Ave., Stinson Beach 94970; (415) 868-1272; parksidecafe.com. Stinson Beach fans have enjoyed the snack bar's burgers and shakes since 1949.

Parkside Cafe, 43 Arenal Ave., Stinson Beach 94970; (415) 868-1272; parkside cafe.com. There's indoor fireside seating or patio seating (dog friendly) for breakfast, lunch, and dinner. The menu is fresh, clean, sustainable California cuisine with local ingredients from the ocean to the grazing lands. Hikers keep coming back for the wood-fired pizzas followed by strawberry-rhubarb cobbler or banana-butterscotch cream pie. You can wash it all down with a frothy root beer float. Don't miss Tues open mic night's spaghetti, salad, and garlic bread buffet.

Stinson Beach to Bolinas Lagoon

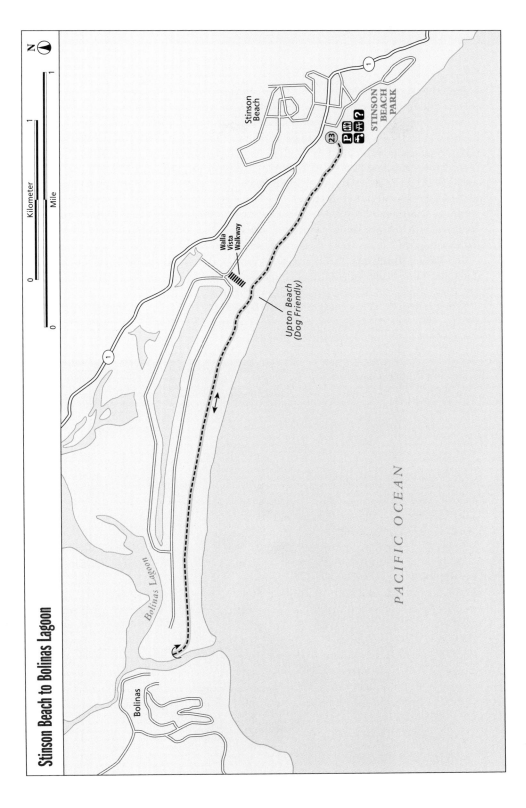

Parkside Coffee Cart, 43 Arenal Ave., Stinson Beach 94970; (415) 868-1272; parksidecafe.com. Whether you're a coffee, tea, or ice cream connoisseur, the new kiosk between the cafe and the snack bar is a stop you'll want to make. The hot beverages pair nicely with the fresh pastries, or just indulge in a scoop of organic ice cream from the local Strauss Family Creamery.

Parkside Marketplace, 43 Arenal Ave., Stinson Beach 94970; (415) 868-1272; parksidecafe.com. The small retail space showcases several local gourmet products including jams, chocolates, and teas.

Sirene Canteen, 3201 CA 1, Stinson Beach 94970; (415) 868-1777; thesirene canteeen.com. It's a snack bar with tasty quick bites including tacos and crepes on the beach in the Golden Gate National Recreation Area parking lot.

Sandpiper Lodging, 1 Marine Way, Stinson Beach 94970; (415) 868-1632; sandpiperstinsonbeach.com. This beach property with a private garden and barbecue areas has rooms, cabins, and cottages with kitchenettes.

Stinson Beach Redwoods Haus B&B, Belvedere and CA 1, Stinson Beach 94970; (415) 868-1034; stinson-beach.com. This small, funky, no-frills property has clean, affordable rooms and some are dog friendly.

Snowy egret scans
a tide pool

24. LIMANTOUR DUNES

WHY GO?

This is one of the most easily accessed trails for a coastal experience in Point Reyes. This hike is a triple-header showcasing Point Reyes National Seashore's phenomenal Limantour Beach, pristine sand dunes, and awe-inspiring estuary.

THE RUNDOWN

Distance: 2.0 miles out and back

Start: Stairs at west end of Limantour Beach parking lot

Nearest towns: Olema and Point Reyes Station

Hiking time: About 1 hour

Fees and permits: None

Conveniences: Restrooms with vault toilets, trash and recycling containers, picnic tables, water and outdoor shower

Beach access: Yes; dogs on leash

Trail users: Hikers on dune trail; horses on beach

Trailhead elevation: 46 feet

Highest point: 46 feet

Trail surface: Sand

Difficulty: Easy

Seasonal highlights: Purple bush lupine in the spring

Managing agency: Golden Gate National Recreation Area, 201 Fort Mason, San Francisco 94123-0022; (415) 561-4700 or (415) 426-5240; nps.gov/goga

FINDING THE TRAILHEAD

From CA 1 at Bear Valley Road in Olema, drive 1.7 miles west on Bear Valley Road to Limantour Road. Turn left on Limantour Road and drive 7.5 miles to the Limantour Beach parking lot. **GPS:** N38 01.73' / W122 52.96'

WHAT TO SEE

Point Reyes National Seashore's 71,000-acre park is steeped in history beginning with the geological forces that shaped the land millions of years ago. Movement of the tectonic plates along the San Andreas Fault has shifted the Point Reyes Peninsula northward from the southernmost Sierra Nevada in the Tehachapi Mountains 350 miles south. The most recent dramatic surge occurred during the 1906 earthquake. The jolt moved Point Reyes 20 feet northwestward. There's an Earthquake Trail near the Bear Valley Visitor Center on the way to Limantour Beach.

Limantour Dunes

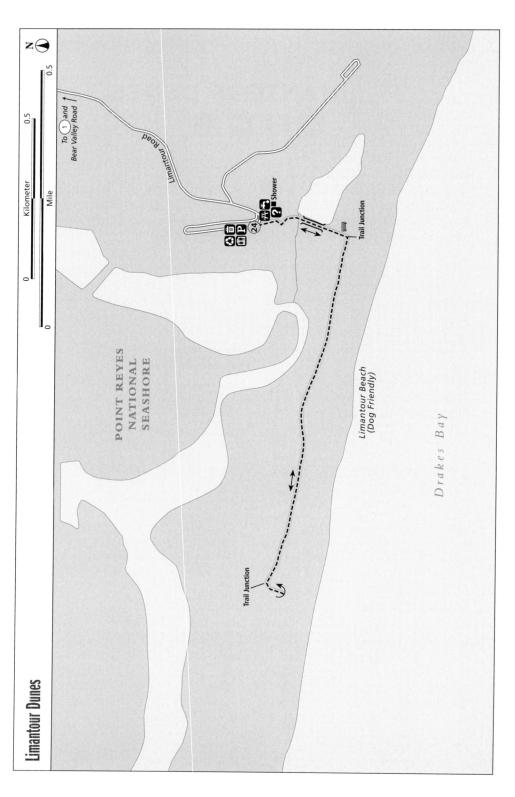

N

Kilometer
0   0.5   0.5

Mile
0   0.5

POINT REYES
NATIONAL
SEASHORE

To (1) and
Bear Valley Road

Limantour Road

24   Shower

Trail Junction

Trail Junction

Limantour Beach
(Dog Friendly)

Drakes Bay

The visitor center also has interesting exhibits about the cultural history of the park. Coast Miwok Indian villages thrived in these parts some 5,000 years ago. Sir Francis Drake was the first European explorer to set foot on this coast from his ship the *Golden Hinde* in 1579. The 1800s brought Mexican ranchos created by the land grants before American settlers began a tradition of ranching and dairy farming.

Talk of acquisition of Point Reyes land by the National Park Service began in the late 1950s, much to the chagrin of local ranchers who opposed the change. President John F. Kennedy signed the bill that protected the first 53,000 acres of Point Reyes under the National Park Service, with the compromise of leasing some land back to the dairy ranchers. Just one look at Point Reyes's emerald pastoral setting in the spring, and you know why California cows are "happy cows."

Point Reyes is a rich and diverse ecosystem on land and sea and part of the Golden Gate Biosphere Reserve. Tule elk and northern elephant seals are star species since they were hunted to near extinction at one time and are now enjoying a successful recovery. The protected coastal waters are rich in nutrients and supply the marine life with an abundant menu that sustains plankton as well as whales.

This is a majestic landscape, and the hike along the Limantour dunes is a sample of the diversity and beauty. Just 0.2 mile after starting on the trail, you turn right on a narrow sandy path on the lagoon side of the dunes. The rolling dunes hide the beach and Pacific from you until about 0.9 mile, when the trail along the lagoon fades into the coastal prairie brush. Bear left uphill and over the ridge of dunes down to the beach. Depending on how much time you have to savor this slice of natural beauty, you can go back to the trailhead the way you came or loop back along the beach. Limantour Beach was named after the French merchant and sea captain Joseph Yves Limantour, whose schooner was wrecked on this beach in 1841.

If you feel like extending your exploration of Limantour Beach, it's another 2 miles north one way to the end of the spit. That beach extension takes you along Drakes Bay to the edge of Drakes Estero (estuary) and looks across to Drakes Beach. The spit and the estuary are closed between March and June to protect the harbor seals that give birth and raise their pups here at that time.

MILES AND DIRECTIONS

0.0 Start at the west end of the parking lot and walk down the steps.

0.1 Walk across the footbridge over the marsh.

0.2 Turn right on the narrow trail across from the bench.

0.9 Bear left and over the top of the dune ridge.

1.0 Arrive at Limantour Beach. Go back to the trailhead the way you came.

2.0 Arrive back at the trailhead.

Walking north through the Limantour dunes

Gazing northward toward Drakes Bay at the turnaround point

BAKERIES, BREWERIES, EATS, AND SLEEPS

Olema is more of a countryside cluster of quaint buildings than a town, but combined with nearby Point Reyes Station's village allure, the two offer the best amenities for exploring Point Reyes National Seashore, with Olema being the closest to the Limantour dunes. There are no breweries in Olema or Point Reyes Station.

Bovine Bakery, 11315 CA 1, Point Reyes Station 94956; (415) 663-9420; bovinebakeryptreyes.com. The list of organic seasonal goodies to enjoy with a cup of Fair Trade coffee, from artisan breads and scones to French pastries and cookies, is endless. Selections include vegan and gluten-free treats as well.

Olema Farmhouse Deli, 10021 CA 1, Olema 94950; (415) 663-8615. The deli is attached to the Point Reyes Seashore Lodge and offers sandwiches, snacks, and provisions to keep you fueled on the hike.

Olema Farmhouse Restaurant, 10021 CA 1, Olema 94950; (415) 663-1264. The historic restaurant and bar began as a stopover tavern for travelers in 1865. Today's vacationers enjoy a variety of fare, with locally sourced seasonal dishes from sea to field including oysters, salads, artisan cheeses, grass-fed beef, and organic chicken complemented by 8 beers on tap from Marin and surrounding North Coast counties. The desserts topped with Straus organic ice cream will not disappoint.

Point Reyes Seashore Lodge, 10021 CA 1, Olema 94950; (415) 663-1264; pointreyesseashore.com. The lodge's 3 acres border Olema Creek and Point Reyes National Seashore. A 0.5-mile path leads to the park headquarters. The well-appointed lodge rooms and 2 cottages open up to a tranquil garden setting. Continental breakfast is included.

Bear Valley Inn Bed & Breakfast, 88 Bear Valley Rd., Olema 94950; (415) 663-1777; bearvinn.com. This B&B has the distinction of being a certified "Green Business."

HI Point Reyes Hostel, 1390 Limantour Rd., Point Reyes 94956; (415) 663-8311; norcalhostels.org/reyes. This eco-friendly hostel is a Wi-Fi and cellular-free retreat with dorm beds and private rooms.

CAMPING

Olema Campground, 10155 CA 1, Olema 94950; (415) 663-8106; www.olema campground.net. It's a clean, private, dog friendly campground in a meadow setting with tall pines for shade. Tent and hookup RV sites.

25. TOMALES POINT

WHY GO?

This is a panoramic hike along a sublime strip of land between the Pacific Ocean and picturesque Tomales Bay. As a bonus, hikers get the unique opportunity to see herds of tule elk as you walk through the Tule Elk Reserve on your way to the point.

THE RUNDOWN

Distance: 9.6 miles out and back

Start: Tomales Point Trailhead in Pierce Point Ranch parking lot

Nearest towns: Inverness and Point Reyes Station

Hiking time: About 5 hours

Fees and permits: None

Conveniences: Trash and recycling containers, telephone, and interpretive panel at trailhead; closest restrooms are at McClure Beach down the road to the left.

Beach access: No

Trail users: Hikers only

Trailhead elevation: 303 feet

Highest point: 537 feet

Trail surface: Dirt, grass, and loose sand

Difficulty: Strenuous

Seasonal highlights: Wildflowers in the spring

Managing agency: Golden Gate National Recreation Area, 201 Fort Mason, San Francisco 94123-0022; (415) 561-4700 or (415) 426-5240; nps.gov/goga

---

FINDING THE TRAILHEAD

From Point Reyes Station at CA 1 and Sir Francis Drake Boulevard, turn west on Sir Francis Drake Boulevard toward Inverness and drive 6 miles to Pierce Point Road. Turn right on Pierce Point Road and drive 9 miles to the Pierce Point Ranch parking lot. **GPS:** N38 11.35' / W122 57.26'

WHAT TO SEE

Point Reyes National Seashore is a 71,000–acre Eden steeped in history beginning with the geological forces that shaped the land millions of years ago. Movement of the tectonic plates along the San Andreas Fault has shifted the Point Reyes Peninsula northward from the southernmost Sierra Nevada in the Tehachapi Mountains 350 miles south. The most recent dramatic surge occurred during the 1906 earthquake. The jolt moved Point Reyes 20 feet northwestward. Don't miss hiking the short interpretive Earthquake Trail at the Bear Valley Visitor Center on the way to or from the Tomales Point Trail.

Wild radish shoulders the trail to Tomales Point.

Tule elk along the trail

The visitor center also has interesting exhibits about the cultural history of the park. Coast Miwok Indian villages thrived in these parts some 5,000 years ago. Sir Francis Drake was the first European explorer to set foot on this coast in 1579. The 1800s brought Mexican ranchos created by the land grants before American settlers began a tradition of ranching and dairy farming.

Talk of acquisition of Point Reyes land by the National Park Service President began in the late 1950s, much to the chagrin of local ranchers who opposed the change. President John F. Kennedy signed the bill that protected the first 53,000 acres of Point Reyes under the National Park Service, with the compromise of leasing some land back to the dairy ranchers. Just one look at Point Reyes's emerald pastoral zone in the spring, and you know why California cows are "happy cows." The intensity and vast panorama of green will blow your mind.

A Vermont legal firm obtained the leases on the original ranches and dairies around 1857. The attorney landlords drew up new leases for the existing tenants and divided the remainder of the 50,000 acres they acquired for new dairy farm tenants and leases. The Pierce Point ranchland was the exception, since it was sold to the Pierce family, friends of the law firm. As you drive along national seashore roads, you will notice that several of the ranch entrances have a letter of the alphabet in addition to the commercial name of the ranch or dairy. The letters were a system devised by the Vermont firm to identify the various ranches. These particular ranches and dairy farms are designated "historic."

Pierce Point's twin dairy ranches and the collective of dairy ranches on Point Reyes were highly successful, and butter with the *PR* (Point Reyes) stamp was considered of the highest quality. At the height of the enterprise in 1867, Marin County produced over 932,000 pounds of butter.

A new century that brought innovation along with eventual overgrazing, the earthquake, and the Great Depression caused many of the original dairies to struggle. Point Pierce Ranch closed in 1973 and was soon incorporated in the newly designated wilderness area, providing a perfect location for the reintroduction of tule elk. The ranch buildings were rehabilitated and opened to the public as an interpretive site in 1985. Pierce Point Ranch is on the National Register of Historic Places. The historic Pierce Point Ranch buildings provide a glimpse into life on a dairy ranch in the nineteenth century.

Point Reyes is a rich and diverse ecosystem on land and sea and part of the Golden Gate Biosphere Reserve. The protected coastal waters are rich in nutrients and supply the marine life with an abundant menu that sustains plankton as well as whales.

Northern elephant seals and tule elk are star species, since they were hunted to near extinction at one time and are now enjoying a successful recovery. One of the highlights of the Tomales Point hike is the opportunity to catch a glimpse of tule elk herds roaming the reserve as you follow the trail across hill and dale on the ridgeline finger of land atop the Pacific tectonic plate straddling the ocean and gorgeous Tomales Bay, created by the San Andreas Fault below. It's geology come to life that

Tomales Point tapers into the sea.

you are standing on the Pacific Plate and looking across to the North American Plate on the east side of Tomales Bay.

The scenic drive to the isolated hilltop trailhead from CA 1 traces Tomales Bay before climbing past forests of pine, cypress, and eucalyptus slopes and across a rolling bucolic landscape punctuated by voluptuous wetlands spilling onto idyllic beaches at the foot of cattle-dotted pastures. The white ranch buildings come into view at road's end and the parking lot for the Tomales Point Trail. There are no restrooms or water at the trailhead or anywhere along the trail. It is an exposed trail with temperamental climate from hot to windy or foggy in the same hour. Wear layers and bring sufficient water.

The hike begins on a dirt and grass ranch road and skirts the base of a nob as you head north into the postcard-perfect setting of ocean, cliffs, and sculpted coastline to the west and the long slice of Tomales Bay to the east against the backdrop of inland mountains and hills. There are several narrow spur trails heading to rock outcrops for picnics, viewpoints, or elk-spotting vantage points. At about 2.0 miles, start scanning for elk. You might just be lucky enough to spot a few herds grazing or resting on the

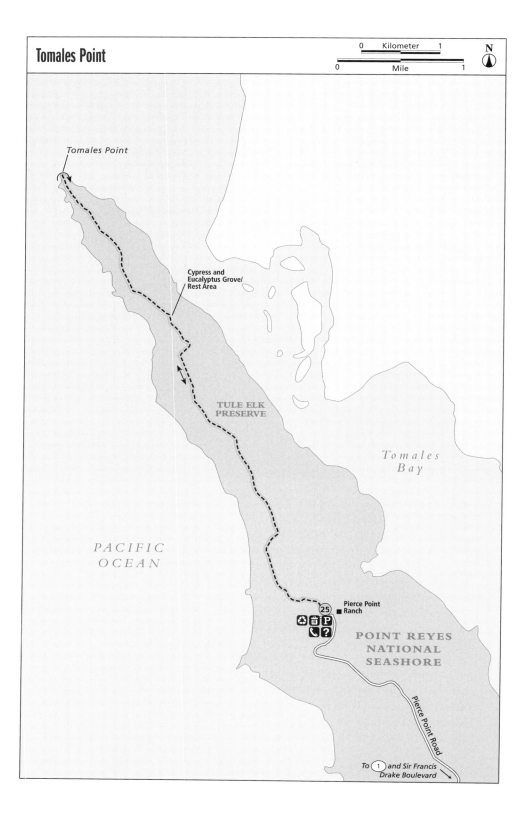

Tomales Point

0 Kilometer 1

0 Mile 1

N

Tomales Point

Cypress and
Eucalyptus Grove/
Rest Area

TULE ELK
PRESERVE

PACIFIC
OCEAN

Tomales
Bay

25 Pierce Point
■ Ranch

POINT REYES
NATIONAL
SEASHORE

Pierce Point Road

To 1 and Sir Francis
Drake Boulevard

slopes. These majestic animals wear their antlers like crowns as they stand peering down at passing hikers.

At 3.2 miles you come to a cypress and eucalyptus grove in a swale and the only shade of the entire hike. It's a perfect destination for a picnic and a turnaround point if stamina or time is an issue. The trail meanders up and down moderate rises and falls as you continue toward the point. At 3.9 miles the trail narrows and becomes loose sand.

Follow the sandy trail as the point of land narrows and begins to gradually descend toward the left edge of Tomales Point. Continue descending as far as you feel comfortable while keeping a safe distance from the eroding edge. Clumps of vegetation cling to the exposed sandstone as the land continues to taper and steepen down to a rocky point. You've arrived at Tomales Point. This last stretch of trail is at the mercy of Mother Nature's whims of wind and rain and continuous sculpting. There are no warning signs or rails, so stay back from the precipitous cliff. Soak up the views and find a comfortable flat perch for a snack and a selfie before going back to the trailhead the way you came.

MILES AND DIRECTIONS

- **0.0** Start at the Tomales Point Trailhead.
- **3.2** Come to a cypress and eucalyptus grove.
- **4.8** Arrive at Tomales Point. Go back to the trailhead the way you came.
- **9.6** Arrive back at the trailhead.

BAKERIES, BREWERIES, EATS, AND SLEEPS

Bovine Bakery, 11315 CA 1, Point Reyes Station 94956; (415) 663-9420; bovine bakeryptreyes.com. The list of organic seasonal goodies to enjoy with a cup of Fair Trade coffee, from artisan breads and scones to French pastries and cookies, is endless. Selections include vegan and gluten-free treats as well.

Cowgirl Creamery and Cantina at Tomales Bay Foods, 80 4th St., Point Reyes Station 94956; (415) 663-9335; cowgirlcreamery.com. It's the story of two University of Tennessee girls who went west after graduation and left their hearts in San Francisco, spending two decades immersed in the city's cutting-edge culinary culture. They discovered the picturesque, historic railroad ranch town of Point Reyes Station in the 1990s and committed themselves to making great cheese and supporting local agriculture. The Point Reyes location is one of their 2 creameries and 4 retail shops in Northern California. The cantina has a fresh hot and cold lunch menu of soups, salads, and sandwiches. The hot and cold beverage menu has its own 6-item Milk Bar.

Station House Cafe, 11180 CA 1, Point Reyes Station 94956; (415) 663-1515; stationhousecafe.com. This mouthwatering hot spot serves breakfast, lunch, and dinner. Breakfast and lunch are available on the patio. The dinner pièces de résistance at

Returning to the trailhead at Historic Pierce Point Ranch

each end of the main course are the hot, fluffy popovers served when you sit down and the golden raisin bread pudding drenched in warm caramel crème anglaise sauce when you finish. Beer lovers wash it all down with a Lagunitas Brewery IPA on tap. Closed Wed.

Inverness Park Market, 12301 Sir Frances Drake Blvd., Inverness Park 94937; (415) 663-1491; perrysinvernessparkgrocery.com. It's the place for an old-style deli sandwich and organic juices and smoothies topped with the best peanut butter cookies in Point Reyes.

Saltwater Oyster Bar & Depot, 12781 Sir Francis Drake Blvd., Inverness 94937; (415) 669-1244; saltwateroysterdepot.com. The menu caters to fresh local oyster lovers, with a few landlubber pleaser items. But the North Coast Brewing Company beers on tap and wines from the Northern California coastal valleys will quench every thirst.

Abalone Inn Bed & Breakfast, 12355 Sir Frances Drake Blvd., Point Reyes Station 94956; (415) 663-9149; abaloneinn.com. The Victorian farmhouse welcomes hikers with 3 guest rooms, cozy casual ambience, a garden for strolling, and hot tub relaxation under the stars.

Tomales Bay Resort & Marina, 12938 Sir Frances Drake Blvd., Inverness 94937; tomalesbayresort.com. Guest rooms overlooking the bay with some pet friendly rooms.

CAMPING

Olema Campground, 10155 CA 1, Olema 94950; (415) 663-8106; www.olema campground.net. It's a clean, private, dog friendly campground in a meadow setting with tall pines for shade. Tent and hookup RV sites.

Dog Friendly Beaches

Rodeo Beach sits on the sand and pebble spit that separates Rodeo Lagoon from Rodeo Cove. It's a great spot for bird watching, but although dogs are welcome to gallivant on the beach under voice control, be ready to snap on Fifi's leash if she is excitable around feathery critters. The beach can be accessed along a sweet trail by the lagoon less than 1.0 mile west of the Marin Headlands Visitor Center (see hike 22), or you can park in the Rodeo Beach parking lot and picnic area down Bunker Road to Mitchell Road west of the Marin Headlands Visitor Center (415-331-1540), Sausalito. Golden Gate National Recreation Area, Building 201, Fort Mason, San Francisco, CA 94123; (415) 561-4700

Muir Beach is part of the Golden Gate National Recreation Area and a highlight in the idyllic coastal hamlet of Muir Beach, with about 200 homes of full-time residents. This voice-control beach boasts offshore surf-sculpted rocks, a creek that forms a lagoon, and wetlands for bird habitat. If you wander north along the beach

Running the surf line
at Upton Beach

to a separate small cove known as Little Beach, you may find sunbathers soaking up vitamin D on their entire body, since clothing is optional in that cove. Muir Beach is accessed off CA 1 at 200 Pacific Way, Muir Beach. The parking lot is at the end of Pacific Way, and a wooden footbridge takes you to the beach and trails. Golden Gate Recreation Area, Building 201, Fort Mason, San Francisco 94123; (415) 561-4700 or (415) 388-2596

Upton Beach is actually a section of beach north of Stinson Beach in the town of Stinson Beach, but few people know about that distinction and generally think of the entire beach and the scenic spit at the edge of the Bolinas Lagoon as all Stinson Beach (see hike 23). This 4-acre-wide band of sand is the only beach where dogs are "officially" allowed, but must be on leash. To access this hidden playground, turn left off CA 1 onto Calle Del Arroyo and park on Calle Del Arroyo before the private Seadrift gated community. Walk up Walla Vista and watch for the pubic pedestrian entrance at the private gated road to Upton Beach. Tell Fido not to worry about the giant flying creatures above the beach—they are just hang gliders coming in for a landing off Mount Tamalpais. Marin County, Marin County Civic Center, 3501 Civic Center Dr., Ste. 260, San Rafael 94903; (415) 473-6387

Limantour Beach is one of two gorgeous beaches that allow dogs on leash in spectacular Point Reyes National Seashore. Respect the posted signs about restrictions during the spring seal pupping season (see hike 24). The beach is accessed from the parking lot at the south end of Limantour Road in Point Reyes National Seashore, Point Reyes Station. Point Reyes National Seashore, 1 Bear Valley Rd., Point Reyes Station 94596; (415) 464-5100; nps.gov

Kehoe Beach's stunning secluded shore of dunes and rocky bluffs extends south and north at the end of a picturesque 0.5-mile dirt and sand trail off of Pierce Point Road. Dogs are not allowed in the snowy plover protected area south of the trail, but leashed dogs can explore the lengthy northern section of the beach with their humans. The beach is accessed from Inverness off of Pierce Point Road in Point Reyes National Seashore. There is a sign for the beach on the west side of Pierce Point Road and parking spaces on the shoulder of the road. Point Reyes National Seashore, 1 Bear Valley Rd., Point Reyes Station 94956; (415) 464-5100

Dillon Beach is privately owned by the Dillon Beach Resort, a rustic cabin resort in a funky beach community overlooking a wide, flat band of firm sand that welcomes day users with "friendly" dogs off leash for a fee. It's a safe playground for bowwows that like to sprint and spin between launching themselves in the surf. The resort has one dog friendly cottage if Fido wants more time on Dillon Beach. The beach is accessed off CA 1 on Dillon Beach Road from the town of Tomales. Dillon Beach Resort, 1 Beach Ave., Dillon Beach 94929; (707) 878-2094

Coastal Attractions

Muir Woods National Monument, 1 Muir Woods Rd., Mill Valley 94941; (415) 388-2595; nps.org. This popular 550-acre redwood park minutes from San Francisco and the Bay Area off CA 1 is a real gem. It may not be home to the tallest of old-growth trees, but such a special oasis protected at the back door of a metropolis should not be missed. Get there early. Parking is limited, but there are also shuttles from the Sausalito Ferry.

Brickmaiden Breads, 40 4th St., Point Reyes Station 94596; (415) 663-1203. Learn about traditional bread-making processes in a day workshop and walk away with your own freshly baked bread, sourdough starter, and pizza dough. Go to brickmaidenbreads.com for a schedule of bread workshops.

Cowgirl Creamery, 80 4th St. at Tomales Bay Foods, Point Reyes Station; (415) 663-9335; cowgirlcreamery.com. Book a tour, tasting, or Cheese 101 class.

Tomales is a dot of a historic community off CA 1 about 13 miles north of Point Reyes. **The Tomales Bakery and Deli/Cafe** are worth the side trip; 27000 CA 1, Tomales 94971; tomalesbakery.com, tomalesdeli.com.

Blue Waters Kayaking, 19225 Shoreline Hwy., Marshall 94940; (415) 669-2600; bwkayak.com. Tomales Bay's 15-mile-long tidal body of water in Point Reyes National Seashore is a pristine kayaking nirvana. Blue Waters offers hourly kayak rentals (2-hour minimum). If you want to extend the adventure, call about the independent overnight camping option and the guided weekend campout excursion.

BEST COASTAL FARMERS' MARKETS

Tiburon Farmers' Market is worth the visit because it's in the chic, charming enclave of Tiburon. Take the ferry from San Francisco or Sausalito and enjoy browsing the 30 vendor stalls. You'll find local honey, microgreens, and freshly roasted peppers. Sip a beer or a glass of wine while watching the local chef demo. The market operates seasonally on Main Street and Tiburon Boulevard late June to late Oct on Thurs from 3 to 7 p.m.; (415) 999-5635; see the Facebook page for more info.

Point Reyes Farmers' Market is in the heart of some of Marin's most fertile land, in one of the quaintest communities in the county. This market's claim to fame is the 20 vendors' organic products. There's music, Asian fusion food to go, and guest chef booths for cooking demonstrations every week. In a region known for its "happy cows," it's no surprise that the market is just as famous for its outrageous grilled cheese sandwiches as the produce. The market is held in Toby's Barn at 11250 CA 1, Point Reyes Station, and operates seasonally late June to early Nov from 9 a.m. to 1 p.m. Visit the Facebook page for specifics.

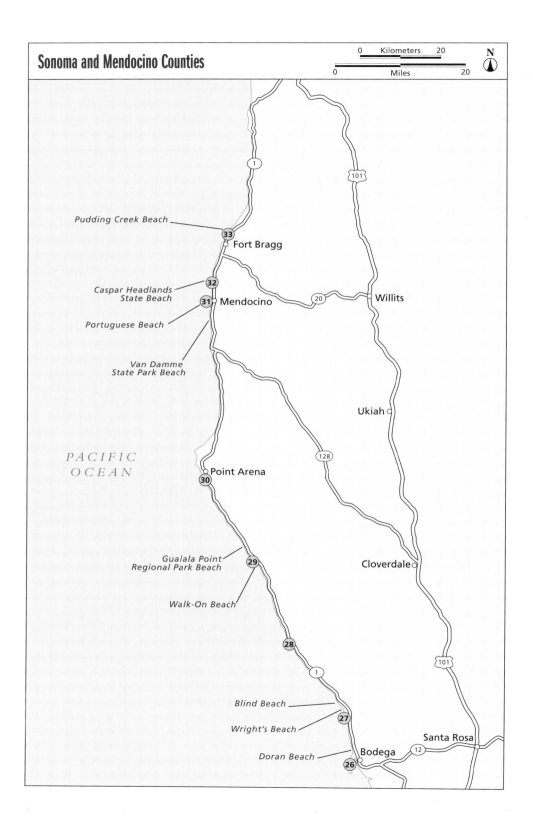

Sonoma and Mendocino Counties

Kilometers

Miles

N

PACIFIC
OCEAN

Pudding Creek Beach

33 Fort Bragg

Caspar Headlands
State Beach **32**

31 Mendocino

Portuguese Beach

Van Damme
State Park Beach

Willits

Ukiah

Point Arena
30

Gualala Point
Regional Park Beach **29**

Cloverdale

Walk-On Beach

28

Blind Beach

27

Wright's Beach

Santa Rosa

Doran Beach

Bodega

26

SONOMA COUNTY

As the California Wine Country's largest producer as well as one of the country's prime agricultural pockets for its fertile land and quality water, **SONOMA COUNTY** is well known among wine fans and foodies. The talents of local brewmasters are also helping to catapult Sonoma County into the spotlight as the new California "Beer Country." Its 76 miles of coastline tucked between Marin County and Mendocino County abound with state marine reserves, and the county's beaches were rated as the cleanest in the state in 2010. The coastal plains and headlands offer the perfect terrain and setting to soak up the Pacific coast's dynamic panorama, and good food complemented by a good vintage or a rich brew is never far away from the trail.

Crabs, starfish and anemones share tide pool

26. **BODEGA HEAD**

WHY GO?

The headlands braced by the Bodega Bay and harbor on one side and the Pacific on the other make the short, dramatic Bodega Head Trail one of the most memorable coastal hikes in California.

THE RUNDOWN

Distance: 1.9-mile loop

Start: Bodega Head Trailhead

Nearest town: Bodega Bay

Hiking time: About 1 hour

Fees and permits: None

Conveniences: Vault toilets and trash and recycling containers at trailhead. Although the gravel trail is ADA wheelchair accessible, in the spring of 2016 some trail segments seemed too eroded to be appropriate for wheelchairs.

Beach access: Yes

Trail users: Hikers and wheelchairs

Trailhead elevation: 75 feet

Highest point: 228 feet

Trail surface: Fine gravel and dirt

Difficulty: Easy

Seasonal highlights: Wildflowers bursting with yellow lupine bush in the spring; migrating gray whales from Dec to Apr

Managing agency: Sonoma Coast State Park, 3095 CA 1, Bodega Bay 94923; (707) 875-3483 or (707) 865-2391; parks.ca.gov

FINDING THE TRAILHEAD

From Bodega Bay on CA 1, turn west on Eastshore Road to Bodega Head. Drive 0.2 mile on Eastshore Road to Bay Flat Road. Turn right on Bay Flat Road, which becomes Westshore Road, and drive 3.5 miles to the Bodega Head parking lot at the end of the road. **GPS:** N38 18.21' / W123 03.87'

WHAT TO SEE

Native Americans were the first to build seasonal encampments on this coast, and they did so for over 3,000 years. But life began to change with the arrival of Russian settlers and fur trappers in the early 1800s, followed by Spanish missionaries and European pioneers lured by gold and the redwood forests' lumber fortunes.

For many it was the 1963 Hitchcock thriller *The Birds* that put Bodega Bay on the destination radar. The movie was filmed in Bodega Bay and the small community of Bodega 5 miles south.

Windswept Bodega Head

This hike highlights Bodega Head and the stunning scenery. Bodega Head marks the entrance to Bodega Harbor and is at the southern end of Sonoma Coast State Park's almost 20 miles of beaches and coves interrupted by rocky bluffs and headlands with craggy cliffs. Bodega Bay is geologically fascinating. Movement along the San Andreas Fault created the natural harbor. More recently the 1906 earthquake caused a 15-foot-long lurch, moving the harbor northward in a straight line.

The loop trail skirts the bluff above sheer cliffs and crashing surf and turns inland across the coastal prairie before dropping back down to the parking lot. The headlands curve southward, creating Bodega Bay's scenic protected harbor. This short trail rewards hikers with a breathtaking panorama of Sonoma's legendary rugged coastline and rolling landscape across the bay.

There are two parking lots for the Bodega Head Trail, but this hike begins at the northern end and takes you south counterclockwise along the bluffs before veering inland on a slight slope and back down to the parking lot. There are a couple of picnic tables and benches along the way as well as a fine gravel wheelchair-accessible trail to the left that stays inland from the bluffs. Follow the dirt trail on the right

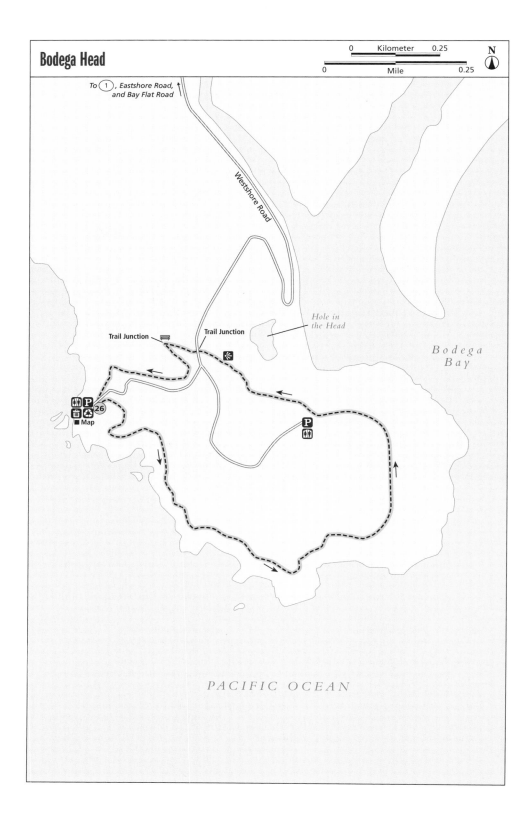

Bodega Head

0 Kilometer 0.25

0 Mile 0.25

N

To ① , Eastshore Road, and Bay Flat Road

Westshore Road

Hole in the Head

B o d e g a
B a y

Trail Junction

Trail Junction

26

■ Map

P

P

PACIFIC OCEAN

closest to the bluffs, but be mindful to stay on the main path and back from the unstable cliff edge.

At 0.5 mile you come to one of the premier picnic spots on the Sonoma coast. The solo picnic table with the million-dollar view is a great excuse to stop for a snack, especially if you happen to be here on a rare windless day.

At 1.2 miles you come to the southern parking lot and restrooms, and you cross the road just 0.2 mile ahead. As you continue walking on the trail, notice the large depression forming a pond below on the right. This is the Hole in the Head and site of excavation for a nuclear power plant that was never built thanks to the protests of local citizens supported by scientists who thought a nuclear plant so close to an earthquake fault was a bad idea. The hearings and court battles raged on for 8 years until the project was abandoned in 1964.

The trail cuts back across the meadow and to a trail junction at a bench on a mellow slope. Turn left at the junction. The parking lot and trailhead where you started are below just ahead. As you step off the trail onto the flat parking area, notice the interpretive panel about the area's geologic history. Coincidentally, if you look more closely at the small cove beach below, you will notice how erosion has devoured a chunk of coastline at your feet and regurgitated a couple of picnic tables, casualties of land in motion.

MILES AND DIRECTIONS

0.0 Start at the Bodega Head Trailhead to the left of the restroom.

1.2 Come to the parking lot and restroom south of the trailhead.

1.3 Come to the Hole in the Head interpretive panel.

1.4 Walk across the road.

1.5 Come to a trail junction at the bench. Turn left.

1.9 Arrive back at the trailhead.

BAKERIES, BREWERIES, EATS, AND SLEEPS

Roadhouse Coffee, 1580 Eastshore Rd., Bodega Bay 94923; (707) 360-8856. This coffee shop makes a good stopover for muffin and cookie snacks with one of their specialty coffees or teas.

Lucas Wharf Restaurant and Bar, 595 Bay Hill, Bodega Bay 94923; (707) 875-3522; lucaswharfrestaurant.com. This is seafood dining on the water with dog friendly outdoor tables. The sautéed calamari and fresh fish tacos go nicely with Lagunitas Brewery's Little Sumpin', one of five Sonoma County beers on tap.

The Birds Cafe, 1407 CA 1, Bodega 94923; (707) 875-2900; thebirdscafe.com. Lagunitas IPA makes the cafe's fish-and-chips a notch above the rest. Vegetarians will love the artichoke tacos. Lunch and dinner daily.

Looking out at Hole in the Head and Bodega Bay

Pelican Plaza Grocery and Deli, 1400 CA 1, Bodega 94923; (707) 875-2522; pelicanplazagrocery.com. Stop for local cheeses; house-made meat loaf; deli sandwiches on fresh-baked sourdough, Dutch crunch, or French rolls; or home-baked gourmet goodies. Manager Sal Hernandez says his wife Kelly's fruit pies just "fly" out the door.

Spud Point Crab Company, 1910 Westshore Rd., Bodega Bay 94923; (707) 875-9472; spudpointcrab.com. Fishing is in the Anello family's DNA. Tony Anello, Spud's owner with wife Carol, is a fourth-generation fisherman going back to his Italian sea-happy roots. Stop by for their award-winning clam chowder or weekend-only crab cakes. Leashed dogs welcome at the outdoor tables.

Bay Hill Mansion Bed & Breakfast, 3919 Bay Hill Rd., Bodega Bay 94923; (877) 468-1588; bayhillmansion.com. If your four-legged furry child has been whining for some quality deluxe vacation time with you, this quiet Victorian perch with ocean views is an idyllic bonding getaway. Pooches are met with organic treats, memory foam beds for sweeter dreams, and other amenities. The top-floor dog friendly Captain's Suite has its own interior staircase so you and Fido can conveniently access the yard during the midnight hours without disturbing other guests. Pet fee.

Bodega Bay Inn, 1588 Eastshore Rd., Bodega 94923; (707) 875-3388; bodega bayinn.com. The inn offers casual dog friendly lodging with king bedrooms—some with bay and ocean views. The common area is appointed with a toaster, coffee machine, and refrigerator for guest convenience. Pick a free flick from the library and popcorn to take to your room, and enjoy a movie night snuggled up with Rover.

CAMPING

Bodega Bay Dunes Campground at Sonoma Coast State Park, 3095 CA 1, Bodega Bay 94923; (707) 875-3483 or (800) 444-park; parks.ca.gov. There are 99 sites for tents and RVs (no hookups and 31-foot max length). Coin showers. Leashed dogs in campground but no dogs on the beach. Bodega Bay Dunes Campground has trees for shade, and many sites are more sheltered from the wind.

Doran Regional Park Campground, 201 Doran Beach Rd., Bodega Bay 94923; Ranger Station, (707) 875-3540; parks.sonomacounty.ca.gov. Tent and RV sites (dump station but no hookups). Dogs must be on leash and have a license. Dogs on leash are allowed on the beach and the grassy dunes trail connecting to the ADA-accessible boardwalk and viewing benches.

Visitor from Canada takes a rest

27. **KORTUM TRAIL TO RUSSIAN RIVER**

WHY GO?

The fact that this section of the California Coastal Trail is tucked between two quaint Northern California communities, Bodega Bay and Jenner, is an added bonus. The panorama is classic rugged Sonoma coast along bluffs punctuated by coves and beaches at the edge of meadows. The mouth of the Russian River at the end of the hike is the scenic pièce de résistance.

THE RUNDOWN

Distance: 9.2 miles out and back

Start: Kortum Trailhead at north end of Wright's Beach parking lot

Nearest towns: Bodega Bay (south) and Jenner (north)

Hiking time: About 5 hours

Fees and permits: None

Conveniences: The first 0.8 mile of trail is wheelchair accessible. Restrooms at Shell Beach and Russian River lagoon parking lot.

Beach access: Yes; dogs on leash on Wright's Beach at the trailhead, Furlong Gulch, Shell Beach, and Blind Beach (see map)

Trail users: Hikers and wheelchairs

Trailhead elevation: 95 feet

Highest point: 341 feet

Trail surface: Compact soil, dirt, grass, and sand

Difficulty: Strenuous

Seasonal highlights: Wildflowers in the spring and whale migration

Managing agency: Sonoma Coast State Park, 3095 CA 1, Bodega Bay 94923; (707) 875-3483 or (707) 865-2391; parks.ca.gov

FINDING THE TRAILHEAD

From the south at Bodega Bay and CA 1, drive 7 miles north to Wright's Beach. Turn west into the parking area to walk the trail north.

From the north at Jenner, drive 5 miles south to Goat Rock Road and turn west. Drive 3 miles on Goat Rock Road to the parking lot at the mouth of the Russian River to walk the trail south. **GPS:** N38 24.09' / W123 05.72'

WHAT TO SEE

The hike described here is from south to north, but can be done in reverse from north to south.

This is one of many highlights along Sonoma Coast State Park's almost 20 miles of spectacular coastline. Named in the 1990s after veterinarian and dedicated environmentalist Bill Kortum, the dirt and grassy trail runs along the bluffs at the edge of the coastal prairie, with CA 1 visible in the distance on its way to the mouth of the Russian River. Both Goat Rock and the Russian River at the end of the trail are significant landmarks. The Russian River is 110 miles long and provided a bounty for the Russian fur trappers from Sitka, Alaska, who trapped river and sea otters for their pelts in the early 1800s. The Russian-American Company operated from Fort Ross 11 miles north of Jenner until they sold the fort to John Sutter in 1841. The Russian River played an important role in the Mexican-American War, gold rush, California statehood, and logging of redwood forests. But prior to the arrival of foreign explorers and exploiters, the river's rich fish population was the star attraction for Native American people. Today several endangered species of salmon still come home to the Russian River.

Humans have also had a hand in designing Goat Rock's history. Prior to the 1920s, Goat Rock was an island. A project to build a jetty at Jenner began with a quarry at Goat Rock. Today the site is an isthmus, which connects Goat Rock to the mainland beach. The jetty project stretched over a couple of decades but was never completed. Mother Nature has largely covered that scar, which remains mostly submerged. Remnants of the narrow-gauge railway that was used to transport the material can still be seen under the shifting sands in the parking area near the mouth of the Russian River at the end of this hike.

The dirt and grassy trail transitions to meandering sections of boardwalk that protect some of the more-fragile riparian meadows. Wooden footbridges cross over narrow gulches carved by seasonal creeks on their journey to isolated coves and beaches.

Except for the momentary shade of a eucalyptus grove at 0.5 mile, the trail is exposed the whole way. The wind can be as punishing as the sun anytime of year and a foggy day can chill you to the bone, so don't leave home without layers for the changing temperatures, sunscreen, and headwear with a brim.

You come to a trail junction at 0.7 mile. The beach is to the left. Bear right to continue on the Kortum Trail. You come to a cul-de-sac parking area and the end of the wheelchair-accessible section of the trail just ahead. Turn left onto the narrow grassy trail to continue your hike along the bluff. If you miss this turn and continue walking across the parking lot on the left shoulder, you can merge back onto the trail at the far end where the road into the parking lot comes off CA 1. The trail is fairly well marked with yellow arrows on wooden posts all the way to the road above Goat Rock.

At 1.1 miles bear left down toward the beach and follow the trail as it curves right across two wooden footbridges at the bottom of Furlong Gulch. The trail then climbs back up to the bluffs. You come to the Shell Beach parking area at 1.8 miles. There is a restroom and trash and recycling containers here, along with a map board identical to the one at the trailhead to help orient you. About 0.2 mile ahead the trail leads to an overlook to the left and a boardwalk straight ahead. Take a minute to check out the overlook before continuing on the boardwalk.

Soak up the open vistas for the next mile before coming to a fractured rock outcrop on the right, where the trail climbs about 200 feet to the top of the hill before dropping down on the other side. If you're not up to the entire length of this hike, there are several great perches for a picnic on this island of rock before going back to the trailhead the way you came. If you are going the distance, follow the trail up to the saddle and back down the other side. You can linger and scamper around the outcrop on the way back. You will have a great view of Goat Rock and Blind Beach from the top of this hill and all the way down to the paved road at 3.6 miles.

Walk along the shoulder of the road past the Blind Beach parking lot. A long, steep wooden staircase leads down to Blind Beach. There are restrooms with vault toilets in the parking lot and picnic tables. You can't miss Goat Rock down below and the long strand of beach at the mouth of the Russian River beyond.

Continue walking on the shoulder of Goat Rock Road for about 1 mile to the trail junction on the right at the sign for the service road stating Authorized Vehicles Only. Turn right down the steps onto the grassy service road to the parking lot for Goat Rock Beach and the amazing Russian River estuary. There are picnic tables, water, restrooms with flush toilets, and trash and recycling containers here. Take the time to walk over the dunes to the expansive beach and the lagoon before going back the way you came.

MILES AND DIRECTIONS

0.0 Start at the Kortum Trailhead above Wright's Beach.

0.7 Come to a trail junction and bear right.

0.8 Come to the end of the wheelchair-accessible section and a parking lot. Turn left onto the grassy trail.

1.1 Bear left downhill toward the beach across Furlong Gulch on two footbridges.

1.8 Come to a parking area and restrooms for Shell Beach.

3.1 Walk past the fragmented rock monolith and follow the trail up and over the hill.

3.6 Come to the paved Goat Rock Road and Blind Beach parking area. Continue walking on the shoulder.

4.5 Come to a trail junction. Bear right and walk down steps off the paved road to the grassy service road.

4.6 Arrive at the Russian River and dunes parking lot. Explore the beach and estuary before going back the way you came.

9.2 Arrive back at the trailhead.

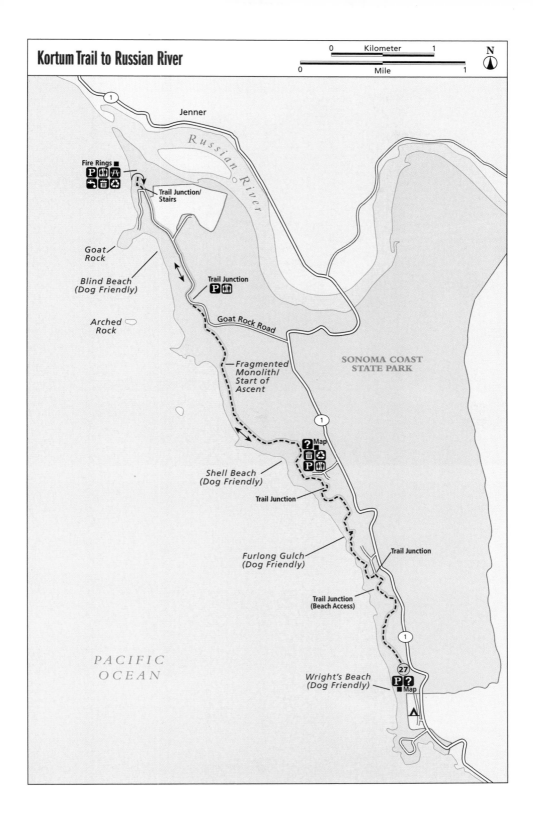

Kortum Trail to Russian River

Kilometer

Mile

N

Jenner

Russian River

Fire Rings

P 🚻 ⛟
🚗 🗑 ♿

Trail Junction/
Stairs

*Goat
Rock*

*Blind Beach
(Dog Friendly)*

Trail Junction
P 🚻

Goat Rock Road

*Arched
Rock*

SONOMA COAST
STATE PARK

*Fragmented
Monolith/
Start of
Ascent*

1

❓ Map
🗑 ♿
P 🚻

*Shell Beach
(Dog Friendly)*

Trail Junction

*Furlong Gulch
(Dog Friendly)*

Trail Junction

Trail Junction
(Beach Access)

*PACIFIC
OCEAN*

1

*Wright's Beach
(Dog Friendly)*

27

P ❓
■ Map

⛺

Winding along creeks and across bridges

Approaching the Russian River lagoon

BAKERIES, BREWERIES, EATS, AND SLEEPS

Roadhouse Coffee, 1580 Eastshore Rd., Bodega Bay 94923; (707) 360-8856. This coffee shop makes a good stopover for muffin and cookie snacks with one of their specialty coffees or teas.

Lucas Wharf Restaurant and Bar, 595 Bay Hill, Bodega Bay 94923; (707) 875-3522; lucaswharfrestaurant.com. This is seafood dining on the water with dog friendly outdoor tables. The sautéed calamari and fresh fish tacos go nicely with Lagunitas Brewery's Little Sumpin', one of five Sonoma County beers on tap.

The Birds Cafe, 1407 CA 1, Bodega 94923; (707) 875-2900; thebirdscafe.com. Lagunitas IPA makes the cafe's fish-and-chips a notch above the rest. Vegetarians will love the artichoke tacos. Lunch and dinner daily.

Pelican Plaza Grocery and Deli, 1400 CA 1, Bodega 94923; (707) 875-2522; pelicanplazagrocery.com. Stop for local cheeses; house-made meat loaf; deli sand-wiches on fresh-baked sourdough, Dutch crunch, or French rolls; or home-baked gourmet goodies. Manager Sal Hernandez says his wife Kelly's fruit pies just "fly" out the door.

Spud Point Crab Company, 1910 Westshore Rd., Bodega Bay 94923; (707) 875-9472; spudpointcrab.com. Fishing is in the Anello family's DNA. Tony Anello, Spud's owner with wife Carol, is a fourth-generation fisherman going back to his Italian sea-happy roots. Stop by for their award-winning clam chowder or weekend-only crab cakes. Leashed dogs welcome at the outdoor tables.

Bay Hill Mansion Bed & Breakfast, 3919 Bay Hill Rd., Bodega Bay 94923; (877) 468-1588; bayhillmansion.com. If your four-legged furry child has been whining for some quality deluxe vacation time with you, this quiet Victorian perch with ocean views is an idyllic bonding getaway. Pooches are met with organic treats, memory foam beds for sweeter dreams, and other amenities. The top-floor dog friendly Captain's Suite has its own interior staircase so you and Fido can conve-niently access the yard during the midnight hours without disturbing other guests. Pet fee.

Bodega Bay Inn, 1588 Eastshore Rd., Bodega 94923; (707) 875-3388; bodega bayinn.com. The inn offers casual dog friendly lodging with king bedrooms—some with bay and ocean views. The common area is appointed with a toaster, coffee machine, and refrigerator for guest convenience. Pick a free flick from the library and popcorn to take to your room, and enjoy a movie night snuggled up with Rover.

JENNER (NORTH END OF THE KORTUM TRAIL HIKE)

Jenner Sea Store, 10444 CA 1, Jenner 95450; (707) 865-2906. Gas station and convenience store for quick snacks and deli provisions.

Fort Ross Store & Deli, 20705 CA 1 (about 13 miles north of Russian River trailhead), Jenner 95450; (707) 847-3414; fortrosslodge.com. Pick up provisions and snacks from this general store and deli across from Fort Ross Lodge.

Fort Ross Lodge, 20705 CA 1 (about 13 miles north of Russian River trailhead), Jenner 95450; (707) 847-3333; fortrosslodge.com. This family-owned-and-operated lodge has 16 rooms on the ocean side of CA 1. Each guest room has a microwave and small refrigerator as well as a charcoal barbecue on the private patio. The 6 hill guest rooms on the east side of CA 1 are "adult only."

Jenner Inn, 10400 CA 1, Jenner 95450; (707) 865-2377; jennerinn.com. The 3-acre property has 21 rooms and 4 cottages (some with kitchens). The restaurant has a lovely patio.

River's End Restaurant and Inn, 11048 CA 1, Jenner 95450; (707) 865-2484; ilovesunsets.com. If romance is what you are looking for at the end of a hike, River's End's scenic setting and techno-free retreat is for you. The are 4 cabins and 1 guest room in the restaurant building. No pets or children under 12. The romance extends to the intimate dining room and deck with views of Goat Rock and the Russian River. The seasonal menus take advantage of local sustainable resources, including fresh catches from the Pacific, poultry farms, ranches, and dairies.

Timber Cove Resort, 21780 CA 1, Jenner 95450; (707) 847-3231; timbercove resort.com. Newly renovated cliff-top property with some dog friendly rooms and hiking trails. Pet fee.

CAMPING

Bodega Bay Dunes Campground at Sonoma Coast State Park, 3095 CA 1, Bodega Bay 94923; (707) 875-3483 or (800) 444-park; parks.ca.gov. There are 99 sites for tents and RVs (no hookups and 31-foot max length). Token-operated showers. Leashed dogs in campground but no dogs on the beach. Bodega Bay Dunes Campground has trees for shade, and many sites are more sheltered from the wind.

Wright's Beach Campground, 7095 CA 1, Bodega Bay 94923; (800) 444-PARK; parks.ca.gov. There are 27 exposed developed sites overlooking the beach for tents and RVs (27-foot max length). No showers (registered campers can use token-operated showers at Bodega Dunes Campground). This campground is convenient to the south trailhead for the Kortum Trail hike. Dogs are allowed on leash on Wright's Beach.

28. SALT POINT TO SENTINEL ROCK

WHY GO?

This trail is not just another one of coastal California's pretty faces with crashing surf at the foot of rugged bluffs and sandy coves. It's all that plus layers of rocky shelves jutting into the ocean from the marine terrace. In the meadow, grassy mounds roll around the scattered sandstone slabs, evidence of the nineteenth-century quarry activity. The trail blends the panorama of tame headlands with the more primeval setting of fern gardens in the shadow of gnarly weather-whipped pine tree tunnels clinging to the cliffs' edge.

THE RUNDOWN

Distance: 7.2 miles out and back

Start: Salt Point Trail at southwest end of parking lot

Nearest towns: Gualala (north) and Jenner (south)

Hiking time: About 4 hours

Fees and permits: Parking fee

Conveniences: Restrooms with flush toilets, sinks, changing rooms, and outdoor shower; picnic tables and trash and recycling containers

Beach access: Yes

Trail users: Hikers and wheelchairs on ADA paved section at the beginning of Salt Point Trail

Trailhead elevation: 65 feet

Highest point: 177 feet

Trail surface: Pavement, compacted soil, and loose dirt

Difficulty: Strenuous

Seasonal highlights: Wildflowers in the spring and gray whale migration

Managing agency: Salt Point State Park, 25050 CA 1, Jenner 95450; (707) 847-3221; parks.ca.gov

FINDING THE TRAILHEAD

From Gualala, drive 20 miles south on CA 1 to Gerstle Cove Campground on the west side of CA 1. Drive 0.7 mile into the campground and follow the signs for the day-use area and visitor center. Continue downhill past the visitor center to the day-use parking lot at the bottom of the hill.

From Jenner, drive 18 miles north on CA 1 to Gerstle Cove Campground on the west side of CA 1 and follow the previous directions to the parking lot. **GPS:** N38 33.99' / W123 19.91'

WHAT TO SEE

The land at Salt Point State Park was originally home to the Kashaya native people who came to fish along the coast during the summer. The Kashaya are considered expert artisans whose exquisite basketry graces museum collections all over the world. Unlike many other Native Americans whose lives were irreversibly disrupted by the arrival of European settlers, many Kashaya descendants remain in the area and keep their traditional culture alive.

Gerstle Campground is named after Lewis Gerstle, who owned the southern portion of Rancho German in the late 1800s. That tract of land included what is now Salt Point. Salt Point State Park is now a majestic 6,000-acre spread and one of California's first underwater parks. Gerstle Cove State Marine Reserve and Salt Point State Marine Conservation Area surround the park, which make the park a stellar site for recreational diving as well as sea kayaking.

The beauty of this hike is that you can call it a day at just about any cove or on any bluff and feel you've had a rich coastal experience. The first couple of miles hug the coastline on a flat exposed trail with pristine panoramic views. The trail narrows and makes a steep descent down to gorgeous Stump Cove Beach before climbing back up to the bluff on an equally narrow and steep trail at the head of the beach. There's a staircase going up to the bluff, but your trail is to the left of the stairs. The stairs connect to a trail that heads back out to CA 1.

Stump Cove Beach's idyllic protected setting makes a perfect destination and turnaround point. But if you're craving more of an adventure, continue walking up to the bluff. The trail crests and you enter a shady pine tunnel at 1.9 miles for about 0.3 mile before emerging back on the exposed headlands. Looking back, you get a spectacular view of Stump Cove Beach.

From here you will walk across a couple of wooden footbridges and rock hop over a couple of seasonal creeks tumbling down over the cliffs. The trail becomes much narrower and more primitive through the pine forest. Watch for small yellow flags planted in the ground to help guide you along. The ocean may disappear from view behind the curtain of trees from time to time but will always be within earshot.

At 3.0 miles you come to a trail junction with an unmarked spur to the right and a sign for Sentinel Rock and Fisk Mill Cove. Bear left to Sentinel Rock. You will pass a picnic table at 3.4 miles just short of the sign for Sentinel Rock to the left. Turn left and follow the narrow trail 0.1 mile up to the top of Sentinel Rock and the viewing platform and bench. This is a splendid perch for a picnic overlooking Fisk Mill Cove. Go back to the trailhead the way you came. But if you want to use a restroom, bear left on the trail when you come down the hill back to the Sentinel Rock and Fisk Mill Cove sign. There is a portable toilet at a parking area off CA 1 about 200 feet up that trail.

Diver access at Salt Point

Open meadow along Salt Point Trail

MILES AND DIRECTIONS

0.0 Start at the Salt Point Trailhead.

0.1 Come to the end of the ADA trail and Salt Point. Turn right on the compacted soil trail.

0.3 Turn left at the bend in the trail to continue along the bluff.

0.6 Come to a T junction at a service road. Turn left along the coastline.

1.8 Arrive at Stump Cove Beach. Follow the sign for the Bluff Trail to the left of the stairs to continue along the bluff.

2.4 Walk across the creek.

3.0 Come to a trail junction and sign for Sentinel Rock 0.5 and Fisk Mill Cove 0.7. Bear left to continue toward Sentinel Rock.

3.5 Come to a trail junction for Sentinel Rock (left) and Fisk Mill Cove (right). Turn left uphill to the top of Sentinel Rock.

3.6 Arrive at Sentinel Rock's viewing platform. Go back to the trailhead the way you came.

7.2 Arrive back at the trailhead.

BAKERIES, BREWERIES, EATS, AND SLEEPS

Twofish Fish Bakery Sea Ranch, 35590 Verdant View, Sea Ranch 95497; (707) 785-2443; twofishbaking.com. Twofish is the successful blend of talents of a former Ritz-Carlton pastry chef and a former imaging operations customer service expert. Margaret the baker and Hilla the manager have created a thriving enterprise that keeps customers coming back for signature products like country wheat baguettes, sticky buns, outrageous toasted granola, and an array of baked cookies. The Sea Ranch location is open Thurs through Sun with lunch items, and Fri is Pizza Night from 5 to 8:30 p.m.

In May 2016 Twofish opened a second North Coast location, 4 miles south of Sea Ranch and north of Salt Point in the historic Stewarts Point Store, 32000 CA 1, Stewarts Point 95480; (707) 785-2011. If you miss the Sea Ranch location's 4-day window of operation, you'll be happy to know that the Stewarts Point Store is open 7 days a week. Check the website for seasonal schedule changes.

Trinks Bakery and Cafe, 39140 CA 1, Gualala; (707) 884-1713; trinkscafe.com. If you love the marshmallow in Rocky Road, don't miss Trinks' version of the treat. The family-operated cafe serves breakfast and lunch daily and gourmet dinners 3 nights a week. Ingredients are pure North Coast sustainable, including seasonal produce from Trinks' garden and orchard.

Surf Market, 39250 CA 1, Gualala 95445; (707) 884-4184. Great source for all your hiking and camping provision needs, from baked goods and local artisan cheeses to deli delights and fresh seafood. There are no breweries in Gualala, but the market carries popular local beers from Mendocino, Anderson Valley, and Bear Republic Brewing Companies.

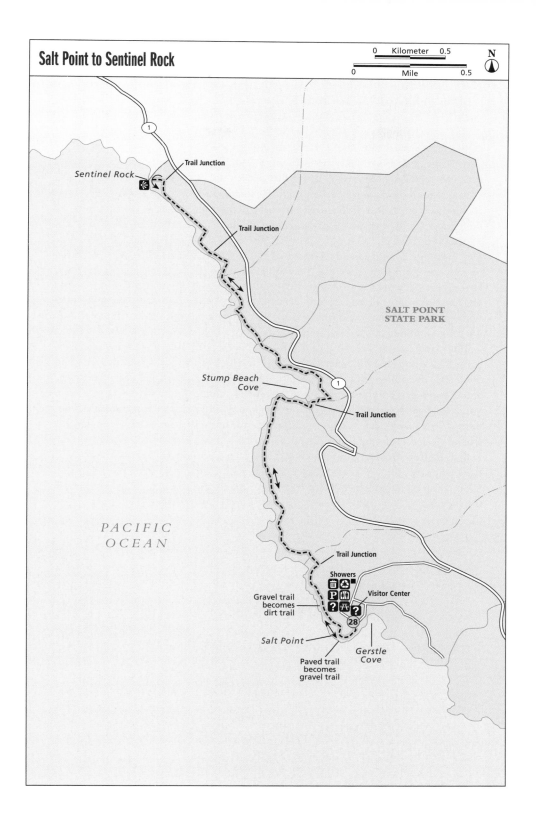

Salt Point to Sentinel Rock

0   Kilometer   0.5

0   Mile   0.5

N

Trail Junction

Sentinel Rock

Trail Junction

SALT POINT
STATE PARK

Stump Beach
Cove

1

Trail Junction

PACIFIC
OCEAN

Trail Junction

Showers

Gravel trail
becomes
dirt trail

Visitor Center

28

Salt Point

Gerstle
Cove

Paved trail
becomes
gravel trail

Black Point Grill at Sea Ranch Lodge, 60 Sea Walk Dr., Sea Ranch 95497; (800) 732-7262; searanchlodge.com. The lodge restaurant serves breakfast, lunch, and dinner. The tavern menu is available in the bar from 11:30 a.m. to 8:30 p.m. Although menus change seasonally, the ever-popular Local Cod Fish & Chips and the Creekstone Angus Burger are here to stay, as are the local brewery beers on tap. The local Pazzo Marco Creamery's artisan gelato flavors take care of the sweet-toothed diners.

Sea Ranch Lodge, 60 Sea Walk Dr., Sea Ranch 95497; (800) 732-7262; searanchlodge.com. This is a dream dog friendly oceanfront resort for overnighting in the perfect blend of rustic elegance, tranquility, and Pacific panorama.

Breakers Inn, 39300 S. CA 1, Gualala 95445; (707) 884-3200; breakersinn.com. The Breakers is conveniently located steps from Gualala's services, with an idyllic cliff-top setting overlooking the mouth of the Gualala River and the Pacific. Rooms are decorated with regional flavor. Whether you are in the Pioneer, Napa, or Denmark room, all have private decks to savor the views. Rooms are appointed with small refrigerators and microwaves, and some luxuries include fireplaces and spa tubs. Continental breakfast is included.

The Surf Motel, 39170 CA 1, Gualala 95445; (707) 884-3571; surfinngualala .com. This good-value '60s, bluff-top, dog friendly, B&B-style lodging upgraded in 2008 and offers a range of amenities. All rooms have a small refrigerator, microwave, and a hypoallergenic featherbed and comforters. Some rooms have ocean views, while others have full kitchens. A full hot and cold breakfast selection complete with fresh-baked scones, biscuits, and waffles and Adirondack chairs for soaking up the Pacific air and views are just some of the perks.

Sea Ranch Beach Rentals, 39200 S. CA 1, Gualala 95445; (707) 884-4235; searanchrentals.com. A beach rental or Sea Ranch vacation home rental offers the most comfortable and convenient base camp for hiking and exploring this part of the Northern California coast. Dog friendly properties available.

Kayakers arriving at
Stump Cove Beach

View from Sentinel Rock toward Fisk Mill Cove

JENNER

Fort Ross Store & Deli, 20705 CA 1, Jenner 95450; (707) 847-3414; fortross lodge.com. Pick up provisions and snacks from this general store and deli across from Fort Ross Lodge.

Fort Ross Lodge, 20705 CA 1, Jenner 95450; (707) 847-3333; fortrosslodge.com. This family-owned-and-operated lodge has 16 rooms on the ocean side of CA 1. Each guest room has a microwave and small refrigerator as well as a charcoal barbecue on the private patio. The 6 hill guest rooms on the east side of CA 1 are "adult only."

Timber Cove Resort, 21780 CA 1, Jenner 95450; (707) 847-3231; timbercoveresort .com. Newly renovated cliff-top property with some dog friendly rooms and hiking trails. Pet fee.

CAMPING

Salt Point State Park Campground, 25050 CA 1, Jenner 95450; (800) 444-7275; parks.ca.gov. Tent and RV sites (check website for max lengths). There are restrooms and drinking water but no showers.

Gualala Point Regional Park Campground, 42401 CA 1, Gualala 95445; (707) 565-2267; sonomacountyparks.org (click on "Reserve a Campsite"). Tent and RV sites (no hookups). There are flush toilets and electrical outlets in restrooms and a coin-operated shower.

29. **BLUFF TOP TRAIL TO WALK-ON BEACH**

WHY GO?
Ranking as one of the best coastal hikes, this trail is brimming with scenic views and opportunities to sample beaches, coves, and picnic perches. But what makes this trail unique is the fact that although it begins in a regional park, by agreement most of it traces the bluffs of a private residential and exclusive resort community. As if that wasn't unusual enough, the trail is also dog friendly for pooches on leash. Even the resort's lodge, Sea Ranch, welcomes overnight canine guests. Fido won't want to miss this one.

THE RUNDOWN

Distance: 8.4 miles out and back

Start: Gualala Point Regional Park visitor center

Nearest town: Gualala

Hiking time: About 4 hours

Fees and permits: Parking fee

Conveniences: Visitor center, restrooms, water, picnic tables, trash and recycling containers, dog waste bag dispenser, and wheelchair-accessible path

Beach access: Yes; dogs on leash (see map)

Trail users: Hikers and dogs on leash

Trailhead elevation: 92 feet

Highest point: 92 feet

Trail surface: Pavement and dirt

Difficulty: Moderate

Seasonal highlights: Wildflowers in the spring

Managing agency: Gualala Point Regional Park, 42401 CA 1, Gualala 95445; Ranger Station, (707) 785-2377; sonoma-county.org/gualala-point. Sonoma County Regional Parks, 2300 County Center Dr., #120A, Santa Rosa 95403; (707) 565-2041; sonomacountyparks.org.

FINDING THE TRAILHEAD

From Gualala, drive 1 mile south on CA 1 and turn right into the Gualala Point Regional Park parking lot. **GPS:** N38 45.55' / W123 31.40'

WHAT TO SEE

The hike begins in Gualala Point Regional Park, at the northernmost end of the Sonoma coast overlooking the picturesque Gualala River estuary, and continues in the Sea Ranch residential community. The park and its residential neighbor share some of the same history, beginning with the Pomo Indians, whose seasonal migration to the shores and lifestyle were gentle on the environment. In the early 1800s the Russians' endeavors of hunting sea otters and logging redwoods left a much less kind imprint. Other Europeans soon followed. The gold rush and the 1906 earthquake fueled growing San Francisco's insatiable appetite for lumber and allowed Captain Bihler's settlement to prosper at Bihler's Landing, where Sea Ranch Lodge now stands. By the time the frenzy abated in the early 1900s, it had taken its toll on the Pomo Indians and the land. Prohibition gave this northern coast a brief jolt of economic stimulation when smugglers came to drop off illegal firewater from Mexico and Canada to quench San Francisco's thirst.

By 1941 the abused landscape had returned to its pastoral condition, and Ed Ohlson acquired Rancho Del Mar's 5,200 acres. The rancher's sheep grazed the coastal meadows for 20 years before architect and planner Al Boeke was seduced enough by the location's beauty to seek investors to get on board with his plans for an environmentally sensitive second-home community.

Thanks to thoughtful opposition and the California legislature in 1968, the Sea Ranch development became a reality in conjunction with dedicated common open space and forest reserve, along with public access to the coast and trails with 200 acres set aside for the Gualala Point County Park and Campgrounds. The scope of

Trail overlooking Gualala Beach

Walking south from
Whale Watch Point

Stairway down to Walk-
On Beach

this development and the controversy and awareness it stirred contributed to the establishment of the Coastal Commission in 1972, which still regulates land use on the California coast.

No lawns, no fences, and salt-washed wooden structures in visual and physical harmony with the natural setting became the Sea Ranch (translated from the Spanish Rancho del Mar) trademark, winning it several architectural and environmental awards. The original 5,200 acres became 2,310 individual building sites on 3,500 acres. Sea Ranch stretches along 10 miles of Sonoma's prized wild coastline. There are six public coastal-access trails across Sea Ranch from CA 1 to the beaches. Only two of these access trails are open to the public as part of an easement agreement with the Gualala Point Regional Park. They connect the north end of the park to the Walk-On Beach parking lot at the south end of CA 1.

The coastal-access parking lots, including Walk-On Beach, have a few parking spots, one restroom, and no water. For the same parking fee, Gualala Point Regional Park has the advantage of a visitor center, flush toilets, and water.

This hike begins behind the visitor center. You make an immediate right onto the dirt path at the bench just past the information board and dog waste bag dispenser. The paved wheelchair-accessible path to the park boundary is a pleasant 1-mile out-and-back stroll if you are short on time or just passing through.

The hike described here follows the dirt trail along the bluff. Your first views are the Gualala River estuary on the right, with Gualala village perched across the river, as you skirt the meadow's grasses with bush lupine and cypress groves laced with California blackberry. You come to a fork at 0.3 mile, with beach access to the right. Bear left toward the restroom and continue on the dirt trail to a fork that takes you to Whale Watch Point and the wind-sculpted tree tunnel. Come back to the fork and follow the bluff trail south.

At 1.0 mile you come to the park and public-access boundary and the sign indicating you are crossing over onto Sea Ranch property. Continue walking toward Walk-On Beach. Notice the Sea Ranch horn logo representing a ram's head in homage to its sheep-ranching history. Stay on the Bluff Trail, respecting the signs for private property.

The next 3.2 miles are a feast of craggy coastline views on the right and Sea Ranch homes' intentionally plain sea-bleached exteriors on the left. If you are hiking in the spring, the yellow bush lupine seems to be the exact touch of color to complement the stark setting. You will cross several narrow gullies on wooden footbridges over seasonal creeks as the trail occasionally weaves through tunnels of wind-battered cypress groves. Stay alert for grazing deer and patrolling herons if you're hiking with an easily stimulated canine pal. There's no drinking water along the way, so make sure you bring plenty for your dog. A foggy start can quickly turn to hot when the sun pops out on this exposed trail.

At 4.0 miles you come to a trail junction. The Walk-On Beach parking lot is to the left. Continue walking straight to Walk-On Beach. You will pass a small beach with a steep stairway that is eroded at the bottom. At 4.1 miles Walk-On Beach is the wider beach at the bottom of the next stairway. Walk down the stairs to the beach. If you have a surf-loving pooch with you, remember that dogs must be on leash. The waves are quite robust here, and Sonoma coast beaches in general are too hazardous for swimming, so that's another good reason to keep your furry friend on leash.

Go back to the trailhead the way you came when you've had your fill of beachcombing. When you arrive back at the Gualala Point Regional Park boundary, you have the option of turning right on the paved path that loops back to the visitor center to shorten the return by about 0.75 mile.

MILES AND DIRECTIONS

0.0 Start behind the Gualala Point Regional Park visitor center on the dirt trail to the right just beyond the information board.

0.3 Come to a fork at the paved trail. Bear left.

0.4 Arrive at a restroom. Continue on the dirt trail.

0.7 Come to a fork. Turn right to Whale Watch Point. Return to the fork and continue walking south along the bluff.

1.0 Come to the end of the park boundary and beginning of public access into Sea Ranch. Continue walking to Walk-On Beach.

2.0 Arrive at a trail junction. Turn right toward Walk-On Beach.

4.0 Come to a trail junction for Walk-On Beach parking to the left. Continue walking straight to the stairs down to Walk-On Beach.

4.2 Arrive on dog friendly Walk-On Beach. Go back to the trailhead the way you came.

8.4 Arrive back at the trailhead.

BAKERIES, BREWERIES, EATS, AND SLEEPS

Twofish Fish Bakery Sea Ranch, 35590 Verdant View, Sea Ranch 95497; (707) 785-2443; twofishbaking.com. Twofish is the successful blend of talents of a former Ritz-Carlton pastry chef and a former imaging operations customer service expert. Margaret the baker and Hilla the manager have created a thriving enterprise that keeps customers coming back for signature products like country wheat baguettes, sticky buns, outrageous toasted granola, and an array of baked cookies. The Sea Ranch location is open Thurs through Sun with lunch items, and Fri is Pizza Night from 5 to 8:30 p.m.

In May 2016 Twofish opened a second North Coast location, 4 miles south of Sea Ranch in the historic Stewarts Point Store. If you miss the Sea Ranch location's 4-day window of operation, you'll be happy to know that the Stewarts Point Store is open 7 days a week. Check the website for seasonal schedule changes.

Trinks Bakery and Cafe, 39140 CA 1, Gualala; (707) 884-1713; trinkscafe.com. If you love the marshmallow in Rocky Road, don't miss Trinks' version of the treat.

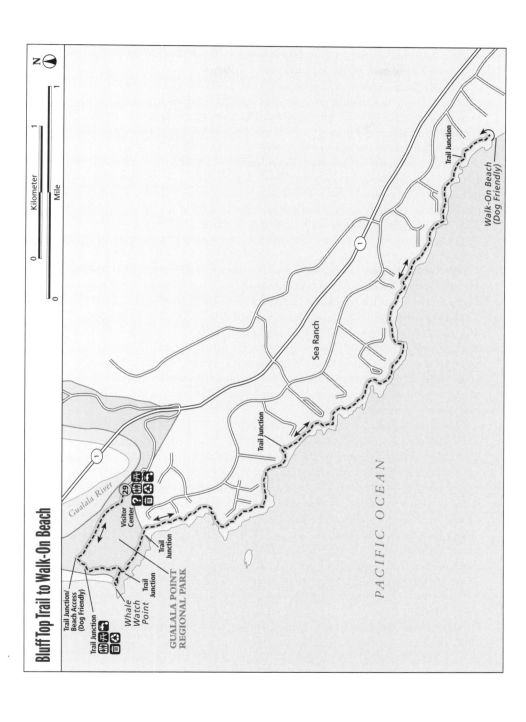

Bluff Top Trail to Walk-On Beach

N

Kilometer

Mile

Gualala River

1

Trail Junction/
Beach Access
(Dog Friendly)

Trail Junction

Whale
Watch
Point

Trail Junction

Visitor
Center

29

GUALALA POINT
REGIONAL PARK

Trail Junction

Trail Junction

Sea Ranch

1

Trail Junction

Walk-On Beach
(Dog Friendly)

PACIFIC OCEAN

The family-operated cafe serves breakfast and lunch daily and gourmet dinners 3 nights a week. Ingredients are pure North Coast sustainable, including seasonal produce from Trinks' garden and orchard.

Surf Market, 39250 CA 1, Gualala 95445; (707) 884-4184. Great source for all your hiking and camping provision needs, from baked goods and local artisan cheeses to deli delights and fresh seafood. There are no breweries in Gualala, but the market carries popular local beers from Mendocino, Anderson Valley, and Bear Republic Brewing Companies.

Black Point Grill at Sea Ranch Lodge, 60 Sea Walk Dr., Sea Ranch 95497; (800) 732-7262; searanchlodge.com. The lodge restaurant serves breakfast, lunch, and dinner. The tavern menu is available in the bar from 11:30 a.m. to 8:30 p.m. Although menus change seasonally, the ever-popular Local Cod Fish & Chips and the Creekstone Angus Burger are here to stay, as are the local brewery beers on tap. The local Pazzo Marco Creamery's artisan gelato flavors take care of the sweet-toothed diners.

Sea Ranch Lodge, 60 Sea Walk Dr., Sea Ranch 95497; (800) 732-7262; searanchlodge.com. This is a dream dog friendly oceanfront resort for overnighting in the perfect blend of rustic elegance, tranquility, and Pacific panorama.

Breakers Inn, 39300 S. CA 1, Gualala 95445; (707) 884-3200; breakersinn.com. The Breakers is conveniently located steps from Gualala's services, with an idyllic cliff-top setting overlooking the mouth of the Gualala River and the Pacific. Rooms are decorated with regional flavor. Whether you are in the Pioneer, Napa, or Denmark room, all have private decks to savor the views. Rooms are appointed with a small refrigerator and microwave, and some luxuries include fireplaces and spa tubs. Continental breakfast is included.

The Surf Motel, 39170 CA 1, Gualala 95445; (707) 884-3571; surfinngualala .com. This good-value '60s, bluff-top, dog friendly, B&B-style lodging upgraded in 2008 offers a range of amenities. All rooms have a small refrigerator, microwaves, and a hypoallergenic featherbed and comforters. Some rooms have ocean views, while others have full kitchens. A full hot and cold breakfast selection complete with fresh-baked scones, biscuits, and waffles and Adirondack chairs for soaking up the Pacific air and views are just some of the perks.

Sea Ranch Beach Rentals, 39200 S. CA 1, Gualala 95445; (707) 884-4235; searanchrentals.com. A beach rental or Sea Ranch vacation home rental serves as the most comfortable, convenient base camp for hiking and exploring this part of the Northern California coast. Dog friendly properties available.

CAMPING

Gualala Point Regional Park Campground, 42401 CA 1, Gualala (707) 565-2267; sonomacountyparks.org (click on "Reserve a Campsite"). Tent and RV sites (no hookups). There are flush toilets and electrical outlets in restrooms and a coin-operated shower.

Dog Friendly Beaches

Doran Beach in Doran Regional Park, 201 Doran Beach Rd., Bodega Bay 94923. This wide 2-mile-long stretch of sand on Bodega Bay is perfect for walking Fido on leash and enjoying a picnic along the way. Sonoma County Regional Parks, (707) 875-3540, parks.sonomacounty.ca.gov

Sonoma County's coastline stretches over 50 scenic miles, of which almost 20 miles are part of the Sonoma Coast State Park beaches interrupted by rocky bluffs and headlands. **Wright's Beach** at the north end of the Kortum Trail (7 miles north of Bodega Bay) and **Blind Beach** (about 6 miles south of Jenner) at the south end of the Kortum Trail (see hike 27) are the two most-accessible dog friendly beaches (on leash) off of CA 1. Sonoma Coast State Park, (707) 875-3483

Walk-On Beach welcomes dogs on leash. The beach sits at the foot of a steep stairway within the private Sea Ranch residential community. Don't let this pretty cove lull you into a false sense of security. The current is strong and waves are powerful on this coast. The quickest way to this beach is from the public-access parking area at 40101 CA 1, Sea Ranch. Walk along a well-marked 0.5-mile path from the parking area to the stairway. The other longer but very pleasant access is from the Gualala Point Regional Park at the north end of Sea Ranch along a 4-mile-long bluff-top trail (see hike 29). Sonoma County Regional Parks, (707) 565-2041, parks.sonomacounty.ca.gov

Gualala Point Regional Park Beach at the northernmost point on the Sonoma coast is a long spit between the Pacific Ocean and the Gualala River. The park is on the south side of the Gualala River at the north end of the Sea Ranch private residential community. You can explore the picturesque driftwood-covered beach with your dog on leash. The beach is accessed from a trail behind the visitor

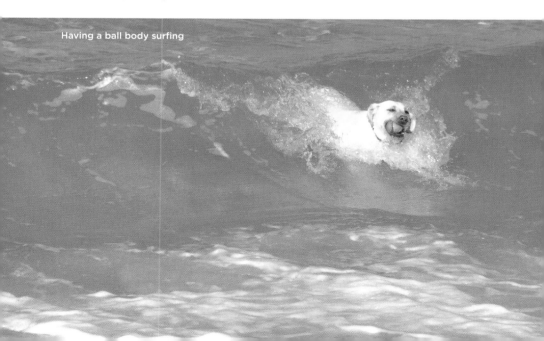

Having a ball body surfing

center (day-use fee), 42450 CA 1, Gualala 95445. Sonoma County Regional Parks, (707) 565-2041, parks.sonomacounty.ca.gov

Coastal Attractions

Bodega, a hamlet 5 miles south of Bodega Bay and 0.5 mile east of CA 1, is best known for the filming of Alfred Hitchcock's *The Birds*. Walk the streets and relive the church and schoolhouse scenes from the 1963 film. Visit the Bodega Country Store and museum for film memorabilia. 17190 Bodega Hwy., Bodega 94922; (707) 377-4056; bodegastore.com

Wild Flour Bread Bakery, 140 Bohemian Hwy., Freestone 95472 (5 miles east of Bodega); (707) 874-2938; wildflourbread.com. Jump start the morning with a stroll around the garden of herbs, flowers, and vegetables while savoring their famous sticky buns and scones. The day unfolds with an amazing daily selection of wood-fired breads available for tasting. Open Fri through Mon.

Vista Mar Trail Viewpoint, northernmost end of Sonoma Coast State Park's beaches and bluffs at the Jenner Grade on the west side of CA 1. This is a mile-long wheelchair-accessible bluff-top loop trail with picnic tables and panoramic views of the sculpted cliffs.

Fort Ross State Historic Park, 19005 CA 1, Jenner 95450; (707) 847-3286; parks.ca.gov. The almost 4,000-acre park preserves North America's southernmost Russian settlement. Back in the late 1700s, parts of Alaska, Hawaii, and California were settlements in the Russian-American colonies under Tsar Paul I. Fort Ross was named after imperial Rossiia (Russia) and was an outpost to grow food for settlements in Alaska and hunt marine mammals such as seals and sea otters for their pelts. The fortress's restored and reconstructed buildings are impressive, as is the setting overlooking the Pacific. The park has a stunning visitor center designed in keeping with the fort's architecture. Walking trails thread the compound and connect to Sandy Cove Beach, the day-use area, and the primitive campground.

Kruse Rhododendron State Natural Reserve, 20 miles north of Jenner next to Salt Point State Park; (707) 847-3221. The 300-acre parcel was donated by the Kruse family, founders of the German Bank in San Francisco. The reserve forest thrives with redwoods, firs, tan oaks, and ferns. But the highlights along the 5 miles of hiking trails are the pink rhododendron blossoms in the late spring (Apr to June).

The short 0.25-mile scenic stitch of path along the bluffs behind Trinks Bakery in downtown Gualala is a hidden little pocket of quiet that celebrates the vision of the California Coastal Trail.

BEST COASTAL FARMERS' MARKETS

Bodega Bay Community Farmers' Market is not the extravaganza of some, but it offers organic produce and local products with live music and a hometown feel. The market is located at 2255 CA 1 (behind the community center) in Bodega Bay and operates on Sun, May through Oct, from 10 a.m. to 2 p.m.

MENDOCINO COUNTY

MENDOCINO COUNTY has quite a natural and cultural résumé. This is where grapes, hops, marijuana, and redwoods meet some of the wildest, most rugged and romantic stretches of Northern California coastline. Wild rivers, thriving estuaries, dreamy beaches, and surf-washed coastal national monuments highlight coastal trails that thread around quaint towns and hidden hamlets.

Note: See map on page 194.

Point Arena harbor
and pier (hike 30)

30. **STORNETTA**

WHY GO?

The almost 1,700 acres of coastal lands managed by the BLM (Bureau of Land Management) were incorporated into the California Coastal National Monument as the "first shoreline unit" in the system of national monuments. Stornetta is an amazing windfall of coastal access for hikers. This hike samples a slice of Stornetta's oceanfront tablelands on cliffs overlooking unusual surf-sculpted arches with wave-worn tunnels through the sea stacks and tidepools on the eroded rocky shelves. The views sweep north to the Point Arena Lighthouse standing on the second-westernmost point in the continental United States and point of land closest to the Hawaiian Islands.

THE RUNDOWN

Distance: 5.4 miles out and back

Start: Point Arena–Stornetta Unit trailhead

Nearest town: Point Arena

Hiking time: About 2.5 hours

Fees and permits: None

Conveniences: Portable toilet

Beach access: No

Trail users: Hikers and dogs on leash

Trailhead elevation: 34 feet

Highest point: 71 feet

Trail surface: Dirt and grass

Difficulty: Easy

Seasonal highlights: Wildflowers in the spring and gray whale migration

Managing agency: Bureau of Land Management, Ukiah Field Office, 2550 N. State St., Ukiah 95482; (707) 468-4000; blm.gov/ca/ukiah

FINDING THE TRAILHEAD

From Point Arena on CA 1/Main Street at School Street, drive 1.5 miles to Lighthouse Road and turn west toward Point Arena Lighthouse. Drive 1.3 miles on Lighthouse Road to the bend in the road and parking area for Stornetta Trailhead. **GPS:** N38 56.42' / W123 43.79'

WHAT TO SEE

Pomo Indian people thrived on the marine and land resources of the area before Europeans made their mark on the landscape with lumber and cattle enterprises.

Lighthouse above Point Arena's chiseled coastline

Beginning in the late 1800s, the Sheppard family operated a dairy farm until about 1924, when A. O. Stornetta purchased the ranch from Joseph Sheppard's widow.

The land underwent various uses and abuses over the following decades. The BLM has been managing the prime spread of oceanfront real estate since 2014, when President Barack Obama designated it part of the California Coastal National Monument. The California Coastal National Monument was established in 2000 to protect 1,100 miles of rocks, reefs, and islands that provide habitat and feeding grounds for seabirds and a diversity of marine life. Stornetta's designation means protection and preservation balanced with recreation.

In addition to the biological and cultural significance of the area, Stornetta's proximity to the Point Arena Lighthouse is what makes this hike especially appealing. The lighthouse is operated by the nonprofit Point Arena Lighthouse Keepers and open to the public for tours. The 115-foot tower is the tallest of the lighthouses you can climb in the country. The grounds, museum, gift shop, and tower just 1 mile up the road from the trailhead are well worth a visit before or after the hike.

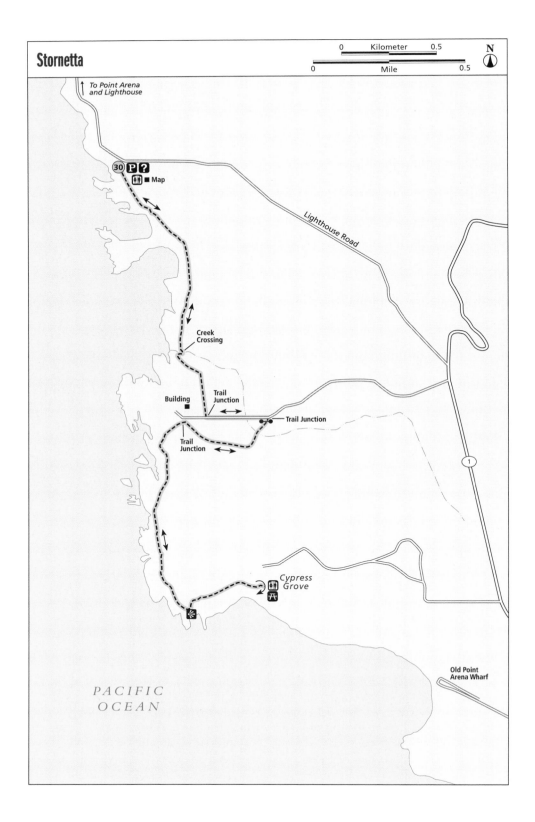

The Stornetta trail begins just off Lighthouse Road and heads south, mostly skirting the eroding sandstone cliffs that look like they were sliced sheer by a carving knife. BLM markers with arrows guide you along the designated trails that are sometimes narrow and faint in the grass. The breadth of the flat exposed landscape intensifies the sense of remoteness. Wave-washed slabs of sandstone and arched monuments gnawed hollow by the sea dominate the coastal canvas. The trail crosses a couple of shallow gullies worn down by seasonal creeks.

At 1.1 miles you come to a paved road. The locked gate to the right is the entrance to the Mendocino College Coastal Field Station. The trail follows the paved road to the left for 0.2 mile before crossing the road at a cattle gate onto a shady pine corridor.

At 1.7 miles you turn left onto an unmarked more-primitive grass trail. The sparse but cushy vegetation has a moor-like quality that adds to the desolateness of the sandstone shelves below the cliffs.

At 2.5 miles the distant view of Point Arena's wooden pier across the harbor is a picturesque contrast to the starkness of the prairie flanked by the ridge of wind-stripped pine woodlands. Just 0.2 mile ahead, you come to a cypress grove with portable toilet and a picnic table on a cement slab. This is your destination and turn-around point just short of the grassy hill. It's a pleasant rest and picnic spot.

The grassy trail continues for another mile over the hill to end behind the Point Arena City Hall. If you have to choose between hiking the last mile to City Hall and getting back in time to visit the lighthouse, which closes at 3:30 p.m. during the winter and 4:30 p.m. during the summer, don't miss the lighthouse.

MILES AND DIRECTIONS

0.0   Start at the Point Arena–Stornetta Unit trailhead.

0.8   Walk across a seasonal creek.

1.1   Come to a paved road and turn left along the road.

1.3   Turn right off the paved road across a cattle guard on a pine-lined trail.

1.7   Turn left onto an unmarked narrow grassy trail.

2.5   Point Arena harbor and pier come into view.

2.7   Arrive at a cypress grove and picnic table. This is your turnaround point. Go back to the trailhead the way you came.

5.4   Arrive back at the trailhead.

BAKERIES, BREWERIES, EATS, AND SLEEPS

Franny's Cup and Saucer, 213 Main St., Point Arena 95468; (707) 882-2500; frannyscupandsaucer.com. The mom-and-daughter experiment has produced a great little spot for pastries, brownies, cookies, and house-made chocolates, along with creative juices.

Pier Chowder House and Tap Room, 790 Port Rd., Point Arena 95468; (707) 882-3400; thepierchowderhouse.net. As the name implies, this is the place for traditional clam chowder as well as their award-winning creative entries at the annual Whale & Jazz Festival Chowder Challenge Championship. The house-made three-fruited cobbler is a local favorite. The Tap Room serves a variety of beers from local breweries, but the Pier Ale brewed specifically for the house by Firestone Brewery in Paso Robles is a must-try for beer lovers. Check the website for upcoming beer tastings and brewery dinners. Your four-legged buddy is welcome on the outdoor deck.

Point Arena Lighthouse Cottages, 45500 Lighthouse Rd., Point Arena 95468; (707) 882-2809; pointarenalighthouse.com. There are 6 renovated units available as vacation rentals: 4 former light keepers' homes (3 three-bedroom/two-bath houses and a one-bedroom cottage), an apartment, and a cozy studio room. Rental fee includes unlimited admittance to the Lighthouse Museum and lighthouse tours. This is a rare opportunity to experience a slice of coastal history with modern comforts and amenities in a stunning location.

Wharf Masters Inn, 785 Port Rd., Point Arena 95468; (707) 882-3171; wharf masters.com. Sleep in a romantic historic home overlooking the ocean. Built in 1865, the original wharf master's home is the oldest house in Point Arena. The inn's 4 buildings house 28 charming rooms. Balconies let you take full advantage of the views, while electric fireplaces provide cozy ambience. The expanded continental breakfast with made-to-order waffles will fuel you up for the day's hike and adventures. Call about dog friendly rooms and policy.

CAMPING

Manchester Beach/Mendocino Coast KOA, 44300 Kinney Lane, Manchester 95459; (707) 882-2375; koa.com. This clean, spacious KOA campground suits tent campers and RV fans as well as those traveling light who wish to rent one of the on-site fully equipped trailers or a cabin (bring your own linens for trailer and cabins). The trailers and some cabins are dog friendly (pet fee). The outdoor "kamping kitchen" is convenient and well appointed for tent campers. RV sites have hookups. The fenced dog park for Fido to romp and sprint around safely is a real boon.

Manchester State Park, 44500 Kinney Lane, Manchester 95459; (707) 937-5804 or (707) 882-2463; parks.ca.gov. The park encompasses 18,000 feet of ocean frontage with dunes, grasslands, and 5 miles of sandy beach. Seasonal steelhead fishing is popular in the park's two streams. There are tent and trailer/RV sites (22-foot/30-foot max length respectively), restrooms, and drinking water. Currently the park hours of operation are restricted to certain days and times of year. Call for updated information on accessing the park and whether reservations are accepted.

31. **MENDOCINO HEADLANDS**

WHY GO?

Mendocino will always be associated with the Angela Lansbury TV series *Murder She Wrote*. The popular series was not the first to pick this picturesque town with a Victorian vibe and its fabulous headlands as a Hollywood set. This hike is the million-dollar-view tour of the coastline. The headlands hug the oceanfront town with a necklace of idyllic coves, arches, and surf-etched sea stacks to the north and the sweeping estuary of the Big River to the south.

THE RUNDOWN

Distance: 4.6 miles out and back

Start: Mendocino Headlands State Park visitor center

Nearest town: Mendocino

Hiking time: About 2 hours

Fees and permits: None

Conveniences: Visitor center; restroom, water, picnic tables and trash container at trailhead and at end of trail

Beach access: Yes; dogs on leash (see map)

Trail users: Hikers and dogs on leash

Trailhead elevation: 86 feet

Highest point: 86 feet

Trail surface: Grass and dirt

Difficulty: Easy

Seasonal highlights: Wildflowers in the spring

Managing agency: Mendocino Headlands State Park, Box 440, Mendocino 94560; (707) 937-5804; www.parks.ca.gov

FINDING THE TRAILHEAD

From CA 1 at Mendocino, turn west on Main Street and drive 0.5 mile to the Mendocino Headlands State Park visitor center. **GPS:** N39 18.29' / W123 48.00'

WHAT TO SEE

Mendocino Headlands State Park's 347-acre belt of riparian meadows and coastal prairie cradles the oceanfront town of Mendocino. The state first acquired headland property in 1957, and Mendocino Headlands State Park was established in 1974.

The Ford House overlooking the Pacific on the headlands and built by Jerome B. Ford, founder of Mendocino in the early 1850s, is home to the Mendocino

Trailhead at Mendocino Headlands State Park visitor center

Headlands State Park visitor center on Main Street and the trailhead for this hike. Back when Mendocino was first settled, the main attraction was the coastal redwoods and the fortunes made from the lumber. Today visitors come for the art galleries, the shops, and the romantic inns' Victorian vibe enhanced by a superb setting perched above these exceptionally scenic headlands.

The visitor center is a great starting point to get acquainted with the area history before setting out on the trailhead to the right of the Ford House through the opening in the white fence. The grassy trail is narrow as you cross the meadow to the bluff and turn right to thread your way along the bluffs. Be aware that Mother Nature is constantly at work reshaping the coastline, and it's important to heed the warnings on posted signs about staying back from the eroding cliff edge.

At 0.4 mile you come to a trail junction for the beach access. The wooden staircase leads down to Portuguese Beach's gray sands strewn with smooth sea-salt-polished driftwood. Take a stroll on the beach if time permits. Otherwise continue past the beach, walking north along the trail. Just ahead you come to the wood and

Portuguese Beach at the foot
of the town of Mendocino

iron-chain remnants of the old wharf. The town's rooflines recede along with the
pods of people who tend to stroll closer to the visitor center.

The headlands zigzag and taper to several promontories along the way, jutting
out to chunks of rocky islands with grassy terraces carved out of the headlands. In
the springtime Mendocino's oceanfront greenbelt is a garden of golden poppies
sprinkled with red and yellow wildflowers. At 1.3 miles you come to a parking lot.
Continue walking past the parking lot along the coastal path. You can see the Point
Cabrillo Light Station to the north.

At 2.3 miles you come to the last parking lot and the end of the headland trail.
There are a few picnic tables, a restroom with flush toilet, and water as well as a trash
container. This is a superb spot to linger, have a picnic, and soak up more coastline
views before going back the way you came.

If time permits when you arrive back at the trailhead, you can continue walking
south along the headlands for about 0.5 mile to a viewpoint overlooking the mouth
of the Big River, where the estuary meets the Pacific. The river's wide sweep where

the waves lap the sandbars paints the mouth of the estuary into one of nature's most sensually organic canvases. There is a wooden staircase down to Big River Beach at the south end of the trail.

MILES AND DIRECTIONS

0.0   Start to the right of the Mendocino Headlands State Park visitor center.

0.1   Come to a trail junction. Turn right on the headlands trail.

0.4   Come to a trail junction for dog friendly Portuguese Beach access. Continue walking along the bluff.

1.3   Arrive at a parking lot. Continue walking along the bluff.

2.3   Come to a parking lot and the end of the headland trail. Go back to the trailhead the way you came.

4.6   Arrive back at the trailhead.

BAKERIES, BREWERIES, EATS, AND SLEEPS

Good Life Cafe and Bakery, 10483 Lansing St., Mendocino 94560; (707) 937-0836; goodlifecafemendo.com. It's the place for great cookies.

Cafe Beaujolais, 961 Ukiah St., Mendocino 95460; (707) 937-5614; cafe beaujolais.com. The cafe's popular French-influenced cuisine for lunch and dinner is no secret. But it's mostly local knowledge that behind the back door of the Victorian farmhouse is a treasure trove of house-made products including fresh-baked bread, cashew granola, and *panforte* (Italian-style energy bars) available between 11 a.m. and 3 p.m.

Harvest Market, 10501 Lansing St., Mendocino 95460; (707) 937-5879; harvest market.com. This family-owned market has a great soup bar and the bakery department carries Kemmy's pies delivered twice weekly from Willits. The apple pie was a flavor flashback to my grandmother's own fresh-cut apple goodies. The market's other fresh-baked goods arrive daily from the mother store in Fort Bragg.

Mendocino Jams and Preserves, 440 Main St., Mendocino 95460; (707) 937-1037; mendojams.com. This gourmet shop will tickle your palate with the flavor of ripe fruit in all 30 flavors of jams and marmalades.

Patterson's Pub, 10485 Lansing St., Mendocino 95460; (707) 937-4782; pattersons pub.com. This is a little Ireland with a lot of brews with over 25 beers on tap, half showcasing regional flavors. Comfort foods and daily specials for lunch and dinner.

Flow Restaurant and Lounge, 45040 Main St., Mendocino 95460; (707) 937-3569; mendocinoflow.com. Enjoy breakfast, lunch, or dinner in one of Mendocino's historic water towers with a bird's-eye view from the deck or the glassed-in dining room. The farm-to-table menu blends comfort staples and clean, fresh flavors with a creative twist. If you're gaga for coconut, try the Coconut Pancakes for breakfast or

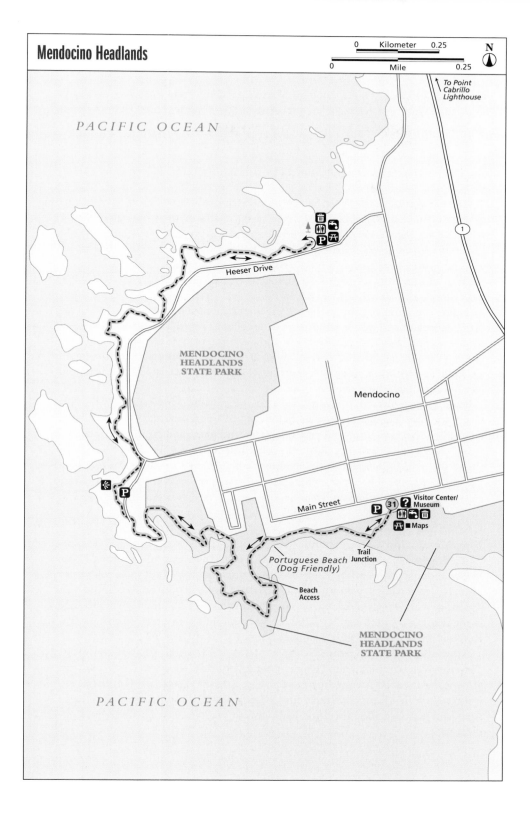

Mendocino Headlands

PACIFIC OCEAN

To Point
Cabrillo
Lighthouse

1

Heeser Drive

MENDOCINO
HEADLANDS
STATE PARK

Mendocino

Main Street

Visitor Center/
Museum

Maps

31

Trail
Junction

Portuguese Beach
(Dog Friendly)

Beach
Access

MENDOCINO
HEADLANDS
STATE PARK

PACIFIC OCEAN

N

0   Kilometer   0.25

0   Mile   0.25

Coconut Curry Mussels for lunch or dinner. The Sticky Toffee Pudding cocooned in caramel sauce and pecans is dessert ecstasy, with a vegan version upon request. Several of the best North Coast brewery beers are available on tap.

Brewery Gulch Inn, 9401 N. CA 1, Mendocino 95460; (707) 937-4752; brewerygulchinn.com. Eco-friendly blends rustic with luxury at this bluff-top Arts and Crafts–style inn built of salvaged redwood. Room rates include organic cuisine for breakfast and dinner.

Hill House Inn, 10701 Palette Dr., Mendocino 95460; (707) 937-0555; hillhouseinn.com. The 44-room Victorian-decor inn sits above town on a quiet hilltop with fabulous ocean views. An expanded continental breakfast with hot and cold cereal and baked goods is included. The in-house restaurant is currently open Sat evenings with a bistro menu, full bar, and local beers on tap.

MacCallum House Inn, 45020 Albion St., Mendocino 95460; (707) 937-0289; maccallumhouse.com. The MacCallum House has a complex of accommodations including 6 charming rooms in the historic Victorian main house built in 1882, cottages, suites, and a couple of vacation rental properties with full kitchens. All lodging includes a gourmet à la carte breakfast. Although the main house guest rooms are not dog friendly (all other accommodations are; pet fee includes a pooch care package in the room), bring Fido's kibbles and enjoy breakfast on the house's wraparound porch overlooking the gardens.

Blair House Inn, 45110 Little Lake St., Mendocino 95460; (707) 937-1800; blairhouse.com. The classic nineteenth-century mansion owned by a Londoner is currently under renovation and projected to receive guests for the summer of 2017. If you were one of the many fans of Angela Lansbury's TV series *Murder She Wrote* (1984–96), you will remember the exterior of Blair House Inn as Jessica Fletcher's Cabot Cove home. Check the website for updates on the reopening of Blair House and any changes in its bed-and-breakfast packages as well as dog friendly policy.

CAMPING

New Mendocino Campground, 9601 N. CA 1, Mendocino 95460; (707) 880-7710; thenewmendocinocampground.com. Teresa Raffo and her husband Chris Hougie bought and transformed the existing campground into a 32-acre soft camping experience with 20 platform canvas tent sites furnished with twin or queen beds dressed in white linens and down comforters. Towels and bath products are provided in the renovated bathrooms. Stock up on provisions in town and enjoy the outdoor barbecue area's gas grills with utensils and tables.

Albion River Campground, 334500 N. CA 1, Albion 95410; (707) 937-0606; albionrivercampground.com. There's nothing intimate about this 100-plus-site, 40-acre, tent and RV campground and marina 10 miles south of Mendocino, but it has a long list of amenities including lodging rentals, kayak/canoe rentals, camp store, and cafe. It is ideal for those who wish to combine hiking with some paddling time.

Mendocino Headlands' sculpted arches with Point Cabrillo Light Station in the distance

Russian Gulch State Park, 12301 N. CA 1, Mendocino 95460; (707) 937-5804; reservations, (800) 444-7275; parks.ca.gov. This small scenic park 2 miles north of Mendocino has 29 tent and RV sites (no hookups, 24-foot max length). There are flush toilets and coin-operated showers. The campground is open Apr through Oct, with reservations between Apr and Sept. Some sites may remain open during the winter. Enjoy forested settings, tidepools, and the beach.

Van Damme State Park, 8001 N. CA 1, Little River 95456; (707) 937-0851 or (707) 937-5804; reservations, (800) 444-7275; parks.ca.gov. This park has 74 developed tent and RV (35-foot max length) sites. There are flush toilets and coin-operated showers. The campground is open Apr through Oct, with reservations between Apr and Sept. The lower loop sites remain open during the winter. The beach access is across CA 1.

32. **POINT CABRILLO**

WHY GO?

It's a treat to find a short accessible hike that is so astoundingly picturesque. Point Cabrillo treats visitors to the romanticism of a restored light station surrounded by soul-stirring coastal views punctuated by craggy bluffs and aquamarine inlets.

THE RUNDOWN

Distance: 3.4 miles out and back

Start: Gravel road to the right of Point Cabrillo Light Station State Historic Park parking lot

Nearest town: Mendocino

Hiking time: About 2 hours

Fees and permits: None

Conveniences: Restroom with flush toilet in building across from parking lot; water, map, and trash container by administrative office; museum and gift shop at lighthouse

Beach access: Yes; dogs on leash (see map)

Trail users: Hikers and dogs on leash

Trailhead elevation: 161 feet

Highest point: 161 feet

Trail surface: Gravel and grass

Difficulty: Easy

Seasonal highlights: Wildflowers in the spring; migrating whales in the spring and fall

Managing agency: Point Cabrillo Light Station State Historic Park, 13800 Point Cabrillo Dr., Mendocino 95460; (707) 937-5804. Point Cabrillo Lightkeepers Association, (707) 937-6122, pointcabrillo.org.

FINDING THE TRAILHEAD

From Mendocino on CA 1, drive 2 miles north to Point Cabrillo Drive. Turn left on Point Cabrillo Drive at the sign for the Point Cabrillo Light Station State Historic Park and make an immediate right. Drive 1 mile on Point Cabrillo Drive and follow the sign for the entrance to Point Cabrillo Light Station. Turn immediately into the parking lot on the left. **GPS:** N39 21.01' / W123 48.79'

WHAT TO SEE

In 1850 the clipper brig *Frolic* hit a reef off the Mendocino Coast and its precious cargo—including a shipment of opium—was lost. Later salvage attempts revealed the unexpected wealth in nearby groves of redwood and Douglas fir trees. These ancestral lands of the Pomo Indians were a treasure trove for enterprising businessmen at a time when booming San Francisco was hungry for lumber. Point Cabrillo Light Station now stands off that reef that led to the discovery of the rich coastal forests that helped grow Northern California's lumber industry and develop Mendocino.

Construction of the Point Cabrillo Light Station and the complex of fifteen structures on 30 acres began in 1908. The project was completed in 1909, and the Fresnel lens was lit in June of that year. Today a 1,000-watt bulb illuminates the restored lens and the beam is visible from 14 miles out to sea. A California Coastal Conservancy grant along with private donations helped with the rehabilitation of the lighthouse in 1991. California State Parks acquired the property in 2002, and the restoration of several structures earned the site the Governor's Historic Preservation Award and the Preservation Design Award.

The cluster of white buildings topped with bright red roofs against the blue Pacific is a striking image easily spotted from the trailhead. It is not surprising to learn that Point Cabrillo has the distinction of being one of the most complete light stations in the United States. Four of the buildings restored in 2006 (the larger light keeper's house and assistant light keeper's house along with two sheds restored as small cottages) are available as vacation rentals. One of the small cottages even welcomes your canine hiking pal.

The trail begins to the right of the parking area along a gravel road that narrows as you approach a grassy trail and junction on the right at 0.4 mile. Turn right toward the cove to a second junction where you turn left. The trail leads to an access to Frolic Beach, named after the ship that wrecked on the reef just north of the cove in 1850. The trail heading right goes back to Point Cabrillo Drive. Follow the trail left to overlook the beach and cove. The short loop traces the bluff above the beach and will take you back to the junction to continue walking straight along the bluff, with the ocean on your right and a sprinkling of private homes on the bluffs across the cove. The interpretive panel describing the *Frolic* incident and its cargo is just ahead on the bluff.

The next mile of trail is the gift that keeps on giving, with sweeping coastal views accented by a stadium of wave-washed rock terraces and jagged cliffs lapped by aquamarine surf.

At 1.4 miles you come to a trail junction at the road to the lighthouse. The lighthouse is on the right. Turn left along the road toward the station houses and then right on a wide gravel road. There are picnic tables on the left. Continue walking straight past the bench on the left and veer right at the wooden post with the faded sign onto a narrow grassy trail at the bend in the gravel road. Follow the grassy trail to the fence.

At 1.7 miles, just beyond the fence, you will see a faint, lightly traveled trail on the left marked with a post and arrow. The park map shows this trail looping back toward the complex of station houses, but that trail was not maintained and had disappeared into the tall grasses at the time of this hike in May 2016. The worn trail continues straight to a tapering bluff edge. This is a lovely overlook and ideal picnic destination for more solitude than the picnic area by the museum and complex of station houses.

Go back to the trailhead the way you came to soak up the views from a different perspective. Make sure to visit the lighthouse and museum on the return if you did not stop earlier. If time is a factor, you can return to the trailhead and parking area along the lighthouse road by turning right at the road in front of the picnic tables and cluster of station houses.

MILES AND DIRECTIONS

0.0 Start at the gravel road to the right of the parking area.

0.4 Come to a trail junction and turn right on the narrow grassy trail.

0.6 Come to a T junction and turn right on the trail.

0.7 Arrive at a trail junction. Turn left toward the cove and the unmarked beach access for dog friendly Frolic Beach at Frolic Cove. Follow the short loop tracing the bluff above the cove before returning to the trail junction at mile 0.6 to continue on the trail. The ocean will be on your right.

1.4 Come to a trail junction at the lighthouse road. Turn left away from the lighthouse.

1.5 Come to a trail junction. Turn right onto a gravel service road and then right onto a narrow grassy trail at the bend in the gravel road.

1.7 Come to a fence and a faint grassy spur on the left marked by a post. That trail is not maintained. The trail for this hike ends just a few yards ahead at a tapering bluff. Go back to the trailhead the way you came.

3.4 Arrive back at the trailhead.

BAKERIES, BREWERIES, EATS, AND SLEEPS

Good Life Cafe and Bakery, 10483 Lansing St., Mendocino 94560; (707) 937-0836; goodlifecafemendo.com. It's the place for great cookies.

Cafe Beaujolais, 961 Ukiah St., Mendocino 95460; (707) 937-5614; cafebeaujolais.com. The cafe's popular French-influenced cuisine for lunch and dinner is no secret. But it's mostly local knowledge that behind the back door of the Victorian farmhouse is a treasure trove of house-made products including fresh-baked bread, cashew granola, and *panforte* (Italian-style energy bars) available between 11 a.m. and 3 p.m.

Harvest Market, 10501 Lansing St., Mendocino 95460; (707) 937-5879; harvestmarket.com. This family-owned market has a great soup bar and the bakery department carries Kemmy's pies delivered twice weekly from Willits. The apple pie was

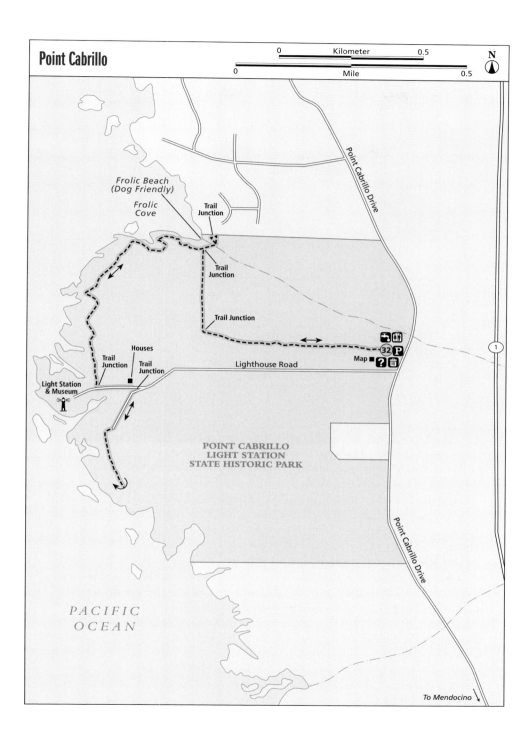

Point Cabrillo

Frolic Beach
(Dog Friendly)

Frolic
Cove

Trail
Junction

Trail
Junction

Trail Junction

Houses

Trail
Junction

Trail
Junction

Light Station
& Museum

Lighthouse Road

Map

32

POINT CABRILLO
LIGHT STATION
STATE HISTORIC PARK

Point Cabrillo Drive

Point Cabrillo Drive

PACIFIC
OCEAN

To Mendocino

0   Kilometer   0.5
0   Mile   0.5

N

Overlooking Frolic Beach

a flavor flashback to my grandmother's own fresh-cut apple goodies. The market's other fresh-baked goods arrive daily from the mother store in Fort Bragg.

Patterson's Pub, 10485 Lansing St., Mendocino 95460; (707) 937-4782; pattersonspub.com. This is a little Ireland with a lot of brews with over 25 beers on tap, half showcasing regional flavors. Comfort foods and daily specials for lunch and dinner.

Flow Restaurant and Lounge, 45040 Main St., Mendocino 95460; (707) 937-3569; mendocinoflow.com. Enjoy breakfast, lunch, or dinner in one of Mendocino's historic water towers with a bird's-eye view from the deck or the glassed-in dining room. The farm-to-table menu blends comfort staples and clean, fresh flavors with a creative twist. If you're gaga for coconut, try the Coconut Pancakes for breakfast or Coconut Curry Mussels for lunch or dinner. The Sticky Toffee Pudding cocooned in caramel sauce and pecans is dessert ecstasy, with a vegan version upon request. Several of the best North Coast brewery beers are available on tap.

Hill House Inn, 10701 Palette Dr., Mendocino 95460; (707) 937-0555; hill houseinn.com. The 44-room Victorian-decor inn sits above town on a quiet hilltop

Point Cabrillo's wild coast

with fabulous ocean views. An expanded continental breakfast with hot and cold cereal and baked goods is included. The in-house restaurant is currently open Sat evenings with a bistro menu, full bar, and local beers on tap.

MacCallum House Inn, 45020 Albion St., Mendocino 95460; (707) 937-0289; maccallumhouse.com. The MacCallum House has a complex of accommodations including 6 charming rooms in the historic Victorian main house built in 1882, cottages, suites, and a couple of vacation rental properties with full kitchens. All lodging includes a gourmet à la carte breakfast. Although the main house guest rooms are not dog friendly (all other accommodations are; pet fee includes a pooch care package in the room), bring Fido's kibbles and enjoy breakfast on the house's wraparound porch overlooking the gardens.

Agate Cove Inn, 11201 N. Lansing St., Mendocino 95460; (707) 937-0551; agatecove.com. Come back to 2 acres of gardens with private cottages overlooking the coast and a dose of luxurious romance after a day of trail and sightseeing. Breakfast will surprise you with a seasonal daily menu of fresh-baked goods, variations on egg dishes, and unexpected delights.

Sea Rock Inn, 11101 Lansing St., Mendocino 95460; (707) 937-0926; searock inn.com. The suites and cottages are the perfect perch complete with feather beds, ocean views, gardens, hillside benches, and a gourmet buffet breakfast. You can even charge your Tesla or other EV on-site.

CAMPING

Casper Beach RV Park and Campground, 14441 Point Cabrillo Dr., Mendocino 95460; (707) 964-3306; casperbeachrvpark.com. This campground is set in a canyon and protected cove across from the beach. There are tent and RV sites (partial and full hookups) as well as convenient amenities including a camp store, a variety of nonmotorized watercraft rentals, and a dog-walking area for your leashed four-legged camper.

New Mendocino Campground, 9601 N. CA 1, Mendocino 95460; (707) 880-7710; thenewmendocinocampground.com. Teresa Raffo and her husband Chris Hougie bought and transformed the existing campground into a 32-acre soft camping experience with 20 platform canvas tent sites furnished with twin or queen beds dressed in white linens and down comforters. Towels and bath products are provided in the renovated bathrooms. Stock up on provisions in town and enjoy the outdoor barbecue area's gas grills with utensils and tables.

Albion River Campground, 334500 N. CA 1, Albion 95410; (707) 937-0606; albionrivercampground.com. There's nothing intimate about this 100-plus-site, 40-acre, tent and RV campground and marina 10 miles south of Mendocino, but it has a long list of amenities including lodging rentals, kayak/canoe rentals, camp store, and cafe. It is ideal for those who wish to combine hiking with some paddling time.

Russian Gulch State Park, 12301 N. CA 1, Mendocino 95460; (707) 937-5804; reservations, (800) 444-7275; parks.ca.gov. This small scenic park 2 miles north of Mendocino has 29 tent and RV sites (no hookups, 24-foot max length). There are flush toilets and coin-operated showers. The campground is open Apr through Oct, with reservations between Apr and Sept. Some sites may remain open during the winter. Enjoy forested settings, tidepools, and the beach.

33. **HAUL ROAD**

WHY GO?

The hike to photogenic Pudding Creek Trestle is much more inspiring than the historic name implies. Oceanfront Haul Road was once a rail transportation artery for hauling logs to the Union Lumber Company mill in Fort Bragg before being converted to a multiuse trail. The trail parallels rural land with some residential and commercial development on the east side. But looking west, the coastal trail's views of tame headlands, tidepools, and snowy plover nesting beaches make this a significant stretch of California Coastal Trail. The trail is also Fido friendly, which is a rare find in a state park.

THE RUNDOWN

Distance: 4.6 miles out and back

Start: Haul Road at Laguna Point parking lot

Nearest town: Fort Bragg

Hiking time: About 2 hours

Fees and permits: Parking fee

Conveniences: Vault toilets, water, picnic tables, and information kiosk at trailhead parking lot. "Pack it in, pack it out" location. Trash and recycling containers near turnaround point.

Beach access: Yes; dogs on leash only at Pudding Creek Beach

Trail users: Hikers, cyclists, wheelchairs, and dogs on leash

Trailhead elevation: 30 feet

Highest point: 41 feet

Trail surface: Pavement; optional boardwalk and sandy trails on parallel bluffs

Difficulty: Easy

Seasonal highlights: Wildflowers in the spring; gray whale migration in the winter and spring

Managing agency: MacKerricher State Park, 24100 MacKerricher Park Rd., Fort Bragg 95437; (707) 937-5804

FINDING THE TRAILHEAD

 From Fort Bragg on CA 1, drive 3 miles north and turn left into MacKerricher State Park. Follow the signs to the Laguna Point Day Use Area.
GPS: N39 29.32' / W123 47.92'

WHAT TO SEE

For thousands of years Pomo Indians and several other native tribes recognized the bounty of these coastal waters, but the Europeans discovered the wealth in the coastal forests thick with prized redwood. Lumber became the backbone industry that sprouted towns like Fort Bragg. The Scottish descent MacKerricher family arrived from Quebec, Canada, in the mid-1800s and purchased 1,000 acres to raise livestock, including draft horses and dairy cows. When a wharf was eventually built at Laguna Point, a deal was cut to allow a railway to carry lumber across MacKerricher's Rancho de la Laguna to be loaded on schooners headed to booming San Francisco.

The State of California acquired the property from the MacKerricher heirs around 1950, and the rancho became the core of MacKerricher State Park's almost 10 miles of shoreline showcasing dunes, sandy beaches, and rocky headlands. A whale skeleton at the park entrance, small visitor center, picnic and camping sites, and a scenic boardwalk across Laguna Point's wetlands enhance the visit to the park and the hike south along Haul Road's multiuse trail.

The hike begins at the southeast end of the Laguna Point parking lot on a gravel path at the split-rail fence. The gravel path quickly merges onto Haul Road's paved surface, where you turn right, heading south. The first 0.5 mile is cradled by a pine woodland before the trail emerges into the open with panoramic views of the coast and beaches to the west.

At 0.4 mile you will see a trail crossing the road from the campground on the left to a narrow trail along a tree-lined corridor on the right. The hike described here is an out-and-back. But on the return, if time permits, turn left onto this trail toward the shore and follow it northward to the boardwalk and Seal Watching Stations visible from the meadow. That return detour to the shore will add about 0.5 mile to the hike. You also have the option of taking the side trip to the boardwalk Seal Watching Stations from the Laguna Point parking area at the end of the hike. It's a very scenic side jaunt with excellent educational panels about the ecology and geology, from ospreys, whales, seals, and intertidal life to earthquake faults and seasonal shifts of beach sand.

Although this hike is described following the historic road converted into a paved multiuse path that you share with cyclists, you can parallel the path on stretches of narrow trails tracing the headlands and across sandy beaches if tides permit.

At 1.3 miles you cross a bridge over a seasonal creek. Notice the interpretive panel on the right about snowy plover breeding and nesting beaches, which is why dogs are not allowed on many of the beaches.

The next landmark is an unattractive aggregate supply yard on the left at 1.6 miles. Less than 0.5 mile ahead you will come to a parking area for trail access on the left. There is a vault toilet in the parking area. The next 0.3 mile is bordered by a couple of two-story motels on the left overlooking the trail and the headlands and beach on the right. The trestle bridge spanning pretty Pudding Creek estuary is just ahead.

Historic lumber road converted
into multiuse trail

Trestle bridge across Pudding Creek

Pudding Creek Beach is a stunning wide, light sand beach reaching from the mouth of the creek at the foot of the headlands. Walk across the unusual, striking trestle and you reach the end of this hike and your turnaround point. Go back to the trailhead the way you came to complete the hike.

MILES AND DIRECTIONS

0.0 Start in the Laguna Point parking lot.

1.3 Walk across a bridge over a seasonal creek.

2.0 Come to a parking lot and restroom on the left.

2.3 Arrive at the end of the trail across the trestle bridge over Pudding Creek, with dog friendly Pudding Creek Beach north of the trestle bridge. Go back to the trailhead the way you came.

4.6 Arrive back at the trailhead.

Option: If you wish to extend this hike, looking south from the trestle bridge, the multiuse trail narrows and continues to the Noyo Headlands above Glass Beach at the end of Elm Street in Fort Bragg. This stretch of trail at the northern end of Fort Bragg was officially inaugurated in the summer of 2016. This new trail segment named Ka Kahleh means "White Water" in the Pomo Indian language and provides the first public access to the shoreline in Fort Bragg since the 1800s. It adds about 3 miles of trail along the town's scenic rocky coast, with interpretive panels about Fort Bragg's logging history. This is phase one of a local project to add new miles to the California Coastal Trail. Phase two, when completed, will connect the Noyo Headlands Trail to the Pomo Bluffs at the south end of Fort Bragg. It's interesting to note that the beach, known as Glass Beach, is actually the former location of three different dump sites between 1906 and 1967, when the last site was closed. Cleanup programs were initiated, and all that remains are the broken pieces of glass and pottery that the waves and sand have tumbled and reshaped into small, smooth, colorful treasures collectors call "sea glass," now popular as jewelry-quality material. Sea glass fans all over the world know of Northern California's Glass Beach. The glass fragments on the Glass Beach within MacKerricher State Park are considered "cultural features" protected by law and may not be removed or disturbed.

BAKERIES, BREWERIES, EATS, AND SLEEPS

Mendocino Cookie Company, 301 N. Main St., Fort Bragg 95437; (707) 964-0282; mendocinocookiecompany.com. This is the in spot for a wide selection of fresh-baked cookies daily.

Laurel Deli and Desserts, 401 N. Main St., Fort Bragg 95437; (707) 964-7812; laurel-deli-desserts.com. Customers flock here for breakfast and lunch. The

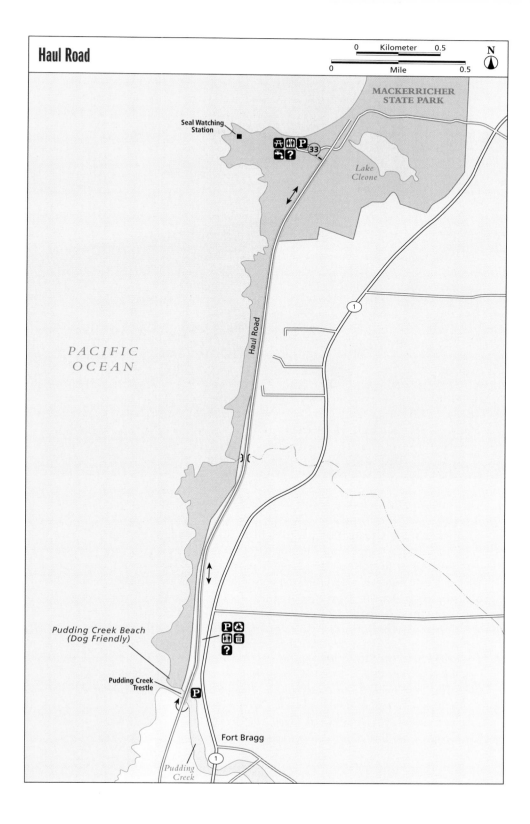

Haul Road

0 Kilometer 0.5

0 Mile 0.5

N

MACKERRICHER
STATE PARK

Seal Watching
Station

Lake
Cleone

33

1

PACIFIC
OCEAN

Haul Road

Pudding Creek Beach
(Dog Friendly)

Pudding Creek
Trestle

P

Fort Bragg

1

Pudding
Creek

Fresh-baked goods are
a treat along the trail.

California Croissant's turkey, bacon, avocado, swiss cheese, and sprouts is a classic staple. All desserts (pies, muffins, and cakes) are baked from scratch daily.

Cowlick's Ice Cream Cafe, 250 N. Main St., Fort Bragg 95437; (707) 962-9271; cowlicksicecream.com. Small batches of handmade artisan ice cream flavors. The long list of flavors runs the gamut from all-time favorites like Cookies and Cream and Rockiest Road to thinking outside the cone with Chai, Egg Nog, and Yellow Cake Batter. The seasonal fruit sorbets are super refreshing.

North Coast Brewing Company and Taproom, 444 N. Main St., Fort Bragg 95437; northcoastbrewing.com. The company's taproom across the street opens at 2 p.m. The taproom is known for its extensive pizza creations and also offers a considerable dinner menu. The scallop salad is a local favorite.

Silver's at the Wharf, 32260 N. Harbor Dr., Fort Bragg 95437; (707) 964-4283; silversatthewharf.com. Good casual spot in Noyo Harbor Fishing Village since the 1950s to enjoy a fresh seafood menu featuring popular dishes like oysters, crab cakes, calamari, crab melts, and fish tacos, to name a few. The chef brothers Silver and Juan blend Mayan and French influences to pan-sear entrees and create tasty sauces with

Boardwalk across meadow off of Haul Road Trail

a kick. The outdoor deck tables are dog friendly, and you can savor lunch or dinner with waterfront views.

Anchor Lodge, 32260 N. Harbor Dr., Fort Bragg 95437; (707) 964-4283; wharf-restaurant.com. This is no-frills, good-value lodging with a deck overlooking the waterfront of Noyo Harbor Fishing Village. The top-floor Captain's Penthouse has 2 bedrooms and full kitchen. Some rooms are dog friendly (pet fee).

Beachcomber Motel, 1111 N. Main St., Fort Bragg 95437; (707) 964-2402; the beachcombermotel.com. The family-owned-and-operated motel has a unique location along the multiuse recreational trail near the pedestrian/bicycle trestle bridge. Of the 69 rooms, 4 have kitchenettes and most have barbecue decks overlooking the ocean. Many of the units also have fireplaces. Rates include continental breakfast. The pooch friendly lodging (pet fee) greets your bowwow with a Welcome Kit. The property's fenced dog run and on-site bicycle rentals are unexpected perks.

Beach House Inn, 100 Pudding Creek Rd., Fort Bragg 95437; (707) 961-1700; beachinn.com. Most of the inn's 30 rooms have decks overlooking the Pudding Creek estuary at the Trestle Bridge. There are 2 barbecue areas for guest use and on-site bicycle rentals. Rates include a continental breakfast served at the inn's sister property, the Beachcomber Motel next door. Some rooms are dog friendly (pet fee).

MacKerricher State Park Campground, 24100 MacKerricher Park Rd., Fort Bragg 95437; (707) 937-5804 or (800) 444-7275; parks.ca.gov. There are over 140 campsites for tents and RVs (35-foot max length, no hookups), flush toilets, and coin-operated showers.

Broken glass and pottery tumbled into sea bling on Glass Beach

Dog Friendly Beaches

Van Damme State Park, steeped in redwood lumber industry history, has a campground and lovely beach in a cove at the mouth of the Little River. Dogs are allowed on Van Damme Beach on leash. The beach is accessed at 8001 CA 1 in the postage-stamp-size town of Little River, 3 miles south of the town of Mendocino. California State Parks, (707) 937-5804, parks.ca.gov.

Portuguese Beach is set in a driftwood cove just off the Mendocino Headlands trail (see hike 31). At low tide there's enough exposed sand for a pleasant on-leash romp to the rock arch at the south end. The slope of the beach is very gentle for pooch to take a dip along the way. The beach is conveniently accessed off the trail at Main and Heeser Streets, Mendocino. California State Parks, (707) 937-5804, parks.ca.gov

Caspar Headlands State Beach is a pretty sandy cove with a gentler lap of the waves than most beaches in the county. It's a sweet spot to walk with your dog on leash. The beach is accessed at 14441 Point Cabrillo Dr., just north of Mendocino. California State Parks, (707) 937-5804, parks.ca.gov

Pudding Creek Beach, below the scenic trestle bridge on the Haul Road trail at the mouth of Pudding Creek (see hike 33), is wider than it is long. The protected cove is deep, offering a generous sandy beach for leashed dogs to walk their humans or take them tidepooling at low tide. The beach is accessed from a parking lot at 1100 N. Main St., Fort Bragg. Walk under the trestle to the beach. MacKerricher State Park, (707) 964-9112, parks.ca.gov

Playtime at Portuguese Beach

Coastal Attractions

Pazzo Marco Creamery, 39250 CA 1, Gualala 95445; (707) 884-9548; pazzomarco .com. An unexpected pleasure in a micro-creamery dedicated to artisan-style gelato and cheese. E-mail Marco for a creamery tour by appointment at marco@pazzomarco.com.

Point Arena Lighthouse, 45500 Lighthouse Rd., Point Arena 95468; (707) 882-2809; pointarenalighthouse.com. In addition to the museum exhibits and gift shop, the daily tours include the opportunity to climb 145 steps past four landings on the way to the top of the tallest lighthouse on the West Coast. Check the website for the schedule of full-moon tours.

Elk, on the Northern California coast, sits isolated between Point Arena to the south and Mendocino to the north. If you blink, you'll miss it. **Bridget Dolan's Pub** (5910 S. CA 1, Elk 95432; 707-877-1820) is housed in a historic home built in 1890. It is the most prominent landmark in Elk and a good place for dinner comfort food and a dose of civilization if you're experiencing civilization withdrawal.

To call the handful of buildings in **Little River** a town is a bit of a stretch. But this once-thriving lumber mill coastal outpost perched above the mouth of the Little River and the Pacific Ocean less than 5 miles south of Mendocino off of CA 1 endures as a tourist hideaway. Among the attractions are the dog friendly (on leash) 1.25-mile Spring Ranch bluff trail, accessed from CA 1 just north of Van Damme State Park, and the dog friendly (on leash) 0.5-mile trail to the geologically intriguing

CA 1 bridge over Russian Gulch Creek Canyon in Russian Gulch State Park

Little River Blowhole, accessed behind the Little River Cemetery off CA 1. Be wary of the poison oak, and keep a safe distance from the blowhole, which is more of a sinkhole created by erosion on a forested trail. See medocinolandtrust.org for more information. As a bonus for film buffs, Little River is home to the renovated, dog friendly **Heritage House Resort & Spa** (formerly the historic Heritage House Inn B&B), 5200 CA 1, Little River 95456, which was the location for the 1978 romantic comedy *Same Time Next Year* starring Alan Alda and Ellen Burstyn.

Catch a Canoe outdoors rental shop makes it possible for you and your furry adventure pal to savor the splendor of the 8-mile Big River tidal estuary, now part of Big River State Park, in a redwood outrigger canoe, traditional canoe, or kayak. Catch a Canoe prides itself on its canine friendly handmade outriggers, which are wide in the center to accommodate four-legged explorers more comfortably. Ask about the canine coaster and the canine cruiser. Catch a Canoe is on the Stanford Inn private property, 0.5 mile south of Mendocino on the east side of CA 1 at 44850 Comptche-Ukiah Rd., Mendocino 95456; (707) 937-0273; catchacanoe .com. Always best to call ahead to coordinate your paddling with the tides.

Russian Gulch State Park, 12301 N. CA 1, Mendocino 95460; (707) 937-5804; parks.ca.gov. This small gem of a park's entrance is 2 miles north of Mendocino across from the Mendocino Headlands. The park's forested headlands boast a scenic gulch laced with trails and a short path overlooking a collapsed sea cave, forming a large blowhole known as the Devil's Punch Bowl. The surging sea washing the vegetated walls in the headland hole is mesmerizing.

Caspar Headlands State Natural Reserve is a small patch of protected rugged coastline on the scenic bluffs shared by a residential community about 4 miles north of Mendocino just south of Caspar State Beach. You must obtain a permit from the Mendocino Sector Office at 12301 N. CA 1, Mendocino 95460 (across from Russian Gulch State Park); (707) 937-5804; parks.ca.gov.

California Western Railroad, 100 W. Laurel St., Fort Bragg 95437; (707) 964-6371; skunktrain.com. Board a historic train for an hour-long ride on the Pudding Creek Express along the creek's lush estuary to the doorstep of the Redwood Empire. Well-behaved dogs are welcome. Check the website for details on the year-round journeys and schedules.

BEST COASTAL FARMERS' MARKETS

Fort Bragg Farmers' Market boasts organic and local produce as well as free-range beef and wild-caught fish. Locals and tourists come for the flowers, artisan cheeses, and baked goods. Sit and enjoy hot food to go while listening to live music. The market is held at 416 Franklin St., outdoors in the summer (Wed 3 to 6 p.m.) and indoors in the winter (Wed 3 to 5 p.m.) in the old Recreation Center Gym on Franklin Street behind City Hall. www.mcfarm.org/fort-bragg.html

Mendocino Farmers' Market is a picturesque venue overlooking Mendocino Bay to shop for seasonal goods. The market operates seasonally (May to Oct) from noon to 2 p.m. at Howard and Main Streets. www.mcfarm.org/mendocino.html

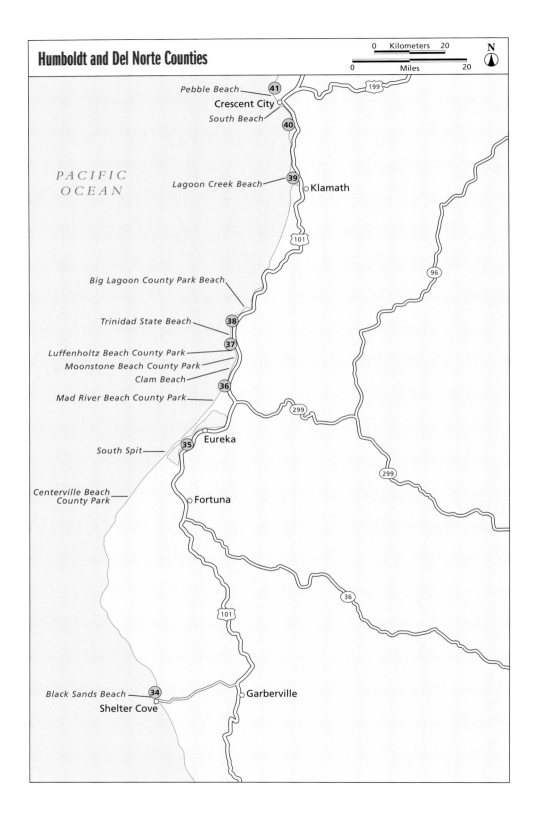

Humboldt and Del Norte Counties

Kilometers 0 20
Miles 0 20

N

Pebble Beach — 41
Crescent City
South Beach — 40

199

Lagoon Creek Beach — 39 ○ Klamath

PACIFIC
OCEAN

101

96

Big Lagoon County Park Beach

Trinidad State Beach — 38

37

Luffenholtz Beach County Park
Moonstone Beach County Park
Clam Beach — 36

Mad River Beach County Park

299

South Spit — 35 ● Eureka

299

Centerville Beach
County Park

○ Fortuna

36

101

Black Sands Beach — 34
Shelter Cove

○ Garberville

HUMBOLDT COUNTY

With over 40 percent of the remaining old-growth coast redwood forests in the state and protected under the banner of national, state, and local public land agencies, **HUMBOLDT COUNTY** is the queen of the Redwood Empire. The county is 200 miles north of bustling San Francisco and the more populated tentacles. Humboldt County's agricultural reputation rests on two main operations: high-quality family-operated dairy farms and equally high-grade marijuana farming. Proposition 215, also known as the Compassionate Use Act of 1996, allows the use of "medical cannabis." In November 2016 Proposition 64 legalized recreational marijuana in California. A university and a college campus keep the bayside communities and their Victorian heritage vibrant. Redwoods stand sentinel along cliffs, and several rivers pour over coastal beaches. Humboldt Bay is California's second-largest natural bay, with 110 miles of coastline (the most of any county), and is the largest protected body of water on the West Coast between San Francisco and Puget Sound. These natural attributes set the stage for some unique coastal trail exploration.

34. **BLACK SANDS BEACH**

WHY GO?

This trailhead is the most accessible portal to the remote and legendary Lost Coast Trail. This hike is a triple treat. The California Coastal Trail runs along Blacks Sands Beach for 25 miles. The hike is a unique opportunity to experience the mystique of the wild and rugged Lost Coast and the King Range Conservation Area, most of which is more suited to the very intrepid. As a bonus, Black Sands Beach Trailhead is in Shelter Cove, one of the funkiest communities of coastal California you'll ever love.

THE RUNDOWN

Distance: 4.2 miles out and back

Start: Black Sands Beach parking lot

Nearest towns: Garberville and Shelter Cove

Hiking time: About 2 hours

Fees and permits: None for day hiking; permits and bear canisters for overnights

Conveniences: Restroom, drinking fountain, picnic table, trash and recycling containers

Beach access: Yes; dogs allowed under voice control

Trail users: Hikers, equestrians, and dogs under voice control

Trailhead elevation: 108 feet

Highest point: 108 feet

Trail surface: Coarse sand and pebbles

Difficulty: Easy

Seasonal highlights: Whale migration

Managing agency: Bureau of Land Management, 1695 Heindon Rd., Arcata 95521; (707) 825-2300. King Range National Conservation Area, 768 Shelter Cove Rd., Whitehorn 95589; (707) 986-5400; blm.gov.

FINDING THE TRAILHEAD

From Garberville at US 101, take exit 639A and drive 2.3 miles on Redwood Drive. Turn left on Briceland-Thorn Road and follow the signs for the King Range National Conservation Area and Shelter Cove. At 13.5 miles bear right onto Shelter Cove Road. Drive 7.5 miles to Shelter Cove and turn left on Machi Road, then drive 1 mile to Mal Coombs Park. From the park drive 1.2 miles along the coast on Lower Pacific Drive to the T intersection and turn left on Upper Pacific Drive. Drive 0.25 mile to Humboldt Loop Road and turn left. Drive 0.75 mile on Humboldt Loop Road to Beach Road. Turn right uphill on Beach

Road and make the first left into the Black Sands Beach Trailhead parking lot. **GPS:** N40 02.72' / W124 04.63'

WHAT TO SEE

To enter the majestic realm of the King Range, also known as the Lost Coast, you must drive 21 snaky miles on a narrow, albeit paved, road. You'll wonder if it's worth it at every curve, and then you'll catch occasional glimpses of the vast forested stadium of mountains stretching in all directions where the road crests before taking another dip and wanting to see more. The road passes through the cool canyon of the John Dewitt Redwood Preserve and rises up.

Although it may be sunny and 90 degrees on US 101, if you are traveling here in late spring to early fall, don't be surprised to drive into a sea of fog as you emerge on the last crest before dropping down into Shelter Cove. The road to Shelter Cove gives you a hint of how isolated and rugged the Lost Coast is. So daunting an engineering challenge was the precipitous wall of mountains rising 4,000 feet above the Pacific that CA 1 detours inland along US 101.

The King Range National Conservation Area, the first conservation area in the country, has been managed by the BLM (Bureau of Land Management) since 1970. It covers 68,000 acres along 35 miles of coastline. Two-thirds of the conservation area was designated as wilderness in 2006.

Black Sands Beach stretches north along the Lost Coast.

Solitude along the Lost Coast

There is a northern section Lost Coast Trail and a southern section Lost Coast Trail. The northern section, which this hike samples, is the more easily accessed of the two. The southern portion of the Lost Coast Trail can only be accessed by remote and rough dirt back roads that become impassable during the winter rains.

The directions to the Black Sands Beach Trailhead purposely route you through the community of Shelter Cove, adding about 2 miles to the driving route, as opposed to taking you directly to the trailhead. The drive can seem brutal if you are not accustomed to mountain roads. A stop in Shelter Cove gives you the chance to refresh your spirit before heading out to the trailhead. If you arrive later in the day, you'll appreciate staying in the campground or checking in at one of the few lodgings to hike the next day.

Shelter Cove has an exceptionally stunning setting and is one of the North Coast's best-kept secrets at the foot of the King Range. It is unfortunate that Shelter Cove's plateau was not preserved more naturally. The upside is that a developed community, funky and rudimentary as it is, provides hikers with some welcome comforts and amenities. One of Shelter Cove's highlights is the Cape Mendocino Lighthouse, which was relocated to Mal Coombs Park in 1999. It is open to the public seven days a week for a few hours between Memorial Day and Labor Day. Shelter Cove is also gifted with tidepools to explore at low tide.

Black Sands Beach Trailhead is the southern terminus to the northern portion of the Lost Coast Trail, which runs from the Mattole Trailhead 25 miles south to Black Sands

Beach in Shelter Cove. There are several long, primitive, and steep hiking trails that rise from the shore to connect to the King Crest Trail and King Peak's 4,088-foot crown.

Although the northern portion of the Lost Coast Trail is more accessible, it is tide sensitive and sections of it are impassable at high tide. The entire trek is typically a three-night backpack with a shuttle back to the trailhead and must be coordinated with the tides. The hike described here allows you to sample the most accessible section of the Lost Coast Trail from a paved road without being affected by the tide.

If the drive down to Shelter Cove is as much of the car you want to see for a while, you have the option of walking to the trailhead from Mal Coombs Park. It will add 2.25 miles (4.5 round-trip) to this hike if you choose to walk to the trail-head from the park. Although you are walking on the street to the trailhead, traffic is practically nonexistent except for a few local vehicles. It's a pleasant first mile along the coast with several opportunities to view the shoreline up close and read some of the BLM's interpretive panels. The last mile winds through the quiet residential neighborhood perched on bluffs at the edge of woodlands.

The trail officially begins in the parking lot following the cement path from the restrooms down to the beach, where you turn right to walk north. The ocean here can be very rough with a stiff undertow, so keep a safe distance from the surf line and sneaker waves. If you take your pooch on this hike, be aware that the coarse sand can injure his feet if his pads are not accustomed to this type of terrain. If any body of water is like a magnet to your furry pal, keep him on a leash. This is not a swimming beach or suitable to play retrieve the ball in the surf.

To start the hike, walk along the sidewalk heading downhill from the trailhead parking. Follow the trail onto the beach and turn right. The beach is black coarse sand with some gravel and cobble sections, which gives your leg muscles a different

Hikers appear out of the fog.

kind of workout. It is hemmed in by crashing surf on the left and steep forested slopes punctuated by stream-eroded ravines on the right. The hike is exposed to sun, fog, and wind, and you will welcome the screen of fog on a warm day. Make sure you pack proper sun protection and bring lots of water. The coast is temperamental, and a foggy morning can melt away under a scorching sun.

At 1.7 miles you come to a colossal boulder sitting on the beach. This is the only significant landmark that interrupts the flat, black sandy landscape that stretches ahead like a mirage.

At 2.0 miles you will pass Horse Mountain Creek flowing down the hillside to the beach. Continue walking 0.1 mile farther to the point where the driftwood rests on a rise. This is as far as you can safely walk at any tide. It becomes impassable at high tide beyond this point. The large driftwood logs make great picnic benches before going back to the trailhead the way you came.

MILES AND DIRECTIONS

0.0 Start at the Black Sands Beach Trailhead parking lot.

1.7 Come to a colossal boulder on dog friendly Black Sands Beach.

2.0 Come to Horse Mountain Creek on the right.

2.1 Come to a driftwood-strewn rise on a point. Go back to the trailhead the way you came.

4.2 Arrive back at the trailhead.

BAKERIES, BREWERIES, EATS, AND SLEEPS

Bon Bistro & Bakery, 867 Redwood Dr., Garberville 95542; (707) 923-2509. Stop in on the way to Shelter Cove for a stash of bagels and cookies. The bistro serves breakfast and lunch. Try the blueberry pancakes, or choose from sandwiches or salads with a smoothie.

Delgada Pizza and Bakery, 205 Wave Dr., #1D, Whitehorn (Shelter Cove) 95589; (707) 986-7672. Shelter Cove is idyllic and remote. Hikers are lucky to have Delgada's to fuel up on made-from-scratch pizza (gluten-free crust available) and lasagna, not to mention house-baked goods. Sara the owner says the brownies, lemon bars, scones, and peanut butter chocolate chip cookies just fly off the shelf. The small eatery is open 4 to 9 p.m. and serves some of Eel Brewing Company's best brews. Fido is welcome at the outdoor tables.

Shelter Cove RV Park and Campground Deli, 492 Machi Rd., Shelter Cove 95589; (707) 986-7474; sheltercoverv.com. The deli provides snacks and some grocery items, but it's the secret house-batter recipe for the most succulent fish-and-chips that makes the stop worthwhile. Unfortunately dogs are no longer allowed on the patio, but you can get food to go and dine with Fido at your campsite or pack it for a picnic just a short walk down to the cove.

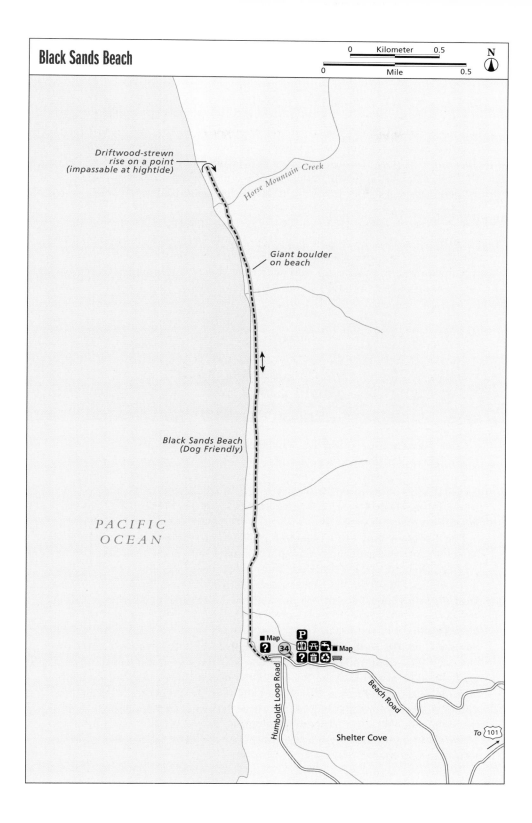

Black Sands Beach

0   Kilometer   0.5

0   Mile   0.5

N

Driftwood-strewn
rise on a point
(impassable at hightide)

Horse Mountain Creek

Giant boulder
on beach

Black Sands Beach
(Dog Friendly)

PACIFIC
OCEAN

■ Map

P

34

■ Map

Humboldt Loop Road

Beach Road

Shelter Cove

To 101

Approaching the turnaround point

Cove Restaurant, 10 Seal Dr., Whitehorn (Shelter Cove) 95589; (707) 986-1197. This local seafood restaurant with some landlubber entrees has outstanding ocean views. It's Shelter Cove's best if not only full-service restaurant. The season, days, and hours of operation are sketchy at best, so call ahead.

Inn of the Lost Coast, 205 Wave St., Shelter Cove 95589; (707) 986-7521; innofthelostcoast.com.

The Spyglass Inn, 118 Dolphin Dr., Whitehorn (Shelter Cove) 95589; (707) 986-4030; spyglassinnatsheltercove.com. These are 4 spiffy suites with ocean views, decks, kitchens, Wi-Fi, gas fireplaces, and in-room Jacuzzi tubs to pamper hikers' weary bodies. Owners/innkeepers Margaret and Richard built Spyglass in 2008 and greet amazing visitors from all over the world to their Shelter Cove haven.

CAMPING

Shelter Cove RV Park and Campground, 492 Machi Rd., Shelter Cove; (707) 986-7474. The rustic campground with tent and RV sites (some hookups) on a grassy meadow overlooking the Pacific and the relocated Cape Mendocino Lighthouse is all about the setting. The shower and restroom building is screaming for some TLC. As of summer 2016, Jack, the congenial owner and local fisherman, had the campground for sale. Call ahead for an update on any changes.

For more primitive camping in the King Range at BLM campgrounds, Google King Range BLM.

35. EUREKA WATERFRONT TRAIL

WHY GO?

This short but thoughtfully developed multiuse trail known as the Hikshari' Trail showcases the Elk River, where it flows into the estuary and south Humboldt Bay. This is a significant scenic stitch in the 4 miles of waterfront trail that will be added to the Hikshari' Trail to create an impressive 6.5-mile waterfront trail around Eureka by 2018.

THE RUNDOWN

Distance: 3.0 miles out and back

Start: Elk River Access Area at north end of Pound Road Park and Ride

Nearest town: Eureka

Hiking time: About 1.5 hours

Fees and permits: None

Conveniences: Trash container and dog waste bag dispenser at trailhead; restroom with flush toilets at end of trail

Beach access: No

Trail users: Hikers, cyclists, equestrians, and dogs on leash

Trailhead elevation: 10 feet

Highest point: 10 feet

Trail surface: Pavement

Difficulty: Easy

Seasonal highlights: Wildflowers in the spring

Managing agency: City of Eureka Parks and Recreation, 1011 Waterfront Dr., Eureka 95501; (707) 441-4241; ci.eureka.ca.gov

---

FINDING THE TRAILHEAD

 From south end of Eureka on US 101, take exit 702/Herrick Avenue/Elk River Road and follow the signs for the Eureka Waterfront Trail. Drive west on Herrick Avenue into the Pound Road Park and Ride parking lot.
GPS: N40 45.52' / W124 11.43'

WHAT TO SEE

Hikshari' is the Wiyot Indian place name for this portion of Humboldt Bay where the Wiyot native people lived for thousands of years. This trail is a sneak preview of what the eventual 6.5 miles of Eureka Waterfront Trail will look like when it is completed in 2018 according to current projections.

The trail begins in the Pound Road Park and Ride lot off US 101. At first glance, there is nothing particularly attractive or promising about this trail. The trailhead here is understated, with no conveniences except a trashcan and a dog waste bag dispenser. But just 0.2 mile ahead, the interpretive panel describing the Elk River Access Area and colorful map board set a different tone. This is one of three access points along the 1.5 miles tracing the Elk River and Wildlife Sanctuary to the mouth of south Humboldt Bay. There are benches and elaborate interpretive panels detailing the ecology and cultural history of the river and bay. The foghorn reminds hikers of the ocean that sits beyond the views of the tidal estuary and extensive marshlands around huge Humboldt Bay, the only deepwater port between San Francisco south and Coos Bay north in Oregon.

The first 0.6 mile follows a riparian corridor of willows and woodland lush with wild California blackberry vines. Just 0.2 mile farther, the Melvin "Cappy" McKinney loop on your left is a 0.2-mile-long gravel path that offers a more intimate experience along the Elk River Wildlife Sanctuary. The loop was named in homage to McKinney's dedication to protecting the area as a sanctuary. The short spur merges back into the main trail 0.2 mile ahead. The parking area at this access has picnic tables.

At 1.3 miles you pass the Hilfiker Lane trail access parking lot. There are picnic tables and trash and recycling containers as well as a dog waste bag dispenser. Notice the wooden posts with painted blue feet across the trail from this access point. These markers lead you on a short spur for a closer view of the river meeting the bay.

At 1.5 miles you arrive at the Truesdale Vista Point and parking area for the north end of the Hikshari' Trail and your turnaround point. There is a restroom with flush toilets and a water fountain in the parking lot, along with picnic tables, benches, and trash and recycling containers. Take the time to read the interpretive panels at the trailhead and enjoy the view across the bay before going back to the trailhead the way you came

MILES AND DIRECTIONS

0.0 Start at the Elk River Access Area sign at the north end of the Pound Road Park and Ride.

0.2 Come to an interpretive panel and map board.

0.3 Walk across the abandoned railroad track and across a tributary on a footbridge.

0.8 Come to a trail junction for the Melvin "Cappy" McKinney loop on the left. Walk straight.

0.9 The McKinney spur rejoins the trail from the left across the Elk River Wildlife Sanctuary access parking lot.

1.3 Come to the Hilfiker Lane trail access parking lot on the right.

1.5 Arrive at the Truesdale Vista Point and the end of the trail. Go back to the trailhead the way you came.

3.0 Arrive back at the trailhead.

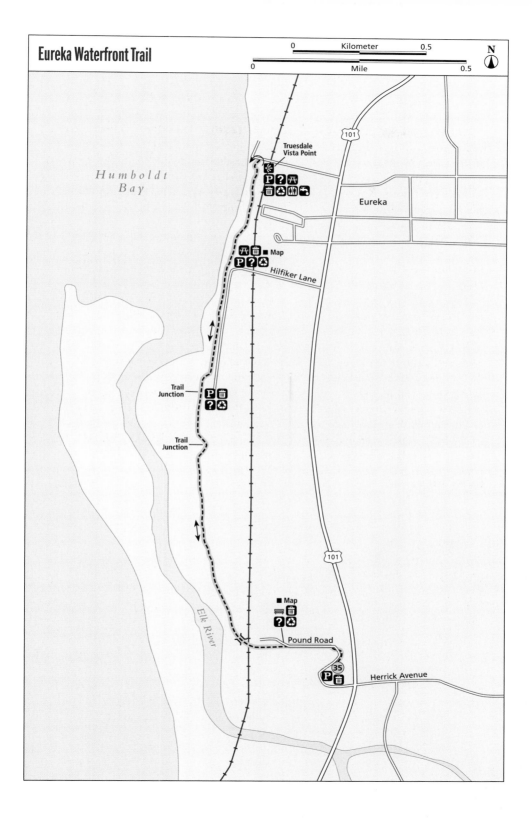

Eureka Waterfront Trail

Humboldt Bay

Truesdale Vista Point

Eureka

101

Map

Hilfiker Lane

Trail Junction

Trail Junction

101

Map

Elk River

Pound Road

35

Herrick Avenue

Wildlife sanctuary in
South Humboldt Bay

The Hikshari' Trail parallels
Humboldt Bay.

BAKERIES, BREWERIES, EATS, AND SLEEPS:

Ramone's Bakery and Cafe, 209 E St., Eureka 95501; (707) 445-2923; ramones bakery.com. The bakery continues to be operated by one of the original owners since 1981, with a bistro cafe that serves breakfast, lunch, and dinner. It's a local go-to place for its cornucopia of baked goodies from pastries and tarts to cakes and pies. Try their variety of cheesecake flavors, and don't leave without one of their mocha chocolate cookies. There are outdoor tables to accommodate four-legged customers.

North Coast Co-op, 25 4th St., Eureka 95501; (707) 443-6027; northcoast .coop.com. This Old Town market is stocked with "local" farm produce and dairy to meat and seafood. They have a large bulk food department and pride themselves in making their deli and bakery goods from scratch with organic ingredients.

Los Bagels Co., 403 2nd St., Eureka 95501; (707) 442-8525; losbagels.com. Besides your traditional bagels and sandwiches, this bagel bakery is a place where you'll find challah bread and knishes alongside empanadas and chorizo.

Lost Coast Brewery & Cafe, 617 4th St., Eureka 95501; lostcoast.com. This brewpub began as a pharmacist's dream in 1986. Barbara Groom brewed her ales and opened the cafe in the 100-year-old building in 1989. The cafe remains in the original building, but the brew house has outgrown two locales and has been most recently relocated to a new state-of-the-art facility at 1600 Sunset Dr. in Eureka. The Lost Coast Brewery's wild and colorful labels are one of its trademarks. The brewery accommodates tours for the public; call (707) 267-9651 for schedule and reservations. The cafe is famous for its Hot Brown roast beef simmered in Downtown Brown beer with hickory-smoked bacon, cheddar, and ranch dressing on a sourdough roll. Lost Coast also claims to have the "best chicken wings in town." Top it all off with a Stout Float for dessert.

Redwood Curtain Brewing Co., 550 S. G Street, Ste. 6, Arcata; (707) 826-7222; redwoodcurtainbrewing.com. Barley being the backbone of the malting process, one of Redwood's highest-quality malts is processed according to German Beer Purity Law in the smallest malting house in North America, located in British Columbia. The brewery's taproom operates in a light commercial complex and does not serve food. The good news is that you BYOF (bring your own food), or savor one of Loco Fishco food truck's several made-to-order brew-compatible dishes. The tacos, fish-and-chips, and daily creative specials all complement Redwood's ever-popular Imperial Golden Ale IGA.

Shamus T-Bones, 1911 Truesdale St., Eureka 95503; (707) 407-3550; shamus tbones.com. What started as a mobile barbecue 15 years ago is now a full-fledged sit-down family restaurant in its own cozy custom building on the banks of Humboldt Bay by the Eureka Waterfront Trail. The old-growth redwood bar, exposed wood crossbeams, fireplace, and outdoor patio create all the ambience to enjoy seafood, pasta, or slow-smoked specialties from the oak pit for lunch or dinner.

Jack's Seafood, 4 C St., Eureka 95501; (707) 273-5273; jacksseafoodeureka .com. Jack's is one of the newest and increasingly popular local kids on Old Town's

Returning to the trailhead along the tidal estuary

waterfront. Jack's menu boasts a long list of fresh seafood dishes and several landlubber favorites. But the word is spreading fast that Jack's is the spot for halibut fish-and-chips and halibut/cod tacos. The granola honey coconut sundae with a berry flambé is a perfect calorie booster after a hike. Furry family members are welcome on the patio.

Café Marina and Woodley's Bar, 601 Starfare Dr., Eureka 95501; (707) 443-2233; cafemarina.net. This nautical-theme restaurant and bar at the largest marina on Humboldt Bay serves breakfast, lunch, and dinner. It's the place for seafood lovers and to feast on fresh crab. There is indoor and outdoor seating with views across the harbor. As a designated protected habitat, dogs are not allowed on the island. Woodley is known for its bird watching and two landmarks: a memorial fisherman sculpture and the home of the relocated Table Bluff Lighthouse.

Carter House Inn, 301 L Street, Eureka 95501; (707) 444-8062; carterhouse. com. The inn's complex of accommodations offers guest rooms, suites, and cottages with kitchens that blend Victorian chic, local charm, and modern amenities. All hotel guests are welcome to enjoy afternoon hors d'oeuvres and wine, evening tea, and a two-course buffet-style morning breakfast. The elegant in-house Restaurant 301, with ingredients from the Carter Gardens, is perfect for a gastronomical splurge. The Carter House Bar on the first floor has a tasty and less indulgent menu, beginning with a daily happy hour at 4 p.m. All rooms are dog friendly (pet fee).

Best Western Plus Bayshore Inn, 3500 Broadway, Eureka 95503; (707) 268-8005; bestwestern.com. The hotel is a stone's throw from the Waterfront Trail and perks include an indoor/outdoor swimming pool, in-room small refrigerator, some rooms with fireplaces, complimentary hot/cold buffet breakfast, and two restaurants nearby (Shamus T Bones and Marie Callender's).

Oyster Beach vacation rentals on North Spit of Humboldt Bay, (707) 834-6555; **redwoodvacation.com.** This is a unique private lodging experience just a few miles by car or bicycle from Eureka. There are 5 separate cabins to choose from for an escape, with most of them Fido friendly, on a 14-acre historic homestead surrounded by wetlands, eucalyptus groves, and a half mile of beach. Oyster Beach is next to Samoa Dunes Recreation Area and the North Jetty for ATV sporting and surfing.

CAMPING

Redwood Coast Cabins and RV Resort, 4050 N. US 101, Eureka 95503; (707) 822-4243; redwoodcoastrv.com. Formerly a KOA campground, Redwood Coast has tent and RV sites along with cabins (linens available upon request). There is a convenience store, seasonal pool, and fenced pooch playground.

Riverwalk RV Park, 2189 Riverwalk Dr., Fortuna 95540; (707) 725-3359; riverwalkrvpark.com. This is a clean, pleasant RV park with full hookups, wooded tent sites with camp kitchen and hot showers, some dog friendly cabins (bring your own linens), and standard amenities. It is conveniently located within walking distance of the multiuse Riverwalk Trail along the east bank of the Eel River and the Eel River Brewing Co. pub and restaurant and Funky Monkey family restaurant for no-fuss bites.

36. HAMMOND TRAIL

WHY GO?

It's the diverse scenery and habitat that makes this section of the California Coastal Trail along the Hammond multiuse trail unique. The trail surface flips back and forth between pavement, gravel, and dirt. The beginning of the trail showcases a shady woodland and fern forest before revealing an expansive estuary and marshland on the way to Clam Beach's broad sandy shore.

THE RUNDOWN

Distance: 8.4 miles out and back

Start: Hammond Coastal Trail at north end of parking lot

Nearest towns: McKinleyville and Arcata

Hiking time: About 4 hours

Fees and permits: None

Conveniences: Restrooms with flush toilets, drinking fountain, picnic tables, playground, trash and recycling containers, dog waste bag dispenser

Beach access: Yes; dogs on leash (see map)

Trail users: Hikers, mountain bikers, equestrians, and dogs on leash

Trailhead elevation: 52 feet

Highest point: 155 feet

Trail surface: Pavement, gravel, dirt, and sand

Difficulty: Moderate

Seasonal highlights: Wildflowers in the spring

Managing agency: Humboldt County Parks, 1106 2nd St., Eureka 95501; (707) 445-7651; humboldtgov.org

FINDING THE TRAILHEAD

From Arcata on CA 1, drive 2 miles north to McKinleyville. Take exit 719 off of CA 1 and turn right on School Road and drive 0.3 mile to Washington Avenue. Turn left on Washington Avenue and drive 0.3 mile to McKinley Avenue. Turn right on McKinley Avenue and drive 0.2 mile to Hiller Road. Turn left on Hiller Road and drive 0.4 mile into the Hiller Park parking lot. **GPS:** N40 56.63' / W124 07.21'

WHAT TO SEE

This trail constructed along parts of the abandoned Hammond Railroad property is a 5-mile stitch in the California Coastal Trail (CCT) thread envisioned to connect

Approaching Clam Beach

the coast from Oregon to California's southern border when it is completed. It's always exciting to step on a trail and see the CCT blue wave logo at the trailhead.

The Hammond Trail begins at the Mad River Bridge about 1 mile south of Hiller Park and runs through Hiller Park before ending at Clam Beach 4 miles north of the park. The Mad River Bridge trailhead is relatively undeveloped except for a small parking lot that sits in a less-traveled corner of McKinleyville. Vehicles are more vulnerable to vandalism at that trailhead, hence the reason for choosing the well-developed and more visible Hiller Park trailhead. The hike described here follows the trail northward to the end at Clam Beach. If time permits when you complete this hike and you want to extend the hike, you can walk the extra mile south (2 miles out and back) from Hiller Park to the Mad River trailhead.

This hike begins on a paved section of the Hammond Trail at the north end of the Hiller Park parking lot. Although this is a coastal trail, the ocean is not visible for almost a mile as you walk along a pleasant shady corridor of spruce trees. You cross a road through a residential neighborhood at 0.7 mile and the estuary appears on the left just 0.2 mile ahead, where the trail splits to the right for mountain bikes and the hiker trail continues straight. Stay on the hiker path and feast on the views

Entering the lush Hammond Trail
Interpretative Footpath

of the estuary and dunes through the trees below the bluff and peeks of the ocean and coastal beaches ahead. You will pass a couple of benches on the bluff above the estuary and spur trails with signs for coastal access.

The trail rises steeply for a few huffs and levels at 1.4 miles at the start of the Hammond Trail Interpretive Footpath. This is an enchanting 0.3-mile stitch that takes you down the steps into another woodland highlighted by a footbridge over Widow White Creek and a carpet of ferns. You emerge out of the woodland, where the paved bike path merges back in from the right.

About 0.5 mile ahead, the trail comes to Letz Road. Walk on the grassy shoulder along the large residential properties with parklike settings on the left and CA 1 on the right. You reconnect with the trail at the cul-de-sac about 0.5 mile farther. The trail continues to alternate between pavement and gravel past a parking area off of CA 1 on the right. There are no services or conveniences at this parking lot. The beach and dunes are in full view on the left for the last mile to the Clam Beach Day Use Area.

At 4.1 miles you cross Strawberry Creek on a footbridge and come to an information kiosk. Continue walking up to the road and bear left heading north for the campground parking lot 0.1 mile past the day-use parking. There are restrooms with vault toilets and water in this small roadside county campground. Trails lead through the dunes onto Clam Beach from the parking lot. A picnic table for day use can be found across the parking lot next to the hitching rail for horses. Clam Beach is an amazing expanse of dunes and hard-packed sand. If your four-legged hiking pal is with you, don't miss the chance to explore the beach and let him take a cool-off dip in the ocean before going back to the trailhead the way you came.

MILES AND DIRECTIONS

0.0 Start at the north end of the Hiller Park parking lot.

0.7 Walk across the street.

0.9 Come to a trail junction for the bike trail to the right and the hiker trail straight ahead. Continue walking straight.

1.4 Come to the Hammond Trail Interpretive Footpath. Turn left down the steps onto the footpath.

1.7 Leave the Hammond Trail Interpretive Footpath. The bike trail merges in from the right. Bear left.

1.9 Come to Letz Road. Follow the road north along the grassy shoulder.

2.4 Come to the Letz Road cul-de-sac and reconnect with the Hammond Trail.

2.7 Walk past a parking lot on the right.

4.1 Walk across Strawberry Creek on a footbridge.

4.2 Arrive at dog friendly Clam Beach County Park and campground parking lot. Go back to the trailhead the way you came.

8.4 Arrive back at the trailhead.

BAKERIES, BREWERIES, EATS, AND SLEEPS

Ramone's Bakery and Cafe, 155 City Center Rd., McKinleyville Shopping Center, McKinleyville 95519; (707) 839-3383; ramonesbakery.com. The bakery continues to be operated by one of the original owners who opened the Eureka

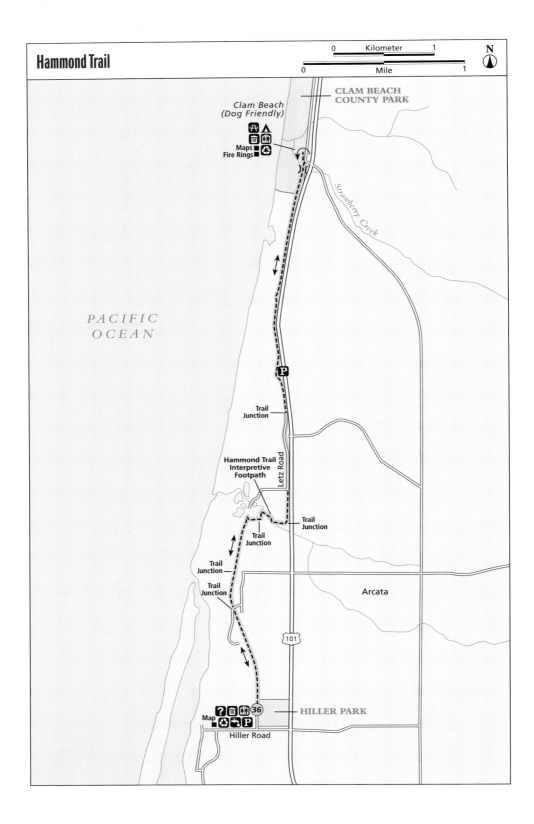

Hammond Trail

0 Kilometer 1

0 Mile 1

N

CLAM BEACH COUNTY PARK

Clam Beach (Dog Friendly)

Maps
Fire Rings

Strawberry Creek

PACIFIC OCEAN

P

Trail Junction

Hammond Trail Interpretive Footpath

Letz Road

Trail Junction

Trail Junction

Trail Junction

Trail Junction

Arcata

101

Map

36 **HILLER PARK**

Hiller Road

location in 1981. The good news has spread to 5 local outlets. The McKinleyville location offers premade sandwiches delivered from the main store daily as well as a cornucopia of baked goodies from pastries and tarts to cakes and pies. Try their variety of cheesecake flavors, and don't leave without one of their mocha chocolate cookies.

Wildflower Cafe and Bakery, 1604 G St., Arcata 95521; (707) 822-0360; wildflowercafebakery.com. The Wildflower has been Arcata's vegetarian favorite for 30 years for breakfast, lunch, and dinner. The menu of quick snack goodies includes fresh corn bread, scones, and vegan thumbprint shortbread cookies with a raspberry center and chocolate drizzle topping.

Wildberries Marketplace, 747 13th St., Arcata 95521; (707) 822-0095; wild berries.com. It's a fabulous market for quality and organic provisions. The juice bar, salad bar, and cafe make eating healthy easy and quick. Ramone's Bakery has an outlet in the marketplace.

Six Rivers Brewery, 1300 Central Ave., McKinleyville 95519; (707) 839-7580; sixriversbrewery.com. This is a happening eatery every day of the week. The extensive menu pleases finicky palates and includes pub favorites like grass-fed beef sliders, fresh halibut and chips, handmade Six Rivers pretzels, the Klamath Quesadilla, and build-your-own stone-baked pizza. Enjoy your brew and grub on the patio with a view.

Humboldt Regeneration Brewing Company, 23220 Central Ave., McKinleyville 95519; (707) 738-8225; humboldtregeneration.com. This is a farmhouse brewery with a 2-acre beer farm for growing its own ingredients. It is the first craft beer operation in California, if not the country, to grow and malt its own hops and grains. The brew house and tasting room welcomes customers with 15 different beers on tap and 8 bottled flavors at their roll-up storefront tucked in at the back of McKinleyville's light commercial complex. Don't miss the chance to cool off at this unique nanobrewery. Grab a bite at the food truck in the parking lot during spring and summer.

Eel River Brewing Co., 1777 Alamar Way, Fortuna 95540; (707) 725-2739; eelriverbrewing.com. Eel River was America's first certified organic brewery in 1995. Some of its most popular craft beers are known for their "citrus-floral" quality. The brewery serves classic pub fare plus its famous on-site stout-smoked Beer-B-Q meats. Vegetarians aren't left out with the Black Bean Burger and Thai Tofu Pasta.

Redwood Curtain Brewing Co., 550 S. G Street, Ste. 6, Arcata; (707) 826-7222; redwoodcurtainbrewing.com. Barley being the backbone of the malting process, one of Redwood's highest-quality malts is processed according to German Beer Purity Law in the smallest malting house in North America, located in British Columbia. The brewery's taproom operates in a light commercial complex and does not serve food. The good news is that you BYOF (bring your own food), or savor one of Loco Fishco food truck's several made-to-order brew-compatible dishes. The tacos, fish-and-chips, and daily creative specials all complement Redwood's

A brewery can be a refreshing stop after a good day's hike.

ever-popular Imperial Golden Ale IGA. If you have time for a stroll, there's a trailhead in the Arcata Wildlife Refuge across the street.

Cafe Brio, 791 G St., Arcata 95521; (707) 822-5922; cafebrioarcata.com. This corner eatery based on principles of organic, sustainability, and seasonal local for breakfast, lunch, and dinner screams of a Paris cafe, with outdoor seating for people watching complete with red-and-white awning. Start the morning with fresh-squeezed orange juice, apple muesli, or the cafe's famous ham and cheese croissant. Lunch features sandwiches on mini baguettes from Brio Breadworks, the cafe's sister business, and the *croque-monsieur* is so ooh la la! Dinner is classic bistro fare with an international twist, whereas the monthly farm-to-table four-course prix fixe dinners are a foodie's dream. Vive la France and Made in America meet with the cafe's popular French macarons and traditional chocolate chip cookies. The wine list is strictly French and local wines.

Lady Anne Victorian Inn, 902 14th St., Arcata 95521; (707) 822-2797; lady anneinn.com. Each of the 6 rooms on this historic property enhanced by a gazebo and gardens has a private bath. The inn's dining room has a small refrigerator for guest convenience. Set 6 blocks uphill from the charming downtown area, the inn is within walking distance of restaurants and services. Rates include a cold cut continental breakfast with fresh-baked treats. Call to find out if one of the select dog friendly rooms is available.

Hotel Arcata, 708 9th Street, Arcata 95521; (707) 826-0217; hotelarcata.com. This historic landmark property (1915) on the downtown plaza is owned by a local Big Lagoon Rancheria Native American tribe. The hotel is dog friendly (pet fee). Rooms have a no-fuss decor, and private bathrooms have claw-foot tubs with showers. You and pooch can stroll downtown for dinner or order room service from Tomo, the downstairs Japanese restaurant.

Redwood Coast Vacation Rentals, (707) 834-6555; redwoodvacation.com. Check this website for vacation rentals in McKinleyville.

CAMPING

Clam Beach County Park, Clam Beach Dr., McKinleyville 95519; (707) 445-7651; co.humboldt.ca.us. There are 9 tent sites and 9 RV spaces (no hookups) in this small campground.

Redwood Coast Cabins and RV Resort, 4050 N. US 101, Eureka 95503; (707) 822-4243; redwoodcoastrv.com. Formerly a KOA campground, Redwood Coast has tent and RV sites along with cabins (linens available upon request). There is a convenience store, seasonal pool, and fenced pooch playground.

Riverwalk RV Park, 2189 Riverwalk Dr., Fortuna 95540; (707) 725-3359; riverwalkrvpark.com. This is a clean, pleasant RV park with full hookups, wooded tent sites with camp kitchen and hot showers, some dog friendly cabins (bring your own linens), and standard amenities. It is conveniently located within walking distance of the multiuse Riverwalk Trail along the east bank of the Eel River and the Eel River Brewing Co. pub and restaurant and Funky Monkey family restaurant for no-fuss bites.

37. **TRINIDAD HEAD**

WHY GO?

This prominent rocky nob covered with lush vegetation boasts one of the most scenic loops on the Northern California coast. The trail follows a mellow grade to the top, and the several spurs are sprinkled with benches at multiple viewpoints, inviting hikers to slow down and soak up the stellar views of the beaches and scan for migrating whales. The sea stacks and rocky islands add a whole new dimension to this coastal setting.

THE RUNDOWN

Distance: 1.6-mile lollipop

Start: Southeast end of Trinidad Head parking lot at the steps

Nearest town: Trinidad

Hiking time: About 1 hour

Fees and permits: None

Conveniences: None at trailhead; restrooms with flush toilets at northeast end of parking lot toward the pier

Beach access: Yes; dogs on leash

Trail users: Hikers and dogs on leash (see map)

Trailhead elevation: 15 feet

Highest point: 322 feet

Trail surface: Dirt, gravel, and pavement

Difficulty: Easy

Seasonal highlights: Whale migration in the spring and fall

Managing agency: City of Trinidad, 409 Trinity St., Box 390, Trinidad 95570; (707) 677-0223; trinidad .ca.gov

FINDING THE TRAILHEAD

From Trinidad on US 101, turn west on Main Street and drive 0.2 mile to Trinity Street. Drive 0.2 mile on Trinity Street to Edwards Street and turn right at the T intersection in front of the mini lighthouse. Drive 0.3 mile downhill to the end of the road into the parking lot at the foot of Trinidad Head. **GPS:** N41 03.40' / W124 08.96'

WHAT TO SEE

The tiny, tidy, and quaint seaside town of Trinidad is a lovely hamlet with one of the most enchanting coastal trails. The natural harbor dotted with picturesque rocks that serve as natural habitat for diverse seabird colonies sits in the sheltering shadow of

Trinidad State Beach

Trinidad Head, a natural landmark. Spectacular beaches to the south and the north also highlight the head.

The trail around Trinidad Head is the best way to fully appreciate this pristine stretch of coastline rimmed by spruce and redwoods and its outstanding beaches. You start at the southeast end of the parking lot near the pier and walk up thirty-six steps to a paved road. This is a service road for the US Coast Guard installations and the Trinidad Head Lighthouse established in 1871. Turn right at the paved road for about 0.1 mile and make a right on the narrow gravel trail. This is the start of the counterclockwise loop that forms a lollipop hike. You will be returning down the paved road to this point to close the lollipop. The bench to the right of the trail is your first invitation to gorge on the views of chiseled sea stacks thrusting out of the surf and the spectacular dog friendly Trinidad State Beach below.

Continue walking up the trail and turn right at the spur along the corridor of ferns and lush coastal chaparral vegetation. The trail rises to a bench and another splendid viewpoint to scan for migrating whales or share a snack with your furry friend. Go back to the junction and turn right up the mellow grade. The views open up in 0.5 mile and the rocky head comes into view. Turn right at the next spur and walk up to a knoll for another perspective of the trail and the coastline and beach to the north.

Back at the trail junction, continue the hike walking right along the corridor lined with yarrow, wild grape, and poison oak as you begin to climb along a mild switchback up the gravel trail to a cross. Walk straight to a small wooden viewing platform from which you may catch a partial glimpse of the Trinidad Head Light-house. The lighthouse you saw at the T intersection when you drove into town is a replica of the tower on the original lighthouse and houses the light's antique Fresnel lens. The light at Trinidad head was automated in 1947.

Walk back to the cross and past a bench. Notice the cell towers on the left. Walk down the gravel service road on the right at the wooden trail sign. Turn right downhill. You will come to the paved road at 1.2 miles. There is a bench and a trash container and a locked gate. Bear left and continue downhill to close the lollipop at 1.5 miles. There is something very Caribbean cove-like about the view of the harbor dotted with anchored boats and rock monuments against the sandy beach background.

MILES AND DIRECTIONS

0.0   Start at the southeast end of the parking lot up the steps.

0.1   Come to a trail junction and turn right.

0.2   Turn right on the spur trail.

0.3   Come to a viewpoint. Go back to the trail junction and turn right.

0.6   Turn right on the spur trail. Walk 250 feet and come to an overlook. Go back to the trail junction and turn right to continue on the trail.

0.9   Arrive at a cross and walk to a wooden viewing platform at the end of a spur. Go back to the cross and continue on the service road on the right.

1.0   Come to a wooden trail sign. Turn right and walk downhill.

1.2   Come to the paved road and a bench. Bear left downhill.

1.5   Close the lollipop and continue downhill to the trailhead.

1.6   Arrive back at the trailhead.

BAKERIES, BREWERIES, EATS, AND SLEEPS

Trinidad Bay Eatery and Gallery, 607 Parker St., Trinidad 95570; (707) 677-3777; trinidadeatery.com. They pride themselves on serving the best clam chowder on the West Coast and cooking with organic trans-fat-free ingredients. There are out-door tables to snack with pooch for breakfast, lunch, or dinner. Browse the local art and gift shop on your way out, and indulge in house-made Rocky Road fudge to go.

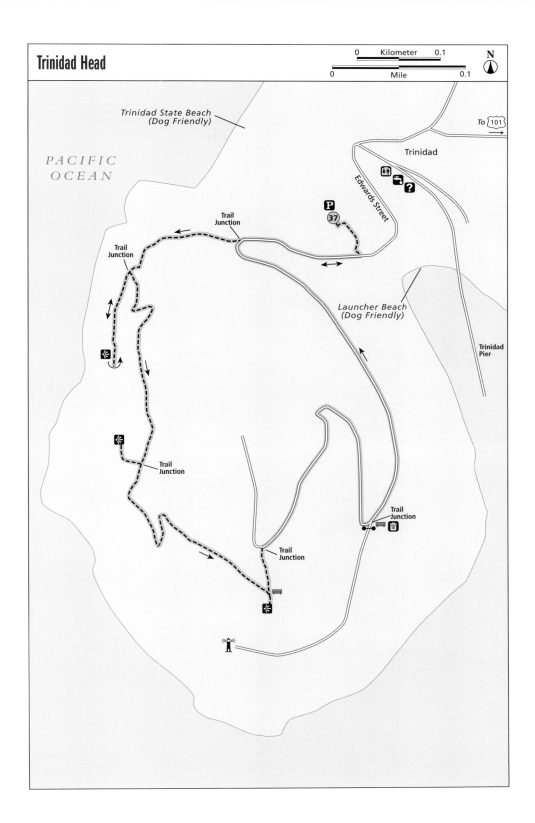

Trinidad Head

0 Kilometer 0.1

0 Mile 0.1

N

PACIFIC
OCEAN

Trinidad State Beach
(Dog Friendly)

To 101

Trinidad

P
37

Edwards Street

Trail
Junction

Trail
Junction

Launcher Beach
(Dog Friendly)

Trinidad
Pier

Trail
Junction

Trail
Junction

Trail
Junction

Trail
Junction

Breathing in the beauty
on Trinidad Head

Trinidad Pier, the northernmost
oceanfront pier in California

Seascape Restaurant at the Pier, Trinidad 95570; (707) 677-3762; seascape -trinidad.com. The restaurant is owned and operated by the local Rancheria Native American tribe. The picnic table with a harbor view is worth getting your food to go and share with pooch. They serve breakfast, lunch, and dinner with a fairly extensive menu from seafood and pasta to sandwiches and burgers.

Trinidad Bay Bed and Breakfast, 560 Edwards St., Trinidad 95570; (707) 677-0840; trinidadbaybnb.com. There are only 4 guest rooms, all with private baths and luxurious beds, in this lovely Cape Cod–style home. The bay views and lovingly tended grounds say it all about quality vs. quantity. Breakfasts feature seasonal menus of baked fruits and comfort food dishes from waffles to egg entrees with warm breads or muffins. There are no TVs to intrude in your Zen space, but there is Wi-Fi if you suffer from techno withdrawal. No pets in room, but if your dog is crate trained, he may be a guest in the garage.

Trinidad Inn, 1170 Patrick's Point Dr., Trinidad 95570; (707) 677-3349; trinidad inn.com. The nonsmoking inn has been a family-owned business since 1960 and is a very relaxing motel-style property on 5 acres with 10 room types. Rooms are appointed with down comforters, cable TV, and Wi-Fi, and some have kitchens. The parklike grounds have picnic tables and fire pits as well as gas and charcoal barbecues for guest convenience. Seasonal fruit with morning coffee is complimentary during the peak season (May through Sept). Some rooms are dog friendly (one dog) with manager approval and pet fee.

CAMPING

Emerald Forest Cabins and RV, 753 Patrick's Point Dr., Trinidad 95570; (707) 677-3554; cabinsintheredwoods.com. The 12-acre redwood spread has 50 RV sites with hookups, 26 tent sites with bathhouses, and 21 housekeeping cabins. The convenience store is stocked with staple provisions. Dogs are allowed in the tent and RV sites (max 3; first one is free with fee for each additional dog). Dogs are allowed in certain designated cabins (pet fee).

Redwood Coast Vacation Rentals, (707) 834-6555; redwoodvacation.com. Check this website for available vacation rentals in Trinidad.

Patrick's Point State Park, 4150 Patrick's Point Dr., Trinidad 95570; (707) 677-3570; parks.ca.gov. This is a beautiful park along the coast, tucked above a broad stretch of sandy beach at the north end and stunning steep cliffs at the south end. There are about 120 developed campsites among 3 campgrounds with water, flush toilets, and coin-operated showers. Agate Beach Campground was adding a few new cabins for the summer of 2016. Reservations accepted May through Sept, (800) 444-7275.

Big Lagoon County Park Campground, 7 miles north of Trinidad off of US 101; www.co.humboldt.ca.us. This small, rustic, lagoon-side campground has 25 tent sites with water and flush toilets. The Big Lagoon between the campground and a spit of sandy beach along the ocean is a kayaker's dream and great beachcombing.

38. **RIM TRAIL**

WHY GO?

This is a lush, shady woodland trail interrupted by spurs to points with sweeping views of the rugged forested coastline highlighted by colossal rock outcrops. This is one of the most picturesque settings of the California Coastal Trail in a developed pocket of coastal land.

THE RUNDOWN

Distance: 5.8 miles out and back

Start: Palmer's Point parking lot

Nearest town: Trinidad

Hiking time: About 3 hours

Fees and permits: Parking fee

Conveniences: Portable toilet, bench, picnic tables, and trash and recycling containers at trailhead, but no water. There is water in the campgrounds along the Rim Trail and at the end of the hike in the Agate Beach day-use area.

Beach access: Yes

Trail users: Hikers

Trailhead elevation: 161 feet

Highest point: 212 feet

Trail surface: Dirt and gravel

Difficulty: Moderate

Seasonal highlights: Azaleas and rhododendron in the spring; migrating whales in the spring and fall

Managing agency: Patrick's Point State Park, 4150 Patrick's Point Dr., Trinidad 95570; (707) 677-3570; parks.ca.gov

FINDING THE TRAILHEAD

From Trinidad at US 101, drive 5 miles north to exit 734 and turn left on Patrick's Point Drive. Drive 0.5 mile on Patrick's Point Drive to the Patrick's Point State Park entrance. Drive 1 mile and follow the signs to the Palmer's Point day-use parking lot. **GPS:** N41 07.78' / W124 09.79'

WHAT TO SEE

The area was home to the Yurok people prior to the arrival of European explorers, starting with Cabrillo and Drake in the sixteenth century. The Russians followed from Alaska in the early 1800s to hunt sea otters for their precious pelts. In the mid-1800s the discovery of gold in Northern California lured many fortune seekers to the area, forever changing the lives of the Yurok people, whose villages spread along the coast between what is now McKinleyville to the south and Crescent City to

Interpretative panel
at Palmer's Point

the north. Those who survived the attacks and the spread of disease were rounded up on reservations.

Unlike other Native American tribes, the Yurok population has managed to recover and revive their language and traditions. They are the most populous tribe in California. A replica of a traditional Yurok village built by a local Native crew is one of Patrick's Point State Park's highlights. You can walk around the Sumeg ("forever" in Yurok language) Village at the east end of the park. The plank houses and dugout canoes are constructed of redwood. Neighboring tribes use the village site as a gathering place for rituals and activities that are part of their heritage.

Patrick's Point was purchased in 1929, and over the years more parcels were acquired to develop the 640-acre park. Back in the 1920s the land was scarred from burning and logging for grazing land. Decades of work have rehabilitated the meadows to a more natural state.

The Rim Trail is a spectacular example of the coast's ecological personality. At this far north end of coastal California, vegetation from ferns to trees looks like it has been on a heavy diet of growth hormones. The forests meet the ocean, and the

The trail weaves through an enchanting forest.

former is as majestic as the colossal rock landmarks that pop out of the rugged coastline like exclamation points to accentuate the drama of the panorama.

The trail hugs the cliff along a lush corridor between the echo of the crashing surf below on your left and the back edge of the campsites on your right. The ocean is always within earshot, and the trail rewards with frequent breathtaking views of the coast through the clearings. Rustic wooden footbridges and short stretches of steep steps cross seasonal creeks and lead to picturesque overlooks at the ends of spur trails.

This hike begins on the Rim Trail at the park's southern trailhead in the Palmer's Point parking lot. Take the time to read the interpretive panels at Palmer's Point before setting off on the Rim Trail to Agate Beach at the northern end of the park.

Walk across two footbridges before coming to a post with the California Coastal Trail blue wave logo. Bear left and cross another footbridge. At 0.9 mile the spur on the left takes you to Rocky Point's terraced promontory facing stunning sea stacks. Go back to the spur junction and continue left to unmarked Patrick's Point just past the rock face on the right. The bench at Patrick's Point is an invitation you should accept. Sit and soak in the views, including the humongous rock outcrop looking north. This is Wedding Rock, and it looks like it is tethered to the Rim Trail by a narrow dirt trail on the narrow saddle.

Loop back to the spur junction and turn left. Be sure not to miss the unmarked spur to Wedding Rock at 1.6 miles. This is the Rim Trail's jewel in the crown of viewpoints. Follow the trail left down the steps, across the saddle, and up the chiseled stone steps to a walled stone terrace. This is a work of art that you can imagine setting up camp on for the night, with its unique view of Patrick's Point across the cove to the south.

Go back to the trail junction and turn left to head to the next unmarked spur. The spur and its steep sets of wooden steps lead to Mussel Rock—another coastal giant. Back at the spur junction you continue walking left and come to the park's paved road at 2.5 miles. Turn left and walk along the road for 0.4 mile to the point overlooking Agate's curving sandy beach named for the semiprecious stones that get tumbled and pounded by the surf. This is your turnaround point at the Agate Beach Campground across from a day-use area with picnic tables, restroom, water, and trash and recycling containers. If time permits, you can walk down the steep set of stairs to the beach before going back to the trailhead the way you came. You can save some time and distance by staying on the Rim Trail and off the spurs or by making the hike a loop walking back to the trailhead along the park road.

MILES AND DIRECTIONS

0.0 Start at the Palmer's Point parking lot and walk back along the road.

0.1 Turn left onto the Rim Trail to Agate Beach.

0.3 Walk across a footbridge over Beach Creek.

0.5 Walk across a footbridge over Penn Creek and bear left at the post with the California Coastal Trail sign before crossing the gully on a footbridge.

0.9 Turn left to Rocky Point.

1.0 Arrive at Rocky Point. Go back to the junction at the main trail and turn left.

1.3 Turn left on the unmarked spur to Patrick's Point.

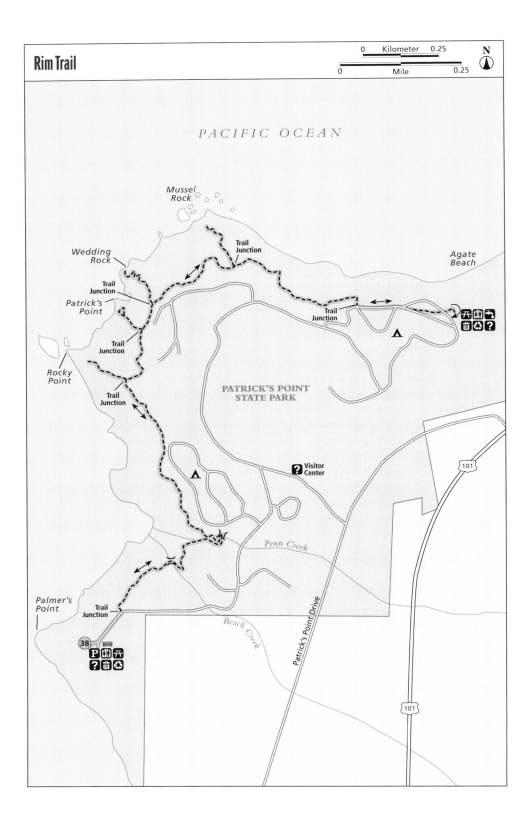

Rim Trail

Kilometer 0 — 0.25

Mile 0 — 0.25

N

PACIFIC OCEAN

Mussel
Rock

Wedding
Rock

Trail
Junction

Trail
Junction

Patrick's
Point

Agate
Beach

Trail
Junction

Trail
Junction

Rocky
Point

Trail
Junction

PATRICK'S POINT
STATE PARK

Visitor
Center

Penn Creek

101

Palmer's
Point

Trail
Junction

Beach Creek

Patrick's Point Drive

101

38

1.4	Come to Patrick's Point. Loop back to the junction at the main trail and turn left.
1.6	Turn left on the unmarked spur to Wedding Rock.
1.7	Come to Wedding Rock. Go back to the junction at the main trail and turn left.
2.1	Turn left on the unmarked spur to Mussel Rock.
2.2	Come to Mussel Rock. Go back to the junction at the main trail and turn left.
2.5	Come to the paved park road. Turn left on the road.
2.9	Come to the Agate Beach day-use area on the right and Agate Beach overlook on the left. Go back to the trailhead the way you came.
5.8	Arrive back at the trailhead.

BAKERIES, BREWERIES, EATS, AND SLEEPS

Trinidad Bay Eatery and Gallery, 607 Parker St., Trinidad 95570; (707) 677-3777; trinidadeatery.com. They pride themselves on serving the best clam chowder on the West Coast and cooking with organic trans-fat-free ingredients. There are outdoor tables to snack with pooch for breakfast, lunch, or dinner. Browse the local art and gift shop on your way out, and indulge in house-made Rocky Road fudge to go.

Seascape Restaurant at the Pier, Trinidad 95570; (707) 677-3762; seascape-trinidad.com. The restaurant is owned and operated by the local Rancheria Native American tribe. The picnic table with a harbor view is worth getting your food to go and share with pooch. They serve breakfast, lunch, and dinner with a fairly extensive menu from seafood and pasta to sandwiches and burgers.

Trinidad Bay Bed and Breakfast, 560 Edwards St., Trinidad 95570; (707) 677-0840; trinidadbaybnb.com. There are only 4 guest rooms, all with private baths and luxurious beds, in this lovely Cape Cod–style home. The bay views and lovingly tended grounds say it all about quality vs. quantity. Breakfasts feature seasonal menus of baked fruits and comfort food dishes from waffles to egg entrees with warm breads or muffins. There are no TVs to intrude in your Zen space, but there is Wi-Fi if you suffer from techno withdrawal. No pets in room, but if your dog is crate trained, he may be a guest in the garage.

Trinidad Inn, 1170 Patrick's Point Dr., Trinidad 95570; (707) 677-3349; trinidad inn.com. The nonsmoking inn has been a family-owned business since 1960 and is a very relaxing motel-style property on 5 acres with 10 room types. Rooms are appointed with down comforters, cable TV, and Wi-Fi, and some have kitchens. The parklike grounds have picnic tables and fire pits as well as gas and charcoal barbecues for guest convenience. Seasonal fruit with morning coffee is complimentary during the peak season (May through Sept). Some rooms are dog friendly (one dog) with manager approval and pet fee.

Wedding Rock is one of the Rim Trail's many highlights.

CAMPING

Emerald Forest Cabins and RV, 753 Patrick's Point Dr., Trinidad 95570; (707) 677-3554; cabinsintheredwoods.com. The 12-acre redwood spread has 50 RV sites with hookups, 26 tent sites with bathhouses, and 21 housekeeping cabins. The convenience store is stocked with staple provisions. Dogs are allowed in the tent and RV sites (max 3; first one is free with fee for each additional dog). Dogs are allowed in certain designated cabins (pet fee).

Redwood Coast Vacation Rentals, (707) 834-6555; redwoodvacation.com. Check this website for available vacation rentals near Trinidad.

Patrick's Point State Park, 4150 Patrick's Point Dr., Trinidad 95570; (707) 677-3570; parks.ca.gov. This is a beautiful park along the coast, tucked above a broad stretch of sandy beach at the north end and stunning steep cliffs at the south end. There are about 120 developed campsites among 3 campgrounds with water, flush toilets, and coin-operated showers. Agate Beach Campground was adding a few new cabins for the summer of 2016. Reservations accepted May through Sept, (800) 444-7275.

Big Lagoon County Park Campground, 7 miles north of Trinidad off of US 101; co.humboldt.ca.us. This small, rustic, lagoon-side campground has 25 tent sites with water and flush toilets. The Big Lagoon between the campground and a spit of sandy beach along the ocean is a kayaker's dream and great beachcombing.

Dog Friendly Beaches

Black Sands Beach is the spectacular coarse sand, tide-sensitive thruway that makes hiking along the Lost Coast possible (see hike 34). If you and pooch are looking for scenic seclusion to bond over a couple-mile stroll and a picnic or games of fetch the ball, stick, or Frisbee under voice control, this is it. Be aware that the untamed ocean here embodies the wild rugged beauty this coastline is famous for. Swimming or flirting with the surf is hazardous and can be deadly. Stay above the beach slope where the beach is wider and sand is dry. If your furry pal is known to get hyper-exuberant around water and throw caution to the wind and waves, be smart and keep him safe and leashed. The beach is accessed off of Beach Road and Humboldt Loop Road in Shelter Cove. King Range National Conservation Area, (707) 986-5400, blm.gov

Centerville Beach County Park has mystique. This 5-mile-long (at low tide) off-the-beaten-path sandy band is the northernmost beach on the remote Lost Coast and stretches north to the mouth of the Eel River. The large white cross on a bluff at the south end of the beach is a California Historical Landmark commemorating the 1860 shipwreck of the mail ship SS *Northerner*. Although many people died, locals rescued 70 passengers and crew after the captain beached the ship on the very sands where your bowwow can kick up his paws under voice control. The beach is accessed off of Centerville Road, 5 miles west of Ferndale. Humboldt County Parks, (707) 445-7651, co.humboldt.ca.us

South Spit is a finger of land straddling the Pacific Ocean and Humboldt Bay. This 4-mile oasis of beach and dunes explodes in yellow lupine during the spring. Dogs are welcome to strut and sniff under voice control Oct through Feb but must be on leash Mar through Sept, when endangered snowy plovers come to nest. It's always safer to call for current information about the snowy plover nesting season. The beach is accessed off South Jetty Road from US 101 at exit 696 near Eureka. Bureau of Land Management, (707) 825-2300, blm.gov

Mad River Beach County Park is an expansive stretch of sand and dunes with opportunities for splashing and swimming. Fido must be on leash in the dunes and on the dry sand above the surf slope, but can be under voice control frolicking on the wet wave slope. Horses are also allowed on the beach, so make sure Fido is up on his "share the playground" manners. The beach is accessed west of US 101 north of Arcata at 1 Mad River Rd., Arcata. Humboldt County Parks, (707) 445-7651, co.humboldt.ca.us

Clam Beach County Park is a wide, expansive beach of dunes and firm-packed sand at the end of a 5-mile multiuse recreational trail (see hike 36). Dogs are welcome on leash on the dry sand above the surf slope, but can be under voice control frolicking on the wet wave slope and in the water. Horses are also allowed on the beach, so make sure your beach-happy pal is up on his "share the playground" manners. The beach is accessed off of US 101 at Clam Beach Drive, McKinleyville. Humboldt County Parks, (707) 445-7651, co.humboldt.ca.us

Unleashed exuberance

Moonstone Beach and Luffenholtz Beach County Parks, north of McKinleyville and south of Trinidad off of US 101, are two beaches that allow Rover to romp under voice control on the surf slope but must be on leash on the dry sand. This is a particularly picturesque stretch of coastline, with the California Coastal National Monument sea stacks peering above the surf just offshore. Moonstone Beach is accessed at 100 Moonstone Beach Rd., Trinidad. Luffenholtz Beach is off of Scenic Drive. Humboldt County Parks, (707) 445-7651, co.humboldt.ca.us

Trinidad State Beach is a stunning stretch of sand running northward from the town of Trinidad in the shadow of Trinidad Head. The main and safest area of the beach to explore with your dog on leash is at the south end. The beach is accessed from a parking lot at the west end of Trinidad at the end of Lighthouse Road. California State Parks, (707) 677-3570, parks.ca.gov

Big Lagoon County Park Beach's expansive sandbar holds the Pacific at bay to create the Big Lagoon. It's a fabulous walking beach with access to the dynamic ocean and the more placid lagoon. Rover can romp under voice control on the surf slope but must be on leash on the dry sand. The lagoon is ideal for kayaking and swimming. Humboldt County, (707) 445-7651.

Coastal Attractions

Avenue of the Giants, Weott 95571; (707) 946-2263; parks.ca.gov, avenueofthegiants.net. This is a 31-mile-long scenic drive paralleling US 101 north of Garberville. It is surrounded by Humboldt Redwoods State Park's more than 50,000 acres of redwood groves and offers the easiest access to admire these ancient noble giants. The state park boasts Rockefeller Forest, the largest remaining stand of old-growth redwoods in the world.

Eureka's Victorian architecture in the Old Town of this historic seaport established in 1850 is a showcase of beautifully restored buildings housing a village of businesses catering to locals and visitors. Take a walking tour of the town or sit back in a horse-drawn carriage. Don't miss the boardwalk at the foot of Old Town overlooking Humboldt Bay.

Loleta Cheese Factory, 252 Loleta Dr., Loleta 95551 (exit 694 off US 101); (707) 733-5470; loletacheese.com. This is a family-founded and -operated cheese factory since 1982. You can watch the process, taste various cheese samples, and savor your purchases in the garden courtyard.

Ferndale is 5 miles west of US 101, south of Eureka, tucked at the north end of the Lost Coast. It gets its name from the giant ferns that grew in the glade that is now the town. It's difficult to believe that this charming little hamlet with exquisite Victorian architecture began with a cabin in a 5-acre clearing. The town's best-kept secret is the **Mind's Eye Coffee Lounge,** 393 Main St., Ferndale 95536, with a backroom manufactory where you can learn how to build your own skin-on-frame sea kayak in Aleutian tradition in one of the workshops led by True North Boats owner/builder Marc Daniels. See mindseyemanufactory.com and truenorthboats.com.

Humboldt Coastal Nature Center, 220 Stamp Lane, Manila, off of CA 255 in Eureka 95503; (707) 444-1397; friendsofthedunes.org. This is an educational center and gateway to 1,000 acres of coastal lands. Leashed dogs are welcome on the trails. Check the website for visiting hours and trail maps.

Fort Humboldt State Historic Park, 3431 Fort Ave., Eureka 95503; (707) 445-6547; parks.ca.gov. Besides being home to young Captain Ulysses S. Grant in the early 1850s, the bluff-top fort overlooking Humboldt Bay was center stage for some of history's saddest chapters of Native American history as gold-crazed settlers poured across their ancestral lands and massacres ensued. There are reconstructed buildings and outdoor machinery displays along with moving exhibits detailing the history of the people around this once-remote military outpost.

McKinleyville totem pole, 1500 City Center Rd. in the McKinleyville Shopping Center, McKinleyville 95519. McKinleyville's claim to fame is the neck-cranking 160-foot-tall totem pole carved out of a single 500-year-old redwood dubbed "the largest totem pole in the world."

Mad River Brewing Company, 101 Taylor Way, Blue Lake 95525; (707) 668-4151; madriverbrewingco.com. It's just 9 miles east of Arcata off of CA 299. The brewing company was on the rise long before the words "craft" and "artisan" were used in the same sentence as "beer" or beer was described as being brewed for a "complex palette of flavors." This famous brew mecca began in 1989 and has grown to boast a beer garden and tasting room and offers public tours.

Thomas H. Kuchel Visitor Center in Redwood National Park, 119441 US 101, Orick 95555; (707) 465-7765; nps.gov. This is the Redwood State and National Parks primo visitor center for its pristine setting with access to the beach and the splendid indoor exhibits and information sources. Orick is also the gateway to the Newton B. Drury Scenic Parkway, which is a fabulous alternative to US 101 for a 10-mile stretch through old-growth redwood forests with access to several trailheads into the majestic realm. It's also a great route to see wild Roosevelt elk herds roaming. Roosevelt elk, named after Theodore Roosevelt, are the largest members of the deer family after moose and the largest of the four North American elk species. They are known for their velvety tan body and dark neck and have the largest antlers (up to 4 feet) of all elk species. They are also known as Olympic elk in the rain forests of the Pacific Northwest. Settlers in Northern California hunted them to near extinction, but the few hundred have grown to thousands thanks to a successful conservation program. Check the website for information about seasonal schedules of days and times when the road is closed to motorized vehicles. This is a unique opportunity to explore the parkway on bicycles.

BEST COASTAL FARMERS' MARKETS

Shelter Cove's secluded hamlet is an unlikely location for a farmers' market, but if you happen to be overnighting here to hike Black Sands Beach, don't miss the vendors at Mario's on Machi Road every Tues from 11 a.m. to 3 p.m. May through Oct. (707) 986-7229

The Arcata Plaza farmers' market is a charming location to shop at 9th and G Streets on Sat from 9 a.m. to 2 p.m. Apr through mid-Nov. The live music starts at 10 a.m. (707) 441-9999

Old Town Eureka's farmers' market at F and 3rd Streets has atmosphere on Tues from 10 a.m. to 1 p.m. June through Oct. (707) 441-9999

DEL NORTE COUNTY

The northernmost county of coastal California bumping into the Oregon border, **DEL NORTE COUNTY** is a titan of rugged and wild natural beauty teeming with land and marine wildlife. Looking east toward the often snowcapped and aptly named Trinity Alps in the Klamath Range while standing above the Pacific staring at some of the most gigantic specimens of ancient coast redwoods, some as tall as 350 feet, Del Norte County seems surreal and so un-California compared to its sibling counties south. Big Foot Country's remoteness is tamed by Crescent City, homeport to local and commercial fishing fleets. Wild scenic rivers, sea-stack-dotted shores, crescent beaches, and historic lighthouses along the coastal trails stoke the imagination and spirit of adventure.

Note: See map on page 256.

Sharing the beach with equestrians

39. **LAGOON CREEK TO KLAMATH OVERLOOK**

WHY GO?

This is a supreme hike that hits several high notes. It's along a section of the California Coastal Trail in Del Norte Coast Redwoods State Park within Redwood National Park, a World Heritage Site and International Biosphere Reserve. Walk in the footsteps of the Yurok people on their ancestral land and on a portion of the Yurok Indian Reservation past a couple of pristine beaches as the trail rises gradually high above the Pacific. Clearings with views of the ocean and secluded coves punctuate the mostly forested trail. The scenic crescendo is the view of the mouth of the Klamath River from the overlook platform at the end of the trail.

THE RUNDOWN

Distance: 9.0 miles out and back

Start: California Coastal Trail at north end of Lagoon Creek parking lot

Nearest town: Klamath

Hiking time: About 4.5 hours

Fees and permits: None

Conveniences: Restrooms with flush toilets, water, picnic tables, trash and recycling containers, interpretive panels

Beach access: Yes; although dogs are not allowed on the trail, Lagoon Creek Beach is dog friendly on leash (see map).

Trail users: Hikers only

Trailhead elevation: 20 feet

Highest point: 565 feet

Trail surface: Dirt, gravel, roots, and pine needles

Difficulty: Strenuous

Seasonal highlights: Wildflowers in the spring

Managing agency: Redwood National and State Parks, 1111 Second St., Crescent City 95531-4198; (707) 465-7335; nps.gov/redw

FINDING THE TRAILHEAD

From Klamath, drive 5 miles north on US 101 and turn west into the Lagoon Creek parking lot. **GPS:** N41 35.67' / W124 05.99'

WHAT TO SEE

The most protected area of the Redwood Coast is a cooperative management project between the National Park Service and California State Parks. The contiguous public lands consisting of three state parks (Prairie Creek Redwoods State Park, Del Norte Coast Redwoods State Park, and Jedediah Smith Redwoods State Park) and Redwoods National Park make up the conglomeration of protected habitat and old-growth forests along the Redwood Coast. The three state parks are linked into Redwood National Park and designated a World Heritage Site and International Biosphere Reserve. This is pretty special territory to say the least, and the vision to save old-growth redwoods from further decimation was a tour de force accomplished by the grassroots activism that created awareness and the cooperation of multiple agencies.

As an added cultural and historical bonus, the coastal trail runs along the Yurok (which means "downriver people") ancestral lands, with a section across the Yurok reservation. The Yurok people, like all Native American tribes, suffered immense losses of life, culture, and land after the arrival of Euro-American pioneers. Miners and settlers invaded Yurok country during the gold rush of the 1850s, sparking conflict that escalated to massacres. Disease also took its toll on the Yurok population, which dwindled by 75 percent. In 1855 a reservation was established with boundaries within a portion of the Yurok's ancestral lands and including most of

Capturing the essence of the Northern California coast

their villages. Some of the Yurok villages date back to the fourteenth century, and the town of Klamath is on the Yurok reservation. More fortunate than other Native Americans, the Yurok were not expelled from their homeland, and they have been able to preserve their culture and language. Several neighboring tribes enrolled in the Yurok Tribe under a 1988 Settlement Act, making the Yurok Tribe the largest group of Native Americans in California.

The hike from Lagoon Creek to the Klamath Overlook is a stellar nature trek along a centuries-old Yurok Indian trail at the western edge of Del Norte Coast Redwoods State Park, established in 1925. But it's also a unique journey back in time on land that makes you feel much like an early explorer. It is not uncommon to come across piles of bear scat along the trail, a reminder of how wild a habitat this coast still is.

The hike starts in the Lagoon Creek parking lot with a scenic bang as you follow the signs for the California Coastal Trail (CCT) to Klamath Overlook across the creek on a wooden footbridge, with Lagoon Creek's salt-bleached driftwood-strewn beach on your right. The trail to Klamath Overlook does not allow dogs, but you can take your dog as far as this beach.

Notice the CCT's blue wave logo on the wooden trail signposts. The trail begins to rise and level on the bluff after the second trail junction. Continue walking on the CCT along the bluff, hemmed in by steep slopes anchored in Sitka spruce on the ocean side and thick woodlands of red alder and Sitka spruce above carpets of fern on the inland side. At 0.6 mile you pass the junction for the Yurok Loop Trail on the left. Continue walking straight on the CCT, but keep the option of taking this short side loop on the return to the trailhead.

At 1.2 miles you come to the trail junction for Hidden Beach on your right. This beach is a perfect place to linger on the return or to call your destination if you are short on time or energy. To complete this hike, continue on the CCT as it rises on a gentle incline over a carpet of spruce needles. The shoulders of the trail broaden, offering clearings with views down the precipitous hillside plunging into the Pacific. The ocean will always be within earshot, even when the lush vegetation obscures the views. At 3.0 miles the bark and low growl of invisible sea lions gets louder and blends with the lonely call of the foghorn on misty mornings. The trail continues on gravel stretches interrupted by tree roots as the terrain dips in swales and across fern-lined ravines. Sitka spruce limbs form tunnels and umbrellas in the forest canopy. The last mile of trail reveals more coastal views in frequent clearings as you continue to bathe in green.

At about 3.5 miles the trail becomes grassier and exposed, with the first hint of the Klamath River mouth ahead as you approach an overlook plateau. The trail has been fairly shady to this point and cool on a foggy day. But don't be fooled. If and when the sun pierces the fog, it can sizzle on that last stretch of exposed trail. Make sure you carry plenty of drinking water, and be prepared to whip your hat and sunscreen from your pack.

Quintessential Northern California coast

River fans will be interested in learning that the Klamath River runs almost 300 miles from Oregon through Northern California before reaching the Pacific. It is the second-largest river in California. The Sacramento River beats it by more than 150 miles on its journey from the headwaters in the mountains of Northern California to San Francisco Bay.

You come to a trail junction at 4.0 miles, where you have the option of turning left uphill to the CCT trailhead or right to the Klamath Overlook down a 0.5-mile exposed, steep, south-facing dirt trail along switchbacks. The Klamath Overlook parking lot about 250 feet up the trail on the left has restrooms with vault toilets and picnic tables. This is a developed scenic viewpoint overlooking the mouth of the Klamath River.

To complete the hike described here, continue walking 0.5 mile down to the gravel platform surrounded by a wooden railing. The views sweep southward to the Klamath River and sandbar. Feast on the views and click some memories before going back to the trailhead the way you came.

On your return to the trailhead, you can turn right at the junction and walk the 250 feet up to the CCT trailhead and Klamath Overlook parking lot to use the restroom and/or enjoy a scenic picnic break before going back to the trailhead. This is a hike you won't soon forget.

MILES AND DIRECTIONS

0.0 Start at the California Coastal Trail (CCT) at the north end of the Lagoon Creek parking lot.

0.1 Come to a trail junction for the CCT and beach access (dog friendly Lagoon Creek Beach) straight ahead. Bear left and cross the creek on a wooden footbridge.

0.2 Come to a trail junction. Bear right on the CCT to the Klamath Overlook.

0.6 Come to a trail junction for the Yurok Loop Trail left and the CCT straight. Continue walking on the CCT.

1.2 Come to a trail junction for Hidden Beach to the right. Bear left to the Klamath Overlook.

3.5 Arrive at the gravel overlook plateau on the right.

4.0 Come to the trail junction for the trailhead with an arrow pointing straight and Klamath Overlook with an arrow pointing right. Turn right.

4.5 Arrive at the Klamath Overlook with views of the Klamath River mouth. Go back to the trailhead the way you came.

9.0 Arrive back at the trailhead.

BAKERIES, BREWERIES, EATS, AND SLEEPS

Vita Cucina, 1270 Front St., Ste. A, Crescent City 95531; (707) 464-1076; vita cucina.com. This small, unpretentious strip mall venue with counter service and a few tables deserves its accolades as Crescent City's best eatery. The Cucina serves breakfast, lunch, and dinner Mon through Fri (closed weekends). The baked goods, salads, daily soups, sandwiches, pizzas, and specials are all freshly made and gourmet quality. The pumpkin chocolate chip bread and oatmeal ranger cookies loaded with coconut, chocolate chips, and pecans are addictive!

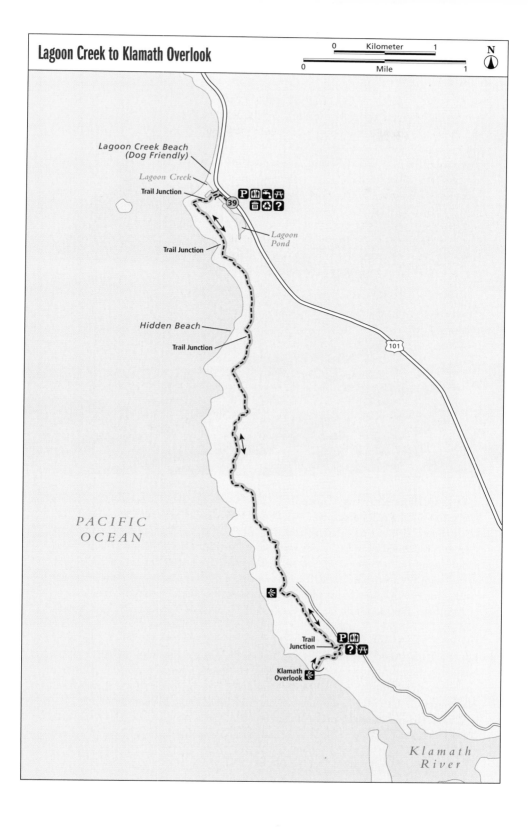

Lagoon Creek to Klamath Overlook

0   Kilometer   1

0   Mile   1

N

Lagoon Creek Beach
(Dog Friendly)

Lagoon Creek

Trail Junction

39

Lagoon
Pond

Trail Junction

Hidden Beach

Trail Junction

101

PACIFIC
OCEAN

Trail
Junction

Klamath
Overlook

Klamath
River

Pristine Hidden Beach

Port O'Pints Brewing Company, 1215 Northcrest Dr., Crescent City 95531; (707) 460-1154; portopints.com. Rick White started as a home brewer in 2002, and by 2015 Port O'Pints was serving from 14 taps (soon to be 27). The Agate American Cream Ale (named after the coast's agate stones) and 11 Bravo IPA (named after the army infantrymen code) continue to be favorites. Rick calls his menu "fresh and clean" with no deep-fried food, instead offering a selection of tasty sandwiches and wraps along with finger foods like the popular pretzel made with local cheese.

Abalone Bar & Grill, in the Redwood Hotel, 171 Klamath Blvd., Klamath 95548; (707) 482-1777; redwoodhotelcasino.com. The grill serves a varied menu for breakfast, lunch, and dinner. The burger roster at lunch is a meat eater's feast, with bison, elk, and Angus beef options. Vegetarians are not left out with the BBC (black bean and chipotle burger) and salad bar. Klamath River salmon is available at dinner year-round. Fri and Sat nights feature prime rib. For the sweet tooth, there's fresh blackberry cobbler during the summer and rich cheesecake during the winter.

Chart Room Restaurant, 130 Anchor Way, Crescent City 95531; (707) 464-5993; ccchartroom.com. This is a casual family restaurant for hearty breakfasts,

Overlooking the Klamath River
flowing into the Pacific

lunches, and dinner specials in addition to seafood favorites. Somehow the food seems to taste that much better if you happen to snag one of the window tables overlooking the picturesque harbor.

Crescent City Crab Shack, Anchor Way, Crescent City 95531; (707) 218-4071. Debbie has been crab fishing with her own boat for over 30 years, and until she opened the Crab Shack in 2012, apart from Safeway, locals had no place to buy fresh Dungeness crab. This is the spot to buy lip-smacking, finger-licking fresh Dungeness crab to go or savor at one of the outdoor picnic tables during the season (typically Dec–July). The rest of the year, pick up locally caught lingcod, rockfish, salad shrimp, oysters, and albacore tuna at the Crab Shack.

Ravenwood Motel, 151 Klamath Blvd., Klamath 95548-1004; (707) 482-5911; ravenwoodmotel.com. This nonsmoking motel has a selection of pleasant rooms and some suites with kitchens. The grounds are nicely landscaped with a barbecue area and fire pit. Room rates include a continental breakfast.

Redwood Hotel, 171 Klamath Blvd., Klamath 95548; (707) 482-1777; redwood hotelcasino.com. The nonsmoking hotel and casino complex built in 2014 on the

Yurok reservation is managed under the Holiday Inn Express banner. It is the newest lodging in the area, with an on-site restaurant (Abalone Bar & Grill). The indoor swimming pool is a nice perk, and room rates include a complimentary hot breakfast. Some rooms are dog friendly (pet fee).

Requa Inn, 451 Requa Rd., Klamath 95548; (707) 482-1425; requainn.com. This historic hotel with the plain facade overlooking the mouth of the Klamath River was built in 1914. It is a unique place to perch yourself for the night, just 1.5 miles from the Klamath Overlook parking at the south end of the Lagoon Creek hike. There are 13 charming guest rooms and 3 cottages with kitchens. The inn's cuisine is seasonal and created from mostly locally sourced organic ingredients. Lodging rates include a voucher toward breakfast, and sack lunches are available for your day hike. Dinners are family style with prix fixe menus featuring several courses of hearty servings of the tastiest food groups, including dessert. You'll deserve chocolate cake with ganache after a full day of hiking.

Crescent Beach Motel, 1455 US 101, Crescent City 95531; (707) 464-5436; crescentbeachmotel.com. This is a clean, comfortable, no-frills beachfront motel. All but 4 of the 27 rooms overlook the beach with either bay windows or sliding glass doors that open to a deck. This is the best value in town for lodging so close to the ocean, you could almost roll out of bed into the surf.

CAMPING

Del Norte Coast Redwoods State Park, 7 miles south of Crescent City on US 101, Crescent City 95531; (707) 465-7335; (800) 444-7275 for reservations between Memorial Day and Labor Day; parks.ca.gov. There are 143 sites for tents and RVs/trailers (31-foot/27-foot max length respectively) with a dump station but no hookups. The campground has flush toilets and coin-operated showers.

Camper Corral RV Park, 18151 US 101, Klamath 95548; (800) 701-PARK; klamathcampercorral.com. This is a sweet place to camp with a tent or RV on 50 riverfront acres with grassy sites and trees for shade. Camper Corral has a limited number of fully equipped trailers for rent. Amenities include a swimming pool, general store, showers, and laundry, plus 25 acres of wooded trails as a bonus. Campsites are dog friendly, and George, the owner of Camper Corral since 2015, is happy to report that most of the canine campers have been very well mannered with responsible owners.

40. **ENDERTS BEACH**

WHY GO?

This is an easily accessible, short, shady stitch of the California Coastal Trail in the precious Redwood National Park. It traces dramatic sheer cliffs and ends with a gradual descent to lovely Enderts Beach.

THE RUNDOWN

Distance: 1.4 miles out and back

Start: California Coastal Trail Last Chance Section trailhead

Nearest town: Crescent City

Hiking time: About 1 hour

Fees and permits: None

Conveniences: Picnic tables to the right of the parking lot, vault toilets at campground junction before Enderts Beach; no water or restrooms at trailhead

Beach access: Yes

Trail users: Hikers only

Trailhead elevation: 213 feet

Highest point: 213 feet

Trail surface: Dirt

Difficulty: Easy

Seasonal highlights: Wildflowers in the spring; whale migration in the spring and fall

Managing agency: Redwood National and State Parks, 1111 Second St., Crescent City 95531-4198; (707) 465-7335; nps.gov/redw

FINDING THE TRAILHEAD

From US 101 at the south end of Crescent City, drive 2 miles south and turn right on Enderts Beach Road. Drive 2 miles to the end of the road and parking area. **GPS:** N41 42.34' / W124 08.57'

WHAT TO SEE

Crescent City is named for the beautiful crescent-shaped sandy beach that stretches south of the harbor. It began as a supply station for the gold miners, and the town was established 1853. The mining boom ended and Crescent City became an important center for the timber industry into the mid-twentieth century. Today the rich waters of the northern coast make Crescent City Harbor homeport to many commercial fishing fleets.

Pioneer and trapper Jedediah Strong Smith was the first white American to travel this coast on foot in 1828. The Redwood Coast was and still is home to Yurok and

Tolowa Nations native people. Smith considered this remote territory "land's end," where the American continent met the Pacific Ocean. His explorations through the West clocked more miles than the famous Lewis and Clark. Smith's exploits remained in the shadows until the 1931 biography was written about him, 100 years after he was killed on the Santa Fe Trail. Jedediah Smith Redwoods State Park at the northern end of the Redwood Coast is one of three contiguous state parks within Redwood National Park. It was established in 1929 and named for the area's early explorer, and protects 7 percent of all the old-growth redwoods left in the world.

The precious Redwood Coast is a cooperative management project between the National Park Service and California State Parks. The conglomeration of protected habitat and old-growth forests along the Redwood Coast is designated a World Heritage Site and International Biosphere Reserve.

This trail to Enderts Beach is at the western edge of Del Norte Coast Redwoods State Park in Redwood National Park and a segment of the California Coastal Trail (CCT). The north end of the trailhead parking lot is nicely developed with a viewing deck overlooking Crescent City Beach toward Crescent City Harbor. The picnic tables are laid out on a grassy belt next to the viewing deck.

The hike takes you along the beginning of the Last Chance Section of the CCT to Enderts Beach for sweeping views of the precipitous coastline. A leafy canopy

Gazing south from the trailhead

shades the flat cliff trail all the way to Enderts Beach and the Nickel Creek Campground junction.

At 0.5 mile you come to the trail junction for Enderts Beach on the right. Walk downhill 250 feet to a junction for the Nickel Creek Campground on the left and the beach straight ahead. Continue walking down toward the beach. You come to an arched rock on the left and Nickel Creek flowing into the ocean. The arched rock has an unusual tunnel opening that you can walk through from one side of the beach to the other for a memorable photo op before going back to the trailhead the way you came.

MILES AND DIRECTIONS

0.0 Start at the California Coastal Trail Last Chance Section trailhead.

0.5 Come to a trail junction. Turn right to Enderts Beach. In about 250 feet, arrive at another trail junction for the campground on the left. Continue walking straight to Enderts Beach.

0.7 Arrive at Enderts Beach. Go back to the trailhead the way you came.

1.4 Arrive back at the trailhead.

BAKERIES, BREWERIES, EATS, AND SLEEPS

Vita Cucina, 1270 Front St., Ste. A, Crescent City 95531; (707) 464-1076; vita cucina.com. This small, unpretentious strip mall venue with counter service and a few tables deserves its accolades as Crescent City's best eatery. The Cucina serves breakfast, lunch, and dinner Mon through Fri (closed weekends). The baked goods, salads, daily soups, sandwiches, pizzas, and specials are all freshly made and gourmet quality. The pumpkin chocolate coffee cake and cookies are addictive!

Port O'Pints Brewing Company, 1215 Northcrest Dr., Crescent City 95531; (707) 460-1154; portopints.com. Rick White started as a home brewer in 2002, and by 2015 Port O'Pints was serving from 14 taps (soon to be 27). The Agate American Cream Ale (named after the coast's agate stones) and 11 Bravo IPA (named after the army infantrymen code) continue to be favorites. Rick calls his menu "fresh and clean" with no deep-fried food, instead offering a selection of tasty sandwiches and wraps along with finger foods like the popular pretzel made with local cheese.

Chart Room Restaurant, 130 Anchor Way, Crescent City 95531; (707) 464-5993; ccchartroom.com. This is a casual family restaurant for hearty breakfasts, lunches, and dinner specials in addition to seafood favorites. Somehow the food seems to taste that much better if you happen to snag one of the window tables overlooking the picturesque harbor.

Crescent City Crab Shack, Anchor Way, Crescent City 95531; (707) 218-4071. Debbie has been crab fishing with her own boat for over 30 years, and until she opened the Crab Shack in 2012, apart from Safeway, locals had no place to buy fresh

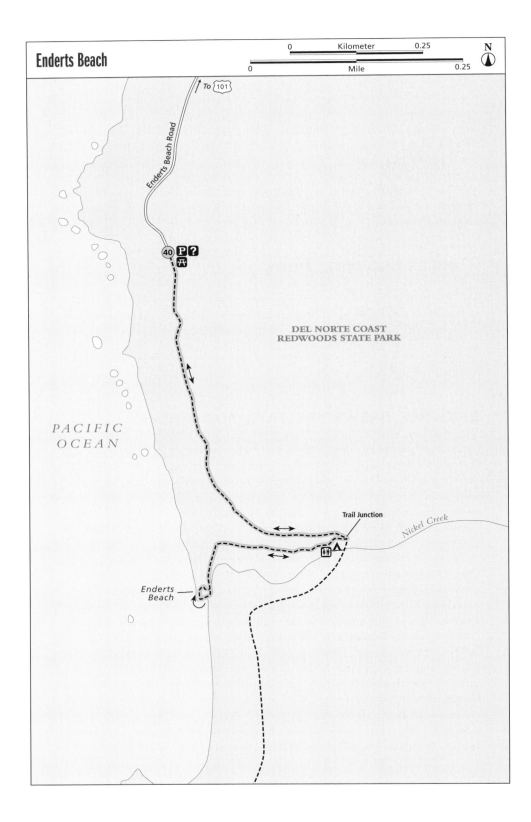

Enderts Beach

0   Kilometer   0.25

0   Mile   0.25

N

To 101

Enderts Beach Road

40 P ? ⚥

DEL NORTE COAST
REDWOODS STATE PARK

PACIFIC
OCEAN

Trail Junction

Nickel Creek

Enderts
Beach

Pathway down to Enderts Beach

Dungeness crab. This is the spot to buy lip-smacking, finger-licking fresh Dungeness crab to go or savor at one of the outdoor picnic tables during the season (typically Dec–July). The rest of the year, pick up locally caught lingcod, rockfish, salad shrimp, oysters, and albacore tuna at the Crab Shack.

Scopa by the Sea, 344 N. Pebble Beach Dr., Crescent City 95531; (541) 944-4156; scopaproperties.com. This 3-king-suite, oceanfront, Craftsman-style home is Patty and Scott Hillier's recent B&B venture. Two years of restoration have created a luxurious haven for guests across from fabulous North Beach. If you thrive on crisp sea air and endless Pacific horizons, you'll love the views from the rooms, the covered front porch, and private garden. Deborah, the Hilliers' indispensable innkeeper, proudly refers to herself as a "Suzie Homemaker." Guests rave about her breakfasts with fresh-baked sourdough bread, homemade jams, German pancakes, vegan creations, and recipes to suit all dietary needs. Although Scopa is not suitable for bow-wow guests, the Hilliers also own the Selah (biblical term for "pause and consider") beach house around the corner as a kid- and pooch-friendly vacation rental.

Solitary fisherman at Enderts Beach

Oceanfront Lodge, 100 A St., Crescent City 95531; (707) 465-5400; ocean frontlodge1.com. This newer hotel on the ocean side of US 101 offers picturesque views, an indoor pool, complimentary hot breakfast, and dog friendly rooms (pet fee and size restrictions).

Crescent Beach Motel, 1455 US 101, Crescent City 95531; (707) 464-5436; crescentbeachmotel.com. This is a clean, comfortable, no-frills beachfront motel. All but 4 of the 27 rooms overlook the beach with either bay windows or sliding glass doors that open to a deck. This is the best value in town for lodging so close to the ocean, you could almost roll out of bed into the surf.

Anchor Beach Inn, 880 US 101, Crescent City 95531; (707) 464-2600; anchor beachinn.com. This is generic motel lodging with bay views and a convenient location to the beach. Useful amenities include in-room refrigerators and microwaves as well as an on-site guest laundry. Your pooch won't mind the lack of curb appeal as long as he's welcome (pet fee).

CAMPING

KOA Crescent City, 4241 N. US 101, Crescent City 95531; (707) 464-5744; koa
.com. This tidy and well-maintained 17-acre campground with standard KOA amenities has tent sites (some with water and electric), RV/trailer sites (full hookups),
and cabin lodging in a redwood forest setting as well as grassy open space. Linens
are available in the cabins with advance notice; some cabins have fully equipped
kitchens, and some are dog friendly. The fancy RV sites have swings on a patio. The
10-acre redwood forest with trails for strolling is as much a perk as the fenced dog
park for off-leash bowwows. Rental bicycles on-site.

Jedediah Smith Redwoods State Park, 1440 CA 199, Crescent City 95531;
(707) 465-7335; (800) 444-7275 for reservations between Memorial Day and Labor
Day; parks.ca.gov. There are 89 developed sites on the Smith River for tents and
RVs/trailers (36-foot max length), with a dump station but no hookups. The campground has flush toilets and coin-operated showers.

Del Norte Coast Redwoods State Park, 7 miles south of Crescent City on
US 101, Crescent City 95531; (707) 465-7335; (800) 444-7275 for reservations
between Memorial Day and Labor Day; parks.ca.gov. There are 143 sites for tents
and RVs/trailers (31-foot/27-foot max length respectively), with a dump station but
no hookups. The campground has flush toilets and coin-operated showers.

Coastal sunsets make
stunning photos

41. POINT ST. GEORGE

WHY GO?

This hike follows a narrow, lush, bluff-top trail bordered by a riparian meadow and overlooks a couple of rocky, driftwood-strewn coves. Jagged sea stacks and rock islands highlight the coastal views. On a clear day, spotting the silhouette of the remote St. George Reef Lighthouse at the tip of a reef 6 miles out from shore is an added bonus to this unique hike.

THE RUNDOWN

Distance: 4.0 miles out and back

Start: Northwest end of parking lot at end of Washington Boulevard

Nearest town: Crescent City

Hiking time: About 2 hours

Fees and permits: None

Conveniences: Trash and recycling containers,

Beach access: Yes; dogs under voice control

Trail users: Hikers and dogs under voice control

Trailhead elevation: 52 feet

Highest point: 76 feet

Trail surface: Dirt and rock

Difficulty: Moderate

Seasonal highlights: Wildflowers in the spring; whale watching in the spring and fall

Managing agency: Crescent City Public Works Department, (707) 464-9506

FINDING THE TRAILHEAD

From the north end of Crescent City at US 101 and Washington Boulevard, turn west onto Washington Boulevard and drive 3.7 miles to the end of the road and parking lot. **GPS:** N41 47.01' / W124 15.15'

WHAT TO SEE

Crescent City, on the breathtaking Redwood Coast, is named for the beautiful crescent-shaped sandy beach that stretches south of the harbor. Crescent City began as a supply station for the gold miners, and the town was established 1853. The mining boom ended and Crescent City became an important center for the timber industry into the mid-twentieth century. Today the rich waters of the northern coast make Crescent City Harbor homeport to many commercial fishing fleets.

Vista point overlooking
Point St. George Beach

The trail traces a rocky cove.

The Redwood Coast was and still is home to Yurok and Tolowa Nations native people. Pioneer and trapper Jedediah Strong Smith was the first white American to travel this coast on foot in 1828. He considered this remote territory "land's end," where the American continent met the Pacific Ocean. Smith's explorations through the West clocked more miles than the famous Lewis and Clark. His exploits remained in the shadows until the 1931 biography was written about him, 100 years after he was killed on the Santa Fe Trail. Jedediah Smith Redwoods State Park at the northern end of the Redwood Coast was established in 1929 and named for the area's early explorer. It protects 7 percent of all the old-growth redwoods left in the world.

Back when roads were rudimentary to nonexistent, lighthouses were crucial to the safe transportation of goods essential to communities' economies. They were often constructed in response to tragic shipwrecks. Battery Point Lighthouse, built in 1855, was one of the first lighthouses built on the California coast and is a registered California Historical Landmark. The isolated St. George Reef Lighthouse was built as a result of the sinking of the coastal steamer *Brother Jonathan* in 1865. Almost 200 people died in the wreck. It took a marvel of engineering and 10 years to build the most expensive lighthouse erected in the United States. It was considered the most dangerous duty in the lighthouse service until the lighthouse was decommissioned in 1975. The original Fresnel lens is now on display in the Del Norte County Historical Society Museum. In the late 1990s the Lighthouse Preservation Society

The spring bloom enhances the California Coastal National Monument sea stacks.

initiated a long, arduous restoration project of the structure, and an automated light now serves as a private aid to navigation.

Crescent City's other claims to fame and infamy include the headquarters of Redwood National Park, which stretches from Crescent City south into Humboldt County east of Trinidad. California's "worst of the worst" criminals are confined in the Pelican Bay State Prison, the only super-maximum state prison in California. Charles Manson was in Pelican Bay's Security Housing Unit for fourteen months in the 1990s. Crescent City is also remembered as the city that was destroyed by four tsunami waves triggered by the Anchorage, Alaska, earthquake of 1964. The seafloor off the coast of Crescent City makes it especially vulnerable to tsunamis. The most recent tsunami damage to the harbor was a result of Japan's 2011 earthquake.

All human and natural disasters aside, Crescent City is an extremely stunning region of coastal Northern California deserving of hikers' attention. The panorama is wild Pacific to the west and forested mountain ranges to the east. In the winter you can see the snow-dusted ridges and peaks of the Trinity Alps rising inland.

The Point St. George trail doesn't boast tourist amenities at a developed trailhead like those associated with the many state parks along the coast. This trail is mostly local knowledge and lightly used. This hike begins at the end of Washington Boulevard just past the former coast guard station, now a private residence, and a cell tower station. You walk around a gate onto a gravel service road for just 0.1 mile before turning left up the slope of the bluff.

Follow the narrow well-worn trail along the bluff, and at 0.3 mile you come to a viewpoint looking out at the spine of a reef stretching northwest offshore. It is interesting to note that at Point St. George, you are standing on the third-westernmost point in the continental United States. The reef you see is St. George Reef, and you might just be lucky enough to spot the silhouette of the lighthouse sitting 6 miles out on the peak of a submerged volcanic mountain nicknamed "Dragon Rocks" in 1792 by explorer George Vancouver. The point has such a mesmerizing view of the reef, and the idea that for 82 years light keepers were stationed on such a precarious perch fifteen stories above the sea at the mercy of storms is almost unimaginable.

Just ahead on the left, the trail skirts the cliffs behind the private residence and cell tower installation. The trail cuts through a thick green riparian carpet of asparagus ferns laced with wild blackberry vines and dotted with white puffs of yarrow and purple lupine.

At 0.6 mile you come to a trail junction. Turn right on the gravel road. Walk 75 feet on the road and turn right on a narrow trail. Continue on the trail for about 0.1 mile and keep a sharp lookout for a faint, steep, primitive trail stepping down to the beach on the right. This hike follows this more adventuresome and tide-sensitive rock beach route for almost 1.0 mile before rejoining the bluff trail. This route is only possible at low tide. If you are hiking Point St. George at low tide but do not feel comfortable with the rocky beach route, stay on the trail that traces the bluff above the beach.

To continue the hike on the rocky beach route at low tide, walk down the narrow steep trail to the beach and continue walking south parallel to the water, threading what looks like a driftwood garden above the heaps of dry seaweed at the shoreline. Notice the isthmus connecting the beach to the rock outcrop. It's alluring, but this is also a tide-sensitive rocky bridge and a dangerous place to get stranded when the tide comes in as swiftly as it does here.

Continue walking up the slope at the end of the beach and rejoin the bluff trail. Follow the trail as it rims the top of the bluff and feast on the sea stacks and offshore rock islands. The rock island south with a green flattop is Castle Island, an important seabird rookery and resting place for sea lions and elephant seals. The island was established as a national wildlife refuge in 1980. The trail dips down to meet the north end of Pebble Beach, which extends south, linking coves for several miles to Battery Beach. If time and tide permit, you can take a stroll on the beach or stop for a picnic break. To continue this hike to the end, turn left before the beach and walk 0.2 mile to the bluff top. Turn around to go back to the trailhead the way you came to complete this hike as an out-and-back.

You have the option of looping back to the trailhead along Washington Boulevard by walking out to the road and turning left, which will shorten your return by 1 mile. You can also follow the bluff trail back to the trailhead and avoid the steep primitive trails up and down the rocky beach route.

MILES AND DIRECTIONS

0.0   Start on the gravel road at the northwest end of the parking lot.

0.1   Come to the bluff and turn left up the slope away from the beach.

0.3   Come to a viewpoint toward St. George Reef and the St. George Reef Lighthouse.

0.4   Arrive at the cell tower on the left.

0.6   Come to a trail junction at the gravel road. Turn right and walk 75 feet, then turn right on the narrow trail.

0.7   Turn right down the slope to the beach on a primitive dirt trail and walk south on the beach.

1.0   Come to a fork. Bear right and walk toward the bluff, then turn right on the gravel road along the narrowing eroding rim above the cove.

1.4   Come to a fork and turn right down a steep, narrow, primitive trail to the rocky shore and walk south.

1.6   Walk uphill to rejoin the bluff trail.

1.8   Come to the north end of dog friendly Pebble Beach and turn left along the bluff trail.

2.0   Arrive on the top of the bluff. Go back to the trailhead the way you came.

4.0   Arrive back at the trailhead.

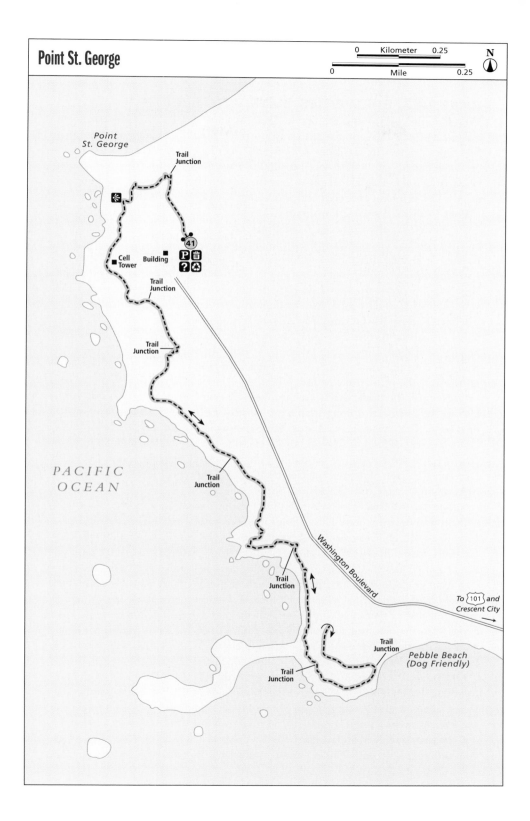

Point St. George

0   Kilometer   0.25

0   Mile   0.25

N

Point St. George

Trail Junction

Cell Tower   Building

41

P

Trail Junction

Trail Junction

PACIFIC OCEAN

Trail Junction

Washington Boulevard

Trail Junction

To 101 and Crescent City

Trail Junction

Pebble Beach (Dog Friendly)

Trail Junction

BAKERIES, BREWERIES, EATS, AND SLEEPS

Vita Cucina, 1270 Front St., Ste. A, Crescent City 95531; (707) 464-1076; vita cucina.com. This small, unpretentious strip mall venue with counter service and a few tables deserves its accolades as Crescent City's best eatery. The Cucina serves breakfast, lunch, and dinner Mon through Fri (closed weekends). The baked goods, salads, daily soups, sandwiches, pizzas, and specials are all freshly made and gourmet quality. The pumpkin chocolate coffee cake and cookies are addictive!

Port O'Pints Brewing Company, 1215 Northcrest Dr., Crescent City 95531; (707) 460-1154; portopints.com. Rick White started as a home brewer in 2002, and by 2015 Port O'Pints was serving from 14 taps (soon to be 27). The Agate American Cream Ale (named after the coast's agate stones) and 11 Bravo IPA (named after the army infantrymen code) continue to be favorites. Rick calls his menu "fresh and clean" with no deep-fried food, instead offering a selection of tasty sandwiches and wraps along with finger foods like the popular pretzel made with local cheese.

Chart Room Restaurant, 130 Anchor Way, Crescent City 95531; (707) 464-5993; ccchartroom.com. This is a casual family restaurant for hearty breakfasts, lunches, and dinner specials in addition to seafood favorites. Somehow the food seems to taste that much better if you happen to snag one of the window tables overlooking the picturesque harbor.

Crescent City Crab Shack, Anchor Way, Crescent City 95531; (707) 218-4071. Debbie has been crab fishing with her own boat for over 30 years, and until she opened the Crab Shack in 2012, apart from Safeway, locals had no place to buy fresh Dungeness crab. This is the spot to buy lip-smacking, finger-licking fresh Dungeness crab to go or savor at one of the outdoor picnic tables during the season (typically Dec–July). The rest of the year, pick up locally caught lingcod, rockfish, salad shrimp, oysters, and albacore tuna at the Crab Shack.

Scopa by the Sea, 344 N. Pebble Beach Dr., Crescent City 95531; (541) 944-4156; scopaproperties.com. This 3-king-suite, oceanfront, Craftsman-style home is Patty and Scott Hillier's recent B&B venture. Two years of restoration have created a luxurious haven for guests across from fabulous North Beach. If you thrive on crisp sea air and endless Pacific horizons, you'll love the views from the rooms, the covered front porch, and private garden. Deborah, the Hilliers' indispensable innkeeper, proudly refers to herself as a "Suzie Homemaker." Guests rave about her breakfasts with fresh-baked sourdough bread, homemade jams, German pancakes, vegan creations, and recipes to suit all dietary needs. Although Scopa is not suitable for bow-wow guests, the Hilliers also own the Selah (biblical term for "pause and consider") beach house around the corner as a kid- and pooch-friendly vacation rental.

Oceanfront Lodge, 100 A St., Crescent City 95531; (707) 465-5400; ocean frontlodge1.com. This newer hotel on the ocean side of US 101 offers picturesque views, an indoor pool, complimentary hot breakfast, and dog friendly rooms (pet fee and size restrictions).

Crescent Beach Motel, 1455 US 101, Crescent City 95531; (707) 464-5436; crescentbeachmotel.com. This is a clean, comfortable, no-frills beachfront motel. All

Stark rock islands dot the coastline.

but 4 of the 27 rooms overlook the beach with either bay windows or sliding glass doors that open to a deck. This is the best value in town for lodging so close to the ocean, you could almost roll out of bed into the surf.

Anchor Beach Inn, 880 US 101, Crescent City 95531; (707) 464-2600; anchor beachinn.com. This is generic motel lodging with bay views and a convenient location to the beach. Useful amenities include in-room refrigerators and microwaves as well as an on-site guest laundry. Your pooch won't mind the lack of curb appeal as long as he's welcome (pet fee).

CAMPING

KOA Crescent City, 4241 N. US 101, Crescent City 95531; (707) 464-5744; koa .com. This tidy and well-maintained 17-acre campground with standard KOA amenities has tent sites (some with water and electric), RV/trailer sites (full hookups), and cabin lodging in a redwood forest setting as well as grassy open space. Linens are available in the cabins with advance notice; some cabins have fully equipped kitchens, and some are dog friendly. The fancy RV sites have swings on a patio. The 10-acre redwood forest with trails for strolling is as much a perk as the fenced dog park for off-leash bowwows. Rental bicycles on-site.

Jedediah Smith Redwoods State Park, 1440 CA 199, Crescent City 95531; (707) 465-7335; (800) 444-7275 for reservations between Memorial Day and Labor Day; parks.ca.gov. There are 89 developed sites on the Smith River for tents and RVs/trailers (36-foot max length), with a dump station but no hookups. The campground has flush toilets and coin-operated showers.

Del Norte Coast Redwoods State Park, 7 miles south of Crescent City on US 101, Crescent City 95531; (707) 465-7335; (800) 444-7275 for reservations between Memorial Day and Labor Day; parks.ca.gov. There are 143 sites for tents and RVs/trailers (31-foot/27-foot max length respectively), with a dump station but no hookups. The campground has flush toilets and coin-operated showers.

Dog Friendly Beaches

Lagoon Creek Beach is a small driftwood-strewn beach just steps from the Lagoon Creek to Klamath Overlook trailhead (see hike 39). Dogs are not allowed on the trail, which is in Redwood National Park, but they are allowed on the beach on leash. Although this beach isn't the epitome of cut-loose excitement, it's a treat for pooch to set paws on national park land off the pavement while you are drinking up the salt air and scenery. The beach is accessed from the Lagoon Creek Picnic Area parking lot off of Redwood Highway/US 101 just 0.1 mile up the Lagoon Creek to Klamath Overlook trail, Klamath. National Park Service, (707) 465-7335, nps .gov/redw

 South Beach, which stretches 3 miles into Crescent Beach south from the Crescent City Harbor, is an incredible wide band of firm sand protected by the jetties. Dogs are allowed on leash, and the slope is gentle for taking Bowser for a run along the surf or just spending half a day beachcombing, surfer watching, and picnicking. The beach is also popular for seasonal horseback rides. Dog owners with canines that have a taste for warm trail muffins should be extra attentive when horses are present. To access the beach, park in the Harbor District off Redwood Highway/US 101 and Anchor Way. City of Crescent City, (707) 464-7483; Crescent City Harbor District, (707) 464-6174

Everybody into the water at South Beach

Pebble Beach stretches from Battery Point in Crescent City north to the bluff trails near Point St. George (see hike 41). The beach strings coves of flat firm sand and pebbled pocket beaches dotted with driftwood. It's a super spot for a long walk with your dog on leash while enjoying the expansive coastal views highlighted by sea stacks and scanning for the small polished agate stones for which this coast is famous. To access the beach, you can park on the street along North Pebble Beach Drive or at the picnic area parking lot across from Brother Jonathan Memorial Park. *Brother Jonathan* was a paddle steamer that hit a reef and sank in 1865. The memorial rock, a California Historical Landmark, stands at the vista point above the beach. City of Crescent City, (707) 464-7483

Coastal Attractions

Yurok Country Visitor Center, 101 Klamath Visitor Center, Klamath 95548; (707) 482-1555; visityurokcountry.com. The Yurok Tribe's attractive visitor center is the first Native visitor center to be funded by the National Scenic Byways Program. The center provides a hub for education with exhibits and material about the tribe's heritage and culture along with a gift shop featuring handcrafted items and jewelry. Visitors can obtain information about driving along culturally and environmentally significant roads designated as Yurok Scenic Byways through their ancestral territory.

Battery Point Light, on Lighthouse Way off of Front Street and US 101, was built in 1856 and was one of the first lighthouses on the California coast. It has an idyllic setting on an islet connected to the mainland by a tide-sensitive isthmus,

Battery Point Light
in Crescent City

which makes tours up to the light tower and the museum only possible at low tide. The museum features the furnished lighthouse keeper's quarters as well as maritime artifacts from the 1850s. The lighthouse is registered as a California Historical Landmark and is listed on the National Register of Historic Places. Call (707) 464-3089 for status of accessibility.

Guided Tsunami Walking Tours are scheduled seasonally from the National Park Service's Crescent City Information Center, 1111 Second St., Crescent City 95531; (707) 465-7335. Free maps for the self-guided Tsunami Walking Tour are available at the Chamber of Commerce Information Center, 1001 Front St., Crescent City; (707) 464-3174.

Del Norte County Historical Society Museum, 577 H St., Crescent City 95531; (707) 464-3922; delnortehistory.org. In addition to Native American artifacts including basketry, the museum displays a collection of photographs and personal accounts of the 1964 tsunami that destroyed large areas of Crescent City following the earthquake near Anchorage, Alaska. One of the museum rooms houses the Fresnel lens from the St. George Reef Lighthouse.

Rumiano 1921 Cheese Co., 511 9th St., Crescent City 95531; (707) 465-1535; rumianocheese.com. Started on a small dairy farm in 1919, this fourth-generation family-owned cheese company is perhaps the oldest family-owned cheese company in California. Taste and buy their selection of organic cheeses that start in the pasture with milk from grass-fed cows. You can watch the cheese process through the facility's large picture window.

BEST COASTAL FARMERS' MARKETS

Crescent City Farmers' Market has grown to showcase 50 to 75 vendors of homegrown food products, locally fished seafood, and handmade arts and crafts. All items sold must be made by the vendors. Independent musicians gather to strum or pick their instruments for added color and ambience every Sat from 8:30 a.m. to 1:30 p.m. from early June to late Oct on the Del Norte Fairgrounds off of US 101, Crescent City. Rural Human Services, (707) 464-7441

APPENDIX A

DAY HIKE CHECKLIST

YOU

- ❏ Sturdy waterproof hiking footwear and sandals for creek crossing and surf walking
- ❏ Bug repellent in sealed plastic bag
- ❏ Sunscreen
- ❏ Sunhat and sunglasses
- ❏ Layers for changing weather and rain-repelling windbreaker for fog and drizzle
- ❏ Pocketknife (Swiss Army–type knife that includes additional tools)
- ❏ Camera

POOCH

- ❏ Collar, harness, leash, and permanent ID tag with home/cell number
- ❏ Flotation vest for safe water fun
- ❏ Health and vaccination certificate
- ❏ Flea and tick application prior to hike (topical or oral available from your veterinarian)
- ❏ Collapsible water bowl and water supply in metal or plastic bottle: 32-ounce bottle for half-day hikes (under 4 hours) and 2-quart bottle for longer hikes (8 ounces of water per dog per hour or 3 miles of hiking)
- ❏ Kibble for your dog at mealtimes on the trail and extra protein snacks for energy boost. Save the yummiest treats for "recalls" on voice-control trails and beaches.
- ❏ Plastic resealable bags for carrying food, treats, medication, and first-aid essentials. The bags can be converted into food and water bowls as well as poop-scoop bags to carry waste out if necessary.
- ❏ Biodegradable poop-scoop bags

YOU AND POOCH

- ❏ First-aid kit (see Appendix B)

APPENDIX B

TRAIL HAZARDS AND FIRST AID

BLEEDING FROM CUTS OR WOUNDS

1. Remove any obvious foreign object.
2. Rinse the area with warm water or 3 percent hydrogen peroxide.
3. Cover the wound with clean gauze or cloth and apply firm, direct pressure over the wound for about 10 minutes to allow clotting to occur and bleeding to stop.
4. Place a nonstick pad or gauze over the wound, and bandage with gauze wraps (the stretchy, clingy type). For a paw wound, cover the bandaging with a bootie. (An old sock with duct tape on the bottom is a good bootie substitute. Use adhesive tape around the sock to prevent it from slipping off. Be careful not to strangle circulation.)

HEAT EXHAUSTION AND HEAT STROKE

Heat exhaustion occurs when humans' or dogs' bodies get too hot. On the trail it is commonly caused by too much physical exertion in hot weather and may be combined with dehydration. Human symptoms can involve heavy sweating, nausea, and headache. Heatstroke is more serious and occurs when human or dog body temperature rises quickly above 104 degrees Fahrenheit. In a dog's case, at this point panting is ineffective to regulate temperature. Don't put your dog at risk during hot weather.

In both human and dog cases, get out of the sun, rest in the shade, drink cool water, and apply water-soaked towels on the head (to cool the brain). Use any available body of water (pond, lake, creek, ocean) to cool off and begin reducing body temperature (no lower than 103 degrees for dogs).

Avoid chilling your dog with icy water while cooling the chest, abdomen, and paws. Swabbing the footpads with alcohol will help.

HYPOTHERMIA

Hypothermia occurs when a human's body core temperature drops below 95 degrees Fahrenheit and your body is losing heat faster than it can produce it. Dogs' normal core temperature is higher than humans' (101 to 102.5 degrees), and they can become mildly hypothermic just under 100 degrees. On the Northern California coast, extended time in the Pacific's mid-50-degree water temperature can cause hypothermia. Swimming is not a popular activity for humans on the North Coast unless you are wearing a wet suit.

Just because dogs have fur doesn't mean they are immune to hypothermia. Certain breeds have a thicker fat layer for cold water, but overall any dog is vulnerable in the cold Pacific. Some dogs will keep running into the ocean for a ball as long as someone is throwing, just as easily as some dogs will run to exhaustion to keep up with their human. Be sensible and responsible. Don't risk your dog's life in the ocean.

Treatment for humans also applies for dogs:

1. Watch for signs of shivering and get him out of the water.

2. Wrap him in a blanket, towel, sleeping bag, your clothing, or whatever you have available. Or if you have access to a clothes dryer, wrap him in warm towels. Fill water bottles with warm water (hot water tap or heated water) and wrap the bottles in a towel and place next to him (bottles directly on the skin can burn). Or hold him close to you for body heat.

3. Have him drink warm fluids.

INSECT BITES

Bee stings and spider bites may cause itching, swelling, and hives. If the stinger is still present, scrape it off with your fingernail or tweezers at the base away from the point of entry. (Pressing the stinger or trying to pick it from the top can release more toxins.) Apply a cold compress to the area, and spray it with a topical analgesic like Benadryl to relieve the itch and pain. As a precaution, carry an over-the-counter anti-histamine (such as Benadryl) and ask your vet about the appropriate dosage before you leave, in case your dog has an extreme allergic reaction with excessive swelling.

A flotation vest is added safety for your dog.

RATTLESNAKE BITES

1. Keep the victim (human or dog) calm (activity stimulates the absorption of venom).

2. Rinse the area with water, and transport the victim to nearest medical aid.

SORE MUSCLES

1. Rest and massage limbs (human or dog).

2. Apply cold-water compresses to tight muscle areas to reduce inflammation.

3. Take an over-the-counter aspirin-based anti-inflammatory (check with your physician), or for your dog, Ascriptin buffered aspirin (check with your vet on dosage for your dog's age, breed, and weight).

SKUNKED

When your dog gets skunked, a potent, smelly cloud of spray burns his eyes and makes his mouth foam. The smell can make you gag, and contact with the spray on your dog's coat can give your skin a tingling, burning sensation. Apply de-skunking shampoo as soon as possible.

De-Skunking Shampoo Mix
1 quart hydrogen peroxide
¼ cup baking soda
1 tablespoon dishwashing detergent

Put on rubber gloves and thoroughly wet your dog, apply mixture, and let stand for 15 minutes. Rinse and repeat as needed.

CARDIOPULMONARY RESUSCITATION

Check with your veterinarian or local humane society for pet CPR classes.

FIRST-AID KIT CHECKLIST FOR YOU AND FIDO

YOU

❑ First-aid book

❑ Band-Aids

❑ Tecnu soap or lotion to wash poison oak oil off skin

YOU AND FIDO

❑ Hydrogen peroxide (3 percent) to disinfect surface abrasions and wounds

❑ Antiseptic ointment

- ❏ Gauze pads and gauze
- ❏ Clingy and elastic bandages
- ❏ Tweezers to remove ticks, needles, or foreign objects in a wound
- ❏ Styptic powder for bleeding
- ❏ Hydrocortisone spray to relieve plant rashes and stings
- ❏ Instant cold pack—helps reduce body temperature if you suffer from heat exhaustion or heatstroke and can save your dog's life if caught on a trail without water to cool him in the unfortunate event of heat exhaustion or heatstroke

FIDO

- ❏ Muzzle—the most loving dogs can snap and bite when in pain. Muzzles come in different styles and sizes to fit all dog nose shapes.
- ❏ Scissors (rounded tips) to trim hair around a wound
- ❏ Sock or bootie to protect a wounded foot
- ❏ Duct tape to wrap around the sole of sock used as a bootie
- ❏ Rectal thermometer
- ❏ Alcohol swabs for dog's footpads and instant cold pack to cool head, neck, chest, and abdomen (dog or human) if caught in an emergency heatstroke situation on a dry trail
- ❏ Ascriptin (buffered aspirin)—older dogs in particular may be stiff and sore at the end of a hike. Consult your vet on the appropriate dosage.
- ❏ Antidiarrheal agents and GI protectants: Pepto-Bismol, 1–3 ml/kg/day; Kaopectate, 1–2 ml/kg every 2–6 hours
- ❏ Indigestion and stomach upset: Pepcid (famotidine) decreases gastric acid secretions, 0.1–2 mg/kg every 12–24 hours
- ❏ Diphenhydramine (Benadryl) dosed at 1mg/lb 2–3 times daily can relieve some allergy reactions exacerbated by the heat.
- ❏ Lemon juice for quick rinse if you don't have ingredients for the deskunking shampoo mix.
- ❏ Your veterinarian's telephone number and the ASPCA National Animal Poison Control Center, (888) 426-4435—tape this vital information inside the kit.

APPENDIX C

USEFUL RESOURCES

SHOPPING FOR THE TRAIL

- adventuremedicalkits.com: Wide selection of first-aid kits
- groundbirdgear.com: Good selection of versatile harnesses/dog packs
- petmountain.com: Good selection of everything dog for travel and trail
- ruffwear.com: Good selection of comfortable harnesses and life jackets
- niteize.com: The DoohicKey tool is tick remover, nail file, burr comb, and bottle opener in one carabiner clip trail tool.
- zukes.com: The power bones by Zuke's are small, healthy energy dog treats in three flavors. Check the website for a Zuke's distributor at a pet supply store in your neighborhood, or go to chewy.com for an online distributor.

COASTAL INFO

- trails.mendocinolandtrust.org/trails: A web source to help locate Mendocino County coastal trails
- coastwalk.org/ccta: Has the most up-to-date information about the progress of the California Coastal Trail (CCT). The Coastwalk office is at 555 South Main St., Ste. 3, Sebastopol 95472; (707) 829-6689.
- californiacoastaltrail.info: This website has maps of the CCT, but the website is not updated consistently.
- ca.usharbors.com: Locate the harbor in Northern California closest to your tide-sensitive trail for the tide chart and schedule of tides that day.
- californiabeaches.com: A web source with additional information about California's beaches
- coastal.ca.gov: This is the California Coastal Commission website, where you can order the latest edition of the *California Coastal Access Guide.*
- *California's Coastal Parks: A Day Hiker's Guide* by John McKinney (Wilderness Press, 2006)

ON THE ROAD

- seemonterey.com: Monterey County tourist information

- santacruz.org: Santa Cruz County tourist information
- smccvb.com: San Mateo County tourist information
- sanfrancisco.travel: San Francisco city/county tourist information
- visitmarin.org; marincoastguide.com: Marin County tourist information
- sonomacounty.com, sonomacoastguide.com: Sonoma County tourist information
- mendocinoguide.com: Mendocino County tourist information
- visithumboldt.com: Humboldt County tourist information
- exploredelnorte.com: Del Norte County tourist information
- redwoods.info: Redwood Coast tourist information

ROAMING WITH ROVER

- bringfido.com: Source for dog friendly lodging and dining
- dogtrekker.com: Source for dog friendly lodging, dining, and activities
- dogjaunt.com: Source for dog friendly public transportation (road, rail, air) including car rentals and San Francisco Bay ferries
- *Traveling with Your Pet: The AAA PetBook,* 17th ed. (AAA publishes new editions annually); aaa.com/petbook **Note:** Membership in the American Automobile Association (AAA) gives you access to free tour books. Northern California tour book and public land campground maps available. Contact (800) JOIN-AAA.
- *The Dog Lover's Companion to California,* 7th ed., by Maria Goodavage (Avalon Travel Publishing)

CAMPGROUND RESERVATIONS

- reserveamerica.com: Campground reservations for state parks
- recreation.gov: Public land campground reservations including national parks and national forests
- koa.com: Network of private campgrounds with standardized amenities

READS FOR THE TRAIL

- *A Walk Along Land's End* by John McKinney (Harper Collins West, 1995)
- *California Coast Trails: A Horseback Ride from Mexico to Oregon* by Joseph Smeaton Chase (BiblioLife, 2009)

HIKE INDEX